Medieval Literature

A HISTORY AND A GUIDE

W. T. H. JACKSON

Medieval Literature

A HISTORY AND A GUIDE

COLLIER BOOKS, NEW YORK
COLLIER-MACMILLAN LTD., LONDON

SECOND PRINTING 1967

Table of Contents

Preface

THIS BOOK is an attempt to provide, in very brief compass, the essential facts about medieval European literature. Although it would clearly be impossible to mention all the works written, I have tried to mention all important works of literature, as distinct from the far more numerous theological, scientific, historical, and philosophical works. More space is devoted to works which I consider significant, but there can be no hope in a book of this size of exhaustive discussion of anything. I have indicated how literature developed in the various countries, and where there is interdependence, I have tried to show it.

The movements originating in France and spreading to other countries have received more attention than those of the Celtic and Nordic areas because I believe that most readers find them more accessible and easier to grasp. I certainly do. It goes without saying that in writing this book I have leaned heavily on those who have written the standard literary histories of the various countries. These are listed at the end of the book, and the reader is referred to them for more detailed information.

A great deal of medieval literature is anonymous, and if no author is mentioned, it may be assumed that none is known. The dates of works are almost always approximate, and there is often sharp disagreement among experts on the dating of even well-known poems. I have tried to give the accepted opinion. Medieval names also constitute a problem. The spelling varies a great deal in the original manuscripts, and the printed editions are often not consistent even within themselves, still less with other editions of the same author. In most cases it is usual to give the modern form of an author's name, *e.g.* Fouquet de Marseilles instead of Folquet de Marseile, Friedrich von Hausen instead of Friderich von Husen, but there is no rule about this. Medieval authors are usually listed in indices under their first name, since the last is often a place with which they are associated rather than a surname. Yet even here there are exceptions, such as Geoffrey Chaucer and François Villon. A medieval author should never be referred to by a name which is a title, such as Andreas *Capellanus* (André the Chaplain), or a place designation, such as Thomas *Aquinas* (Thomas of Aquino).

It will be noted that many titles have been translated, sometimes with the original form in parentheses, sometimes not. Here again, it is impossible to be completely consistent. Most readers do not need to have *Chanson de Roland* and *Nibelungenlied* translated, and *Song of Roland* and *Song of the Nibelungen* are both misleading, but the meaning of *Jeu de la Feuillée* is by no means obvious. It should be remembered that libraries normally list the work under its original title, although there may be cross references to a translation.

In the last few years there has been a welcome improvement both in the number of translations of medieval works available and in their quality. Lyrics are still poorly represented, and there is no way of reading the great medieval French or German dramas in a modernized version. The narrative works, however, are easily accessible in good paperback versions in English, although it is often preferable to read a modernized form of the original vernacular.

To understand medieval literature, it is useful to have some background of medieval history and culture. *Medieval History* (New York: Macmillan, 1963) by Norman Cantor is a most useful work of this kind.

Introduction

THE TERM "MEDIEVAL" is an arbitrary one, implying as it does an age between two other ages, classical antiquity and the Renaissance. It is, unfortunately, very hard to determine when these two ages ended and began respectively. The civilization of classical antiquity did not end with the fall of Rome, nor did the advent of Boccaccio and Petrarch usher in the Renaissance for the whole of western Europe. Any limits set can easily be shown to be wrong in one particular or other. For the purposes of this book, we shall regard the death of Boethius (524) as marking the end of classical antiquity and 1500 as the end of the Middle Ages.

Only in the history of Europe and in particular western Europe does the expression "Middle Ages" have any significance. We shall therefore confine our discussion of the literature to the works produced in western Europe within the period already mentioned. A great deal of this work was written in Latin, not the highly formalized language of Livy and Cicero but a more practical, loosely constructed, and flexible Latin which was constantly increasing its stock of words in order to act as an effective instrument for philosophy, theology, history, law, and public administration. It is a mistake to regard medieval Latin as "vulgar Latin," "church Latin," or "monk's Latin." Although it did not conform to all the classical rules of grammar and rhetoric, the language as it appears in the works of philosophers and literary men is polished and accurate according to its own standards. It is unfair to judge it by the entries made in account books and records of real-estate transactions.

Many of the literary histories of the Middle Ages, particularly those concerned with Latin literature, regard all written works as their province and include in their account history, philosophy, and didactic works of every kind. This book will confine itself to literature as that term is usually employed in writing histories of modern literature. Works which fall outside this category will be discussed only insofar as they have a bearing on the literary works mentioned.

TYPES AND GENRES

It may be well at this point to mention the most important types of medieval literature and give some definition of each.

There was little literary prose in the Middle Ages, particularly in the vernacular languages. The early centuries saw Latin literature almost completely dominant on the literary scene. Most of the works produced were imitations of the classical Latin types, particularly epic, lyric, and occasional poetry. Christian hymns, of course, were written in large numbers, and saints' lives formed an important part of the output in prose. Against this the vernacular languages had little to show. There was no doubt a considerable amount of orally transmitted literature among all peoples, but the earliest extant works in vernacular languages were written in the British Isles in Anglo-Saxon (often called Old English). Much of this work was religious in nature and was often little more than adaptation of Latin originals, but some lyrics and in particular the narrative poetry was of great originality and high literary quality.

Although the extant versions of these narrative poems date from a period after the conversion of Britain, they are based on earlier material and contain many features of style and content which clearly belong to a common Germanic past. This tradition is to be found in a few scattered remains on the continent of Europe, and later the oral material was reworked into a large body of prose and verse narrative in Scandinavia and Germany. In the Germanic-speaking and the Celtic-speaking countries, the stories tended to concentrate on a small group of chosen heroes—Dietrich, Siegfried, Gunther, and Hagen in Germanic literature, Cuchulain and Finn in Celtic literature. The great figure of Welsh literature, Arthur, is known principally from works in other languages.

Vernacular literature appeared later in France than in Britain and Germany and at first offered only the usual adaptations of religious works, but from the beginning of the twelfth century it took over a dominating position in the literature of medieval Europe. Both in quantity and in originality it outstrips all the other vernaculars, although this does not by any means imply that the best works within any given literary type were written in French. Several major genres emerged in France in the twelfth century. The first in point of time was the *chanson de geste*, a narrative poem whose heroes belong to the period of history when France was governed by Charlemagne and his immediate successors. Action is most important in this type, loyalty and physical bravery the principal characteristics of its heroes. Most of the important *chansons de geste* were written during the twelfth and thirteenth centuries, but imitations and prose versions continued to appear until the late Middle Ages, not only in France but in all the countries of western Europe.

The most important type of narrative poetry in the Middle Ages was undoubtedly the romance. It is a genre hard to define, since it includes works of widely differing style and subject matter, but it may be said that in general it was written for entertainment, not instruction; that its personages were idealized; that it did not shrink from the introduction of the exotic and magical; and, perhaps most important, that love was one of its principal themes. All these statements could be challenged by reference to particular poems, but in general they are true. By far the most important cycle of romances is that which tells stories connected with King Arthur and the knights of his court. Although a great deal of the material is Celtic in origin, France again would appear to be the home of the earliest Arthurian romances, but the type was extremely popular and romances were written in all the countries of western Europe. It could scarcely be disputed that the greatest narrative works of the Middle Ages, if we except the *Divina Commedia* of Dante, were romances.

Allegory is often felt to be the most typical expression of the medieval spirit in literature, and a case could be made for such a contention, since almost all major works contain some allegorical elements. Formal allegory—that is, a long work, usually in poetry, whose characters are personifications of abstract qualities—flourished during the thirteenth and fourteenth centuries. Although such works contained passages of great poetical merit, the aim of their authors was undoubtedly didactic and the allegory was felt to be the most effective and also the most accurate method of imparting ideas, particularly on the subject of love. Many works, including some by Chaucer, are partly allegorical, that is, they can be read as narrative but are best understood when interpreted allegorically.

The existence of a national epic poetry in Germany and Scandinavia has already been mentioned. A similar national epic existed in Spain too, with the personality of Rodriguez Bivar, known by his Arabic title of Cid, the principal focal point.

Not all narrative poetry, however, was concerned with

heroes, whether fictional or otherwise. The fabliaux, short poems of a few hundred lines, usually recounted the adventures of much more mundane characters and for the most part delighted in tales of intrigue which told of loves far different from those of the romances. Many of the stories were old tales in new guises, and the fabliaux in their turn were developed by later authors, of whom Chaucer is the best example, into brilliantly witty stories in verse. In the later Middle Ages, prose versions of them appeared, of which the best known are those in the *Decameron* of Boccaccio.

It is hardly necessary to add that in all countries there existed short narrative poems, and later, prose works, which tried to tell an amusing or instructive story. Such works existed in Latin before they appeared in the vernaculars, and collections of them were made, often with the avowed intention of providing moral instruction, called the *exempla*, which served as source material for the later works which appeared for popular consumption.

Until the twelfth century, virtually the only lyric poetry still extant was written in Latin. Most of it was little more than imitation of classical models, using classical meters and language. Only gradually did there appear a new kind of lyric whose meter was based on stress rather than quantity and whose themes were topical and occasionally personal. The eleventh and twelfth centuries were the great age of the secular Latin lyric. Vernacular lyric may be said to begin in the early twelfth century, and in a surprisingly short time a mastery of language and rhythm was developed which has rarely been equaled. Southern France led the way, especially in the formal love song, in which the lady was celebrated by a singer who usually despaired of ever attaining her and consequently spent much of his time complaining of her cruelty and analyzing his own feelings toward her. Such poetry was often of extreme complexity of thought and language and, indeed, often hard to understand. It was widely imitated in Germany, northern France, and Italy, which developed schools of their own. During the later Middle Ages insistence on rigid canons of form tended to produce lyrics which were facile or arid, although there were great exceptions, Villon in France and Petrarch in Italy.

Under the term "lyric" we may also classify the numerous poems of social and political comment written at all periods, but particularly from the end of the twelfth century. The earliest and in many ways the most successful were written in Latin, but there is no lack of them in the vernaculars, especially in France and England.

The rich heritage of classical drama was very largely lost to the Middle Ages. Although the names of the Greek playwrights were known, their plays were not—and even the Latin authors, whose works were available in manuscript throughout the period, were little read and even less understood. Only Terence had any vogue, chiefly because of the purity of his Latin style. It should hardly surprise us, therefore, that imitations of Latin comedies and tragedies are rarely found. There can be no doubt that there were popular presentations in dramatic form in all areas of Europe, a number of which have survived until the present day, but these cannot be called true drama.

Certain features of the liturgy began to develop dramatic elements relatively early during the Middle Ages, and gradually there emerged a dramatic form of spectacle in which certain events of the Holy Year, particularly those of the Passion and Easter, were represented. Saints' lives, too, were good subjects. By the end of the Middle Ages a highly complex series of dramatic spectacles had been developed in all the countries of western Europe except Scandinavia, many of which dealt with the whole history of Christian salvation in a large number of different scenes. The only unity was provided by the fact of Christianity itself. Except for the plays on saints' lives already mentioned, few other subjects were treated. The moralities presented edifying material, often in allegorical form, and there were a few plays on such events as the siege of Troy. Comic scenes developed within some of the religious plays, but there were some other, slapstick plays, popular in origin and formless in construction, which barely qualify as drama. From them much sixteenth-century popular comedy took its origin.

One form of narrative deserves separate mention. The beast epic, as it is usually called, is concerned mostly with the adventures of Renard the fox and his enemy Isengrim the wolf. Many of the adventures are undoubtedly of popular origin, and some come from literary sources, particularly fables. Versions are to be found in French, Dutch, Low German, and Latin, as well as in English, but there can be little doubt that the home of the beast epic was in the Low Countries, northern France, and northwestern Germany. In the later Middle Ages several prose versions appeared. The earlier beast epics, as might be expected, were in verse.

GEOGRAPHICAL AND LINGUISTIC
DIVISIONS

When we think of modern literature, we almost invariably associate it with national groups. English literature does not include American, and there is even hesitation in including Austrian literature under German. In the Middle Ages such national groups either did not exist at all or existed only in a rudimentary form. We can speak only of works written in a particular language. Thus what would now be the area of French literature was divided, during a considerable period of the Middle Ages, into the area of the *langue d'oc*, frequently though inaccurately called Provençal, and the *langue d'oïl*. The former was a literary language of southern France, but it was sometimes used in lyric poetry by persons living elsewhere—Richard the Lion Heart in England and early Italian troubadours. The *langue d'oïl* was a group of northern French dialects which were employed by the *trouvères* and narrative poets of the French court. The *langue d'oc* ceased to be of importance after the thirteenth century. In Germany one dialect, Low Alemanic, spoken in southern Germany, developed a literary language which, with very slight variants, was used by all German poets, whatever their origin, in the late twelfth and thirteenth centuries.

The emergence of Tuscan as the most important dialect of Italy took place considerably later, and in England there was no dominant dialect before the end of the Middle Ages, although much of the greatest work, *e.g.* Chaucer's poems, was written in East Midland. Political circumstances in the Iberian peninsula ensured the dominance of Castilian and Catalan as literary languages. The incapsulated culture of Iceland has preserved most early Scandinavian works in its dialect, although there is much influence of the dialects of the mainland. The relatively scanty remains of medieval Celtic literature are, of course, written in the medieval languages of Ireland and Wales.

It should never be forgotten that one literary language

transcended all national boundaries—medieval Latin. While it would be wrong to say that there was no difference in the Latin used in various countries, the variations offered no difficulty in comprehension. It is often impossible to decide in which country an anonymous medieval Latin work was written. Medieval Latin works and vernacular works were not, however, merely the same types in different languages. The great period of medieval Latin literature antedates the emergence of the vernaculars as fully developed literary instruments. (Use of Latin as the vehicle of learning for philosophy, theology, and science naturally continued.) Furthermore, medieval Latin literature is always consciously learned. It follows classical models closely, it is very conscious of rhetorical rules of style, it is rarely personal or deeply emotional and very rarely nationalistic. Nevertheless the models it offered in style and structure were of the very greatest importance to the developing vernacular literatures.

GENERAL INFLUENCES ON MEDIEVAL LITERATURE

The forces which determined the development of medieval literature naturally varied through the many centuries of its development, but it is possible to indicate some influences which, in varying degrees and manners, affected literature throughout the period. These are the Christian religion, the literature of classical antiquity, the legendary and historical material of the individual peoples, and the mass of orally transmitted stories, often of Eastern origin, available to medieval writers.

The Christian Religion

We are, of course, right when we assume that every writer in western Europe in the Middle Ages was a Christian (except for the early anonymous writers of Germanic materials). We are not right in assuming that all such Christians were pious, ascetic, and orthodox. Christians were just as assorted then as they are now, and orthodoxy was not easy in a period when dogma and even observance were much less clearly defined than they have been since the Council of Trent. The twelfth century in particular seems to have been very liberal —even secular-minded—and formal observance of doctrine

seems to have been enough. Nevertheless, Christianity at all
periods of the Middle Ages was probably more important
than at any later period because it dominated education,
reading, and habits of thought.

Anyone who was given formal education in the Middle
Ages—and most known writers did have considerable formal
education—was instructed by men of the Church. The schools
were primarily designed for potential clerics, and stress was
therefore placed on the study of the Bible, the fathers, and
certain classical authors. The number of works available for
study was inevitably very small, and they were known thoroughly. Knowledge of certain parts of the Bible is obvious in
many writers whose attitudes otherwise are not particularly
Christian. Much more important, however, than particular
verbal knowledge were certain typically Christian attitudes.
The contrast between the City of God and the City of the
World, between the eternal and the temporal, true joys and
vanity, in short between the ideal and the real was firmly
fixed in Christian thought, largely influenced as it was in the
earlier Middle Ages by the towering figure of St. Augustine.
This contrast was felt not only in religious matters but in all
forms of literature, however secular in thought and content
they might be.

Training in Christian ways of thinking had another important result. The terminology of Christianity was so familiar to
any educated man that it was used also in secular matters.
This is particularly true of the terms of biblical exegesis.
Greek and Hebrew scholars had developed techniques of ex-
plaining the texts of Homer and the Scriptures in the light
of customs and morality different from those prevailing when
the works were originally written. These techniques were
taken over by the Christian fathers and developed with great
skill. The Old Testament was interpreted in terms of the New,
and all sacred writings were regarded as having different levels
of meaning. The identification of similar types in the Old and
New Testaments may be called typology; the interpretation
of the sacred writings on different levels is allegorization. The
best-known description of the various levels of scriptural interpretation is to be found in the letter of Dante to Can
Grande. In speaking of the *Divina Commedia*, Dante points
out that a work may be read literally (*ad litteram*), that is,
accepting only the surface meaning, and allegorically, that is,

interpreted according to accepted techniques. Most medieval writers accepted four divisions: literal, allegorical, spiritual, and anagogical. The last two referred to Christian conduct and Christian doctrine.

Clearly such interpreting of texts need not be confined to sacred writings. Stories from pagan literature and popular material could be made to serve a religious and didactic purpose if they were interpreted correctly. The books of *exempla* or moral tales are full of such allegorization, the methods and results of which border on the fantastic. Even more important, perhaps, is the fact that writers and readers of purely secular literature were trained in allegorization, and in reading medieval romances and lyrics we are justified in seeking for meanings which are not obvious. This does not, however, mean that every medieval work is an "allegory" and *must* be interpreted. It may be mentioned that the genre we call "allegory" does *not* need to be interpreted in this way. The author is setting up a general situation by deliberately using personified abstractions. The framework of the allegory is what determines the interpretation to be used (*e.g.* if the terminology is from hunting, the events are to be interpreted in the light of hunting techniques). Such allegories probably became popular precisely because they seemed to be of general application and needed no interpretation.

It hardly need be added that the terminology of Christian thinking, of mysticism, and even of formal theology tended to appear in secular works too. Similarly, the commonly used figures of Christian thought, black and white for evil and good, red for passion and white for innocence, are so common that we must assume that virtually all members of the audience understood them. Nor should we forget that, at least among the educated, there was a knowledge of saints' lives and of apocryphal material which far exceeded what we should expect in a modern layman. Even the drama, a popular rather than learned genre in the late Middle Ages, depends for its effects on such knowledge.

On the other hand we should beware of the facile assumption that all medieval writing is dominated by Christian thought. There was religious, even ascetic, writing in all periods, of course, but the literature of the twelfth and early thirteenth centuries is markedly secular in tone, and much of it pays only lip service to Christianity. For much of the

Middle Ages and at all times for a large fraction of the population, religion was a matter of observance. Preaching and moral instruction were not common until revived by the Dominicans and Franciscans in the early thirteenth century. Doctrine was by no means so clearly determined as it became after the Counter Reformation, and there was a good deal of latitude permitted, especially to laymen, provided that they did not practice doctrines which had been declared heretical. Even such rules as the celibacy of the clergy were not rigidly enforced in the early Middle Ages.

Education and Knowledge

We have already stated that the works of classical authors and those of the Christian fathers formed the basis of formal education. By late classical antiquity liberal education had largely assumed the form which it was to retain throughout the Middle Ages. After learning to read and write, a student studied the subjects of the trivium: grammar, rhetoric, and logic. These terms are rather deceptive, for in the course of his training the student spent a great deal of time on what would now be called literary studies, including prosody and practice in writing prose and verse in Latin. The course in logic was based, in the high Middle Ages at least, on the then known works of Aristotle, the Lesser Organum. Its character changed to some extent as more philosophical works became available. The quadrivium consisted of sciences which were basically mathematical—music, astronomy, arithmetic, and geometry. All of these were more broadly interpreted than would be usual in modern times. The study of music was mostly theoretical and was based on Greek theory until well into the Middle Ages; astronomy included astrology.

Any further study after the completion of the quadrivium was specialized. As the universities developed in the twelfth and thirteenth centuries, they regarded the trivium and quadrivium as a basic arts course, to be succeeded by study in the higher faculties of law, medicine, and philosophy. The highest study of all was theology. A common graphic representation of the process of learning shows a tower with figures at windows indicating the various ascending branches of knowledge, and at the very top is theology.

That many of the writers of secular works in the Middle Ages passed through parts of this educational process is cer-

tain, but it is by no means easy to determine how many
or where they acquired the additional knowledge needed.
It is clear that the men who wrote the poems of the *Edda*,
the Anglo-Saxon epics and lays, the highly complex verse
forms of the troubadours, must have received special training. Yet we have little more than hints of the existence
of schools of secular vernacular poetry until the fourteenth
century. Famous poets no doubt took pupils and passed on
their skills; but as often happens, the advent of real schools
of poetry, particularly in German, led to sterile repetitions
and imitation.

It would be very useful for us to know the extent of the
knowledge of some writers. Interpretations based on "influences" and assumptions of familiarity with works, particularly
theological works, of an earlier era are unconvincing unless
it can be shown that there is at least a reasonable chance of
the author's having read the works in question. Far too often,
modern critics in their enthusiasm ascribe to medieval authors
an amount of recondite learning which would not disgrace a
modern specialized scholar.

Whatever learning a medieval author acquired was assimi-
lated by methods which we would now regard as extremely
clumsy. Books were expensive, slow to produce, and consequently hard to obtain. A good library might contain six hundred volumes, a high proportion of which would be religious
works. Not until the fourteenth century was a method of
effective commercial manuscript production evolved which
could approach that of classical antiquity. The results of this
shortage of books were interesting and important for literature. All writing was designed to be heard. Lyric poetry was
sung, the earlier Germanic epics were recited, and in both
cases oral transmission was the rule. The courtly romances
were probably "book epics" in the sense that written versions
of them were made as soon as they were created, but the audiences probably heard readings by either the author or a professional reciter. Even if a man read them himself, he read
aloud. Hence rhythm and sound were very important. Another
result of the importance of oral delivery and transmission was
considerable variation in texts. Passages were added and
omitted, the order of strophes in lyrics was changed, and
there were a host of minor variations which are best explained
by careless listening and inadequate memory. Even when

a text was copied directly, the copyist was likely to repeat the words aloud and then write them down. Obviously he might well change the spelling in such a procedure or even write the words in his own dialect. The constant turning away from the text led inevitably to the omission of words and whole lines. In the course of a few copyings, major changes could and did appear in the texts. Very rarely is it possible to say with any certainty that a particular text represents what the author actually wrote.

One additional feature of the transmission of medieval works should be mentioned. The formal organization of the modern book—author, title, place, and date of publication—is absent from a medieval manuscript. The title and author often appear at the head of the writing, especially if the work is a classical text, but the dating of a manuscript of a literary work is rare until the fourteenth century. In vernacular works up to the thirteenth century the naming of the author is the exception rather than the rule. If the name appears at all, it may well be found in the text itself. A large number of works have no indication of their author or even, if they are Latin works, of the country in which they were written. Dates are equally uncertain. The style of handwriting will usually determine approximately the date on which the earliest extant version of a work was written down, but naturally there could have been a large number of earlier versions of the same work. Latin poetry is particularly hard to date, since the language does not exhibit the changes which give us a clue to the dating of a vernacular poem. Hence the reader will not be surprised that the large majority of dates given for works in this book are approximate.

We have noted the formal learning available to medieval writers, but it should not be forgotten that the informal knowledge they acquired was equally important. The stories, legends, myths, fairy stories, and tales of adventure which were known to everyone from nobleman to serf came from a large number of different sources. No one knew them all, and every story existed in a large variety of forms. Names and details of plot, setting, and time were often different even when a story was fundamentally the same over a wide area. Many attempts have been made to show that certain branches of medieval literature were deeply influenced by the myths, folklore, and pseudohistory of a particular people. Although some success can be achieved on these lines, the possibility always exists that similar stories from different sources may have been known to the writer. We shall here indicate some of the principal sources of what may be called popular knowledge without attempting to show what precise influence they had on a particular literature.

The most primitive and most persistent source of stories is also the hardest to define. It consists of the mass of mythical material, much of it perhaps nature symbolism, which sometimes becomes part of the formal religion of a people but more often, or at least to a greater extent, develops into fairy stories, superstitions, and old wives' tales. A relatively small number of themes may be found in numerous forms—the lonely voyage, the fool setting out on a journey, the realm of the dead, the contest between light and dark, the fatherless exile. The origins and wide proliferation of such themes have been demonstrated many times by anthropologists, and the attempts to show that a particular theme belongs to a certain ethnic group have usually proved unsuccessful. It hardly needs to be emphasized that the transmission of information of this sort was almost always oral.

Not far removed from the last category, but more formalized and more artistically conceived, were the pseudohistories of the various western European peoples. All the extant accounts show some admixture of historical "fact"—that is, of events whose occurrence can be independently verified—and widespread anthropological motifs. The historical events and their chronology are often distorted and confused, but the existence of some historical background is clear. Much of the material of the so-called national epics falls into this category.

Still further removed from primitive anthropological material but in the last resort still dependent upon it were the "Eastern tales" which were widespread in western Europe in the Middle Ages. We know that all classes of society in Hellenistic and Roman times enjoyed a large number of Greek romances whose chief attractions were the plight of romantic lovers and exotic settings and journeys. Very few of these have survived, but they were transmitted in whole or in part by wandering performers, and sometimes portions were incorporated into respectable and even religious literature. They had themselves drawn heavily upon Near Eastern stories, and thus much Semitic material became known in western Europe even before such collections as the *Thousand and One Nights* were translated. Even the story of the Buddha was well known in the Middle Ages under the title of *Barlaam and Josaphat*.

It is very doubtful whether we shall ever know the relative importance of the various sources of knowledge for medieval writers. We naturally tend to stress the importance of material which we can check, which means written material, particularly since the facile explanation that a particular motif owes its origin to "a lost source orally transmitted" is rightly suspect among scholars. But we cannot afford to forget that for every written work now extant, many have been lost, and that there was such a thing as oral transmission. Every identification of a source, unless the author specifically states it, must remain tentative. And even an author's own statement cannot always be trusted. We are on safer ground if we attempt to show what use an author made of a motif rather than to determine where he found it.

Medieval Literature

A HISTORY AND A GUIDE

Early Germanic Literature

GENERAL

THERE ARE SEVERAL REASONS for beginning a survey of medieval literature with the earliest literature of the Germanic peoples. The most obvious is that they were the first people to produce literature in a vernacular language after the end of the Roman Empire in the west. In the Romance-speaking countries Latin changed slowly into the medieval forms of the modern Romance languages, and it was some time before these languages were felt by the speakers to be independent enough to be used for a literature of their own. Until the tenth century, Latin was the literary language of France, Italy, and those parts of Spain not dominated by the Arabs. Most of the literature was religious and didactic. The secular works were usually little more than imitations of classical models. Something will be said about these later.

The massive wanderings of the Germanic tribes from the third to the sixth centuries produced much material which passed into literature and also a great deal of social and intellectual ferment. No doubt there were in existence a large number of orally transmitted lays of gods and heroes, but modern scholarship avoids the wholesale attempts at reconstruction which the nineteenth century found so attractive. The extant remains of the heroic literature are small and are all of much later date than their earliest versions. It will be convenient to consider them in the following order: Anglo-Saxon literature, Old High German literature, and Old Norse literature. Before treating these separate literatures, we may examine some features which they have in common.

The Hero and His Code

It is dangerous to think of "Germanic" heroes as different from those of other races, but we must remember that we are here attempting to determine the characteristics of the hero as he appears in works of literature. From the relatively limited material at our disposal, it is possible to state with some certainty what qualities were regarded as essential. Firstly he had to be physically strong. No hero could hope to survive unless he could vanquish all human opponents. Even more important, perhaps, was his ability to show courage when his situation was hopeless. One of the commonest themes in Germanic literature is that of the hero, hopelessly outnumbered or overpowered, defying his enemies and with them fate and dying with a laugh on his lips. Such was the supreme test of the hero—his ability to face danger not only calmly and with courage but even with bravado.

This defiance of fate was one aspect of the hero's code of honor. It involved the maintenance of external reputation rather than internal honor in the modern sense. Honor depended on the estimate of others, and hence it was essential to observe strictly certain social obligations. One of these was the bond of blood kinship. Failure to avenge the blood of a kinsman involved certain loss of honor. Even more important was the bond of loyalty to the chief. Tacitus lays great stress on this in his book on the Germans (*Germania*), written at the end of the first century A.D., and the evidence of the extant epics confirms it. The conflict of loyalties was a favorite theme in Germanic literature, for the audience for which it was written could conceive of no greater problem than to be faced with the choice between loyalty to one's kinsman or adopted blood brother and loyalty to one's chief.

It is worthy of note that in none of the Germanic epics is love between the sexes of any significance. The hero's conduct is never affected by considerations of affection for women (other than his blood relations). If he is married, it is family loyalty which sways him, and the highest compliment to his wife is that she behaves like a fellow warrior.

Formal religion is of little importance in the extant Germanic works. *Beowulf*, as we shall see, shows some Christian influence, but the *Hildebrandslied* is entirely secular in tone. The songs of the *Older Edda* are in part concerned with mythology and the gods, but not with any morality which these gods represent. The hero's code is one based entirely on the mores of his society, not on any sense of sin and repentance or the possibility of reward and punishment hereafter.

Prosody and Style

It would be a mistake to regard Germanic poetry as primitive. It shows a very high degree of sophistication, both in language and verse form. If its structure appears loose and discursive to us, we should remember that tastes vary considerably from one generation to another.

The Germanic verse form which is found in the major narrative works of Anglo-Saxon, Norse, and Old High German is based upon the heavy stress accent in each word common to all the Germanic languages. The line contains a fixed number of such stresses, but the number of unstressed syllables may vary widely. There is no end rhyme but a fixed pattern of alliteration of stressed syllables. The verse form of *Beowulf*, which is also that of many other major narrative works, has four main stresses in each line. The line is invariably divided into two half lines with two main stresses. The initial consonant of the third main-stress syllable must alliterate with at least one other stressed syllable in the first half line. Usually it alliterates with more than one. It is possible to show patterns of stresses in the half lines, of which the most common are the descending /x and the rising x/, but such patterns may well be accidental. More important is the theory that each half line may have had a definite musical length—two full beats—with stressed syllables counting as a quarter or half beat and unstressed syllables a quarter or eighth. This theory also envisages quarter-beat pauses at the caesura between the two half lines and at the end of a line. These pauses may have been marked by a note or chord on a harp. There were definite rules about the position of noun and verb in the half lines (noun before verb) and doubtless some rhythmic subtleties which we cannot appreciate.

A further distinguishing mark of Germanic poetry was its use of kennings, or noun substitutes. These usually consisted of two nouns, one possessive, to describe a noun. Neither could be the noun itself. Many of these are well known, such as "whale's path" for "ocean," but they existed in great variety and presupposed some degree of sophistication on the part of the audience as well as of the poet. Circumlocution is as characteristic of Germanic poetry as it is of most early writing. A great deal of the writing was descriptive, and variation was regarded as important.

We may now turn to the literatures of the individual Germanic-speaking countries, beginning with that of Anglo-Saxon England.

ANGLO-SAXON LITERATURE

The Germanic invaders of Britain brought with them a number of stories, which they had learned in their European homeland, and the techniques of Germanic verse-writing.

Before any of their literature could be written down, the various tribes were at least formally converted to Christianity. Britain enjoyed a period of relative stability in the eighth and early ninth centuries, and its monasteries were famous throughout Europe as centers of learning. Even during the Danish invasions, King Alfred of Wessex (849–99) encouraged learning and the use of the vernacular.

There was considerable variation between the Anglo-Saxon dialects of Northumbria, Mercia, Wessex, and Sussex. For prose purposes late West Saxon (of the time of Alfred) is regarded as standard, but the dialects in which the poetry has come down to us vary.

A great deal of the Anglo-Saxon literature which has survived is fragmentary, largely because it has been accidentally preserved when parts of the manuscript on which it was written were used for binding later works. The works which have survived whole or in large part are to be found in four manuscripts. *Beowulf* is in Cotton Vitellius A XV in the British Museum; Caedmon's poems (probably imitations of his style) are in the Junius MS in the Bodleian Library at Oxford; *Widsith* and other short works are in the Exeter Book in Exeter Cathedral, while the Vercelli MS contains among other poems *Andreas* and the *Dream of the Rood*. Of these poems *Beowulf* is by far the most important. The others are interesting as cultural monuments, but even the hot enthusiasm of some scholars cannot make them into great poetry. *Widsith*, written probably between 650 and 700, is an account by a *scop*, or minstrel, of his highly imaginary wanderings. The name means "Far Traveler." It is little more than a list of names. *Waldere* (c. 750) is a fragment of the German Walter of Aquitaine story (see *Waltharius*, p. 124f.), which was found on the flyleaf of a religious manuscript. The poem consists of two speeches, one by Hildeguth, Walter's betrothed, encouraging him, and one of defiance by Walter himself. A similar fragment is the *Fight at Finnsburg*, a short extract from an account of a blood feud between Danes and Frisians mentioned also in *Beowulf*. It also dates from the mid-eighth century.

Beowulf

Beowulf is one of the great poems of the Middle Ages. It has come down to us in only one manuscript, and even this was damaged in the eighteenth century, fortunately after a copy had been made. It is interesting to speculate how many such manuscripts did not survive. The manuscript was written in the tenth century, but the poem is much earlier. Critics are of differing opinions about details, but it is fairly generally agreed that the extant version was written down sometime in the eighth century in Mercia or Northumbria. Certain references in the poem can be dated, particularly the allusion to Hygelac, whose defeat at the hands of the Franks is mentioned by the French historian Gregory of Tours in his *History of the Franks* as taking place in the year 520. Thus the poem must have been written down after this.

The story is concerned with three episodes in the life of the hero, Beowulf, two of them in his youth and the other his last exploit. A considerable amount of other material appears in the numerous digressions. The story opens with an account of the ancestry of Hrothgar, chief of the Scyldings, who has built a great hall, Heorot. The joyous life here is disturbed by the incursions of Grendel, a monster from the lake bottom, who snatches sleeping men from the hall and devours them. Beowulf, son of Ecgtheow, a Geat from southern Sweden, hears of this and brings his men by sea to Hrothgar's lands in Denmark. He is challenged by the coast guard but well received by the king. Only when Unferth attempts to discredit him is his anger aroused enough to make him boast of his own exploits. When Grendel comes in the night, he devours one warrior before Beowulf, disdaining the use of weapons, tears out his arm, wounding him mortally. The monster returns to his lake to die and the warriors celebrate by feasting and listening to the tales of Sigmund, Heremod, and Finn.

But the next night their rejoicing ceases, for Grendel's mother comes to the hall to avenge her son. She seizes Aeschere, a close friend of Hrothgar, and returns to her lair. Beowulf, who has not slept in the hall, hears of this and sets out in pursuit. With a fine sword, Hrunting, offered by Unferth, he plunges into the horrors of the lake and is pulled by Grendel's mother into her waterless cave. The borrowed sword proves useless, and Beowulf is in difficulties until he seizes a huge sword from the wall and kills the monster. The blade melts, and the hero brings back to his despondent followers only the hilt and the severed head of Grendel. Once again there is joy in Heorot. Loaded with gifts, Beowulf returns to Hygelac, his king, and shares his gifts with him. He prophesies the coming of internal strife in Denmark.

The second part of the poem shows a completely different situation. Hygelac is dead and so is his son Headred. Beowulf has ruled the Geats wisely for fifty years. Now a dragon, angered at the pilfering by an escaped slave of a treasure he was guarding, ravages Beowulf's lands, and the aged hero must once again defend his men. With an iron shield to defend him against the beast's fiery breath, he attacks the dragon. All his followers except Wiglaf flee, but together the two kill the dragon. But Beowulf is mortally wounded. He gives his armor and ornaments to the faithful Wiglaf, orders the treasure to be given to the Geats, asks for cremation near the sea, and dies. Wiglaf pours scorn on the men who had deserted them and carries out all Beowulf's commands, except that the treasure is once again buried.

It is clear that the principal interest of *Beowulf* lies in the character and prowess of its hero. He is a great man, magnificently endowed with physical strength, courage, the power of leadership, generosity, and loyalty. Great care is taken by the poet to introduce episodes which will illustrate these characteristics. Further, in his last battle, he shows the most important of all qualities for a Germanic hero, contempt for certain death. The central character holds the story together through all its digressions. Yet only three incidents in his very long life form the main substance of the poem. These incidents are exemplary. They show the power of the young, strong man to overcome evil as personified in monsters vaguely described. As often happens, the second encounter is a repetition of the first but on a more terrible scale. The last incident shows an old man who is the shepherd of his people and must fight to save them, not to gain glory as the younger Beowulf had. This method of selection is highly effective, for it shows us the complete warrior-king.

Yet there is more to the epic than this. Clearly we see throughout the struggle between the forces of light and darkness, good and evil. The bright feasting hall, Heorot, is contrasted with the outer darkness of the mere of Grendel, the king and his thanes with the monsters of the deep. These islands of civilization are constantly under pressure from the forces of destruction, not least those which are in their own hearts. Beowulf's own death is actually due to the greed for money of one of his subjects. Buried treasure was traditionally associated with the devil even by Christians, and there is no reason to doubt that the dragon which sleeps guarding the treasure but is aroused to ravage when the hoard is pilfered was thought by the poet to be the power of evil which lurks in gold.

The messenger who reports Beowulf's death muses on the coming destruction of the Geats by the Swedes. There is a foreknowledge of decline throughout the poem—of the destruction of the Scyldings, of the end of the Geats. For the people cannot stay strong unless there is a great leader, as we see when they run away when Beowulf is not there to hold them at the mere or when he appears lost at the dragon's cave.

Beowulf, for all its concentration on one man, is a political and didactic poem, as Homer's *Iliad* is political and didactic. It holds up for examination heroes and peoples and warns by example. It contrasts men who are great and petty, worthy and weak. The author believes strongly that only with great leaders can a people be great.

There has been much discussion of the relation between the pagan and Christian elements of the poem. It should be stated at once that the culture and morality are thoroughly Germanic. Beowulf is buried in accordance with pagan rites. There are references to Cain, to the "true religion," to "God," but none specifically to Christ, to the Trinity, or to basic Christian concepts. No doubt the author knew about Christianity—he could hardly avoid such knowledge—and he may well have been a Christian. But he was working with non-Christian material and, unlike some later authors, he did not attempt to reshape it. Possibly Beowulf's character shows more charity than might be expected of a Germanic warrior, possibly the incident of the dragon's hoard shows the influence of Christian hatred of avarice. But such incidents are at least equally well explained by pre-Christian beliefs. It is certainly true that the poet seems to assume a monotheistic religion and a hero who realizes his debt to his Creator. But the God he describes is closer to the one of the Old Testament than to the one of the New. In any case Beowulf has no doubt that it is his career on this earth which is important. Humility, meekness, and poverty are not virtues which he seeks.

The author was a master of the elements of Germanic poetry. His use of meter and epithet is superb. Many of his descriptions—particularly the sea voyage and arrival of Beowulf among the Scyldings—are excellent. He was a master poet, and from every point of view *Beowulf* ranks very high among the epic works of the Middle Ages.

Religious and Miscellaneous Verse

As might be expected in a people converted relatively recently to Christianity, the great bulk of literature produced by Anglo-Saxon authors—who were themselves almost invariably clerics—was religious and didactic in tone and purpose. It is not of very great interest as literature to a modern reader, except for a few lyrical poems. In point of both time and importance Caedmon (c. 650–80) should be mentioned first. Bede tells the story of how the humble lay brother at a monastery in Northumbria was ordered in a dream to sing the praise of the Lord and how his songs so impressed the experts that he was assumed to have a divine gift. He joined the abbey at Whitby and composed until his death. The nine-line hymn mentioned by Bede is extant. Several other poems ascribed to Caedmon in the manuscripts are probably by imitators.

Among the "Caedmonian" poems is a long account of the war in Heaven, the fall of Lucifer, Creation, the fall of Adam and Eve, and other events up to the incomplete sacrifice of Isaac. Although it is called *Genesis*, much of the material is taken from the Apocrypha. Actually it consists of two distinct parts, *Genesis* A (lines 1–234 and 852–2935) and an interpolation (lines 235–851), called *Genesis* B, which is not of the Caedmon school. The inserted portion is concerned with Satan and is a powerful narrative. A Caedmonian *Exodus* tells of Moses, who has many characteristics of a Germanic chief, and his struggle with the Egyptians. *Daniel* A (c. 700) and *Daniel* B (ninth century) and *Christ and Satan* are also Caedmonian poems.

The other great name in lyric and elegiac poetry is Cynewulf, whose name appears in runic letters in four works. He was an Anglian cleric of the late eighth century, but nothing more is known of him. The poems which bear his name are *The Fates of the Apostles*, versified lives of the twelve, *Christ II*, an account of the Ascension, *Juliana*, a poem based on the life of St. Juliana, martyred during the reign of

Maximian, and *Elene*, an account of the discovery of the True
Cross by Helena, mother of Constantine.

Cynewulf's work is distinguished by its use of allegory and
metaphor. He is fond of the traditional figures of life as a
voyage and the attempt of evil to capture the fortress of
virtue, and he handles these with skill and fervor.

Several poems are extant which may be called "Cyne-
wulfian." Even if they are not by him, they are written in
his style. *Guthlac* is another life of a holy man, this time
English; *Christ I* and *Christ III* deal respectively with the
coming of Christ in eleven Advent hymns and with Dooms-
day, a popular subject with early poets. The *Dream of the
Rood* is an account of a dream in which the Cross itself tells
the history of the Crucifixion and begs the dreamer to be
aware of the importance of the Rood. The *Physiologus* is a
fragmentary version of the account of allegorized animals
found all over Europe, and the *Phoenix* is an allegorical poem
where the ever rejuvenated bird stands for the immortal soul.

A few anonymous narrative and elegiac poems and fragments should be included to complete this survey of Anglo-
Saxon poetry. The *Andreas* of about 800 is an account of how
St. Andrew rescued Christians from the cannibal Merinedo-
nians and then converted the heathens. It has many elements
of Germanic poetry in style and action. *Judith* (ninth century)
is a 350-line fragment of a poem about the Jewish heroine
who killed Holofernes. *Deor*, a poem of six stanzas of the late
ninth century, is an account of famous misfortunes of Germanic history, which the poet recites as a kind of consolation
for his own loss of patronage. *Wanderer* and *Seafarer* are
both allegorical voyage poems.

Two battle poems of vigor came out of the Danish warfare of the tenth century—*Battle of Brunanburh* of about 937
and *Battle of Maldon* of about 991. The former describes
Athelstan's victory over the Scots and Norsemen, the latter
the glorious defeat of Byrhtnoth of Essex by the Vikings.

Apart from some riddles in the Exeter Book, magic charms,
and gnomic verse, this is the total of Anglo-Saxon verse. It is
probably a fraction of what was actually composed. As might
be expected, the literary worth of many of the extant poems
has been exaggerated. Only *Beowulf* is a really important
work, but some of the lyric and elegiac material is good
enough to prove the existence of competent poets and a tradi-

tion of style and craftsmanship worthy to compare with any contemporary literature and with all but the best of what was to follow.

Anglo-Saxon prose is not strictly literature. Its most famous monuments are the translations of King Alfred, the Anglo-Saxon Chronicle, and the religious homilies of Aelfric (c. 955–1020) and Wulfstan, who died in 1023 after a distinguished ecclesiastical career.

OLD HIGH GERMAN LITERATURE

As might be expected, there are marked resemblances between the literatures of the Anglo-Saxons and those of the Continental Germans. Both were deeply influenced by the traditions of their common Germanic past and the artistic forms it had developed. Both used literature in large part for Christian didactic purposes. But the Continental Germans were converted to Christianity much later than the inhabitants of England—actually by Winfrith, or Bonifatius, himself from England—and they remained in a state of political chaos for a much longer period. There is no doubt that Germanic lays existed on the Continent as they did in Britain, but it is not until the relatively short period of political stability under Charlemagne and his immediate successors that any literature began to be written down.

A great deal of what survives from the late eighth and early ninth centuries merely indicates how recently the conversion of many tribes had taken place, for it consists mostly of prayers, catechisms, and vernacular versions of gospel harmonies. There is no need to dwell further on them. Some of the religious pieces have literary merit, and we shall speak of those later. By far the most interesting as well as the most ancient monument of Continental Germanic literature is the *Hildebrandslied*. After that it will be best to consider the longer religious poems and then the minor religious and didactic works.

The *Hildebrandslied*

A lucky accident preserved a 67-line fragment of the *Hildebrandslied* in the flyleaf of the *Liber sapientiae* at Kassel. After World War II both leaves disappeared, and only one was recovered. Fortunately there are ample facsimiles.

The text of the poem has probably produced more controversy and discussion than any work of comparable length in any European language. The text is clearly corrupt, for it exhibits an extraordinary mixture of dialect forms ranging from Upper German to Anglo-Saxon. However, there are many theories about the original, for some critics believe it to be basically High German with Low German forms imported by the scribe; others believe exactly the opposite. One theory holds it to be Langobardic, which is possible but hard to prove, since we have very little literary material in that dialect. It is quite certain that the form we possess is a third, fourth, or tenth copy of the original and that this original itself is a version of a much older, orally transmitted poem. The corruption of the language has also distorted the verse form. There is no doubt that the poem is written in four-beat alliterative Germanic verse, but there are more and greater irregularities than can be accounted for by carelessness or even incompetence.

The story is derived from the period of the tribal wanderings, and its main characters appear frequently in Germanic legend. The essential conflict, however, is much older and can be found in the legends of many cultures. It is the meeting of father and son on the field of battle after they have been separated for many years and the fatal consequences of this encounter.

A few lines are almost certainly missing from the *Hildebrandslied*. Hildebrand and his son Hadubrand are shown meeting, each the chosen champion of his army. In accordance with custom Hildebrand asks the young man about his family and learns to his horror that he is facing the son whom he left behind as an infant when he fled with his lord Theodoric (Dietrich) from the wrath of Odoacer (Ottakar). Now he is fighting with Theodoric in the army of Attila the Hun. Hildebrand, without revealing his identity, attempts to conciliate Hadubrand but is scorned. He laments the hard fate which forces him to kill his son or be killed himself, and the fight begins. The poem breaks off, but later versions show that the boy is winning until his father shouts his battle cry, and the boy drops his guard and is killed.

The conflict here, as so often, is between two loyalties, that of blood and that of duty. Hildebrand cannot refuse to fight his son, because he has been chosen to represent his army, and refusal would be tantamount to defeat—unless there is mutual agreement not to fight. Hildebrand fails to achieve this agreement and has to fight.

The poem is in many ways more dramatic than narrative. Its style is terse, and it is composed largely of dialogue. A great deal of action and recapitulation is compressed into its 67 lines, and this very economy shows that the lay is a different type from an epic. No author could have composed an epic like *Beowulf* merely by stringing together lays like *Hildebrand*. There is the *material* for an epic here, but it would require the epic expansion which characterizes *Beowulf*.

Brief though the poem is, it contains a great deal of the material of which Germanic legend was composed. The setting of strife between Attila and some German tribes is, of course, historical. But it took place in the second quarter of the fifth century. Dietrich, the greatest of German heroes, is here shown, as often, in the service of Attila, having been exiled by Ottakar. Historically Ottakar or Odoacer was defeated by Theodoric or Dietrich, who ruled Italy for the first quarter of the sixth century as Theodoric the Great. This historically inaccurate representation of the most important figures of the tribal wanderings persists throughout medieval Germanic literature. It is worth noting, however, that Attila's character varies. Poems in the southeastern, Gothic tradition show him as a kindly, beneficent ruler. Those in the northwestern and particularly Scandinavian tradition depict him as a bloodthirsty tyrant.

Religious Works

The *Hildebrandslied* is the sole survivor of its type. There is a story that Charlemagne had the lays of his Germanic ancestors collected but that the collection was destroyed by Louis the Pious. It may be so. In any event the remaining Old High German literature is almost all of a pious, didactic nature. Two long poems, the *Heliand* (c. 830) and the *Evangelienbuch* (c. 870) of Otfried of Weissenburg are alike in telling the life of Christ in vernacular form. They both use Latin gospel harmonies or lives of Christ made up from the three synoptic gospels as their base. Yet in other respects they are widely different: The *Heliand* uses the meter and language of the Germanic lay and concentrates on incidents in the life

of Christ, particularly on incidents in which His heroic stature
can be emphasized. Some critics have thought that the poem
is an attempt to make Christ appear as a Germanic hero and
thus more palatable to newly converted chiefs. This is unlikely. The author was so steeped in the traditions of Germanic epic that he could probably not write any other way.

Otfried's work is much more formally religious. It is written in four-beat rhyming couplets clearly based on Latin meter
and is the work of a monk trained in theology. It includes a
great deal of formal allegorization or explanation of biblical
incident in the light of theology. Otfried is conscious of being
a pioneer in the use of vernacular for religious poetry, and
it must be said in his favor that his handling of language and
rhyme improves as he gets deeper into the poem.

A few other short poems deserve brief mention. The
Muspilli is a fragment telling of the end of the world and
the battle of Antichrist and Elijah. The elements of description have been variously viewed as coming from Germanic,
Slavic, or even Hebrew sources. Certainly the description of
the Day of Judgment is very powerful. The *Ludwigslied* is a
neat historical poem telling of the victory of Louis III over
the Norsemen in 881 at Saucourt. Since he died the next year,
while the poem shows him still alive, an exact dating of the
work is possible. Louis is shown as gaining his victory entirely
because of his dependence on and faith in God, but the
action is well described.

There are some Old High German translations of prose
works, such as the gospel harmony of Tatianus, but the only
prose work worth recording is the pedagogical writing of
Notker Labeo. In his commentaries on Boethius and Martianus Capella he was forced to find vernacular equivalents
for the technical terms of theological Latin. He is thus in a
sense the father of German prose.

Relatively little was written in the eleventh century in Old
High German, a period during which the language underwent
major changes. The works of the twelfth century show us a
different language and a different spirit.

OLD NORSE LITERATURE

It is convenient to discuss Old Norse literature at this
point because a considerable amount of it is connected with

the heroic tradition represented in the *Hildebrandslied* and *Beowulf*. Nevertheless it must be recognized that the extant written remains date from the thirteenth century on. Most of our knowledge of Old Norse literature comes from works written in Iceland. The reason for this is that there was a large immigration of nobles from Norway to Iceland in the reign of Harold Fairhair. The immigrants were conservative— they had fled because they resisted Harold's desire for central authority—and they remained pagan longer than other parts of Scandinavia. Musicians and poets were held in high honor among them and the nobles themselves wrote poetry. Hence Iceland preserved and cherished a great deal from the past, and even when it had become Christian, scribes wrote down pagan works in numerous manuscripts.

Eddas

Of these by far the most famous are the *Older* or *Poetic Edda*, a manuscript of about 1270 containing twenty-seven songs of gods and heroes, and the *Younger* or *Prose Edda* of Snorri Sturluson. The *Older Edda* is a collection of poems of very different periods whose dating is a source of contention among scholars. The earliest probably go back to the eighth century, the latest scarcely precede the making of the collection. The collection falls into two parts, mythological poems and heroic poems. The mythological group deals with the adventures of some gods, *e.g.* Thor and figures such as Wayland the Smith, but there is no attempt at a complete mythology. The *Völuspá*, a prophecy, is a kind of cosmogony or description of creation and its ultimate destruction, but it is not easy to interpret clearly. Some of the poems are didactic, consisting of sayings, like *Hávamál* ("Sayings of Odin"). More easily placed in context are the songs of heroes, for many of them have parallels elsewhere. The great majority of them go back to the migrations of the Germanic tribes for their subject matter and spirit. Even though they may be original Icelandic compositions, their existence postulates knowledge of old, perhaps Norwegian versions. The three lays about Helgi are thought to be Norwegian. They tell how he won his bride Sigrún, a valkyrie, but only at the cost of killing her father and brothers. A surviving brother, with Odin's help, kills Helgi, and Sigrún dies of grief. The other heroic lays are all, in one way or another, connected with

Sigurd the Volsung. *Reginsmál* and *Fáfnismal* tell of his killing the dragon and gaining possession of the hoard of cursed gold. He gains the power to understand birds by eating Fafnir the dragon's heart. In the *Sigrdrífumál* he awakes the sleeping valkyrie who may or may not be the same as Brynhildr. In another song, the *Grípisspá*, Sigurd meets Brynhildr at a house and has a child by her. He is made to forget her by a potion given by Guthrún's mother, Grimhildr. Then he rides through the flame wall and wins Brynhildr for his brother-in-law Gunnar. Later Brynhildr and Guthrún quarrel and the former brings about Sigurd's death. She commits suicide in the flames of his pyre. Guthrún marries Atli, who kills her brothers when they visit her and upon whom she exacts frightful vengeance, serving him his son to eat and then killing him.

Several things should be noted about these poems. Firstly, they often overlap in subject matter (for example *Atlamál*, the longest of them, and *Atlakvitha*). Secondly, they are by no means entirely narrative. A great many of them contain precepts and didactic sayings, of which perhaps the most striking example is the stream of advice given by Sigrdrífa to Sigurd when he wakens her. Thirdly, the poems are terse to the point of obscurity. If it were not for the prose introductions and our knowledge of their content from other sources, they would be almost impossible to understand. Although they use various forms, all their verse is based on the alliterative principles mentioned in connection with Anglo-Saxon poetry. There is a tendency to stanzaic form. Kennings, as might be expected, are common.

Because of the similarity of its subject matter, it will be convenient to mention here the very different *Younger* or *Prose Edda*. This is a work by an author about whom we know some facts. Snorri Sturluson was of a prominent and wealthy family. The youngest of three brothers, he was born in 1179 and educated by Jón Loptsson of Oddi, son of a Norwegian princess. He married at twenty and, with rich estates, was able to live well and take his full share in politics. In 1218 he was in Norway and Sweden, where he mediated a family quarrel. Later, when Earl Skúli Bártharson rebelled against Hákon of Norway, he unfortunately took the wrong side, fled to Iceland, but was murdered at Hákon's orders in 1241. His works certainly include the *Prose Edda* and the *Heimskringla* ("Earth's Circle") and perhaps *Egils saga*.

The *Prose Edda* is a sophisticated work, designed to provide instruction for professional poets. It includes sections on mythology and diction and a key to meters. The latter two are highly technical demonstrations, in verse, of the rhetorical and metrical material available to the poet, but the part on mythology contains almost all the material about gods and heroes which we think of in connection with Norse literature —the story of Baldr, of Odin, of the death of the gods. Further it contains a much more lucid account of the stories of Sigurd and Brynhildr than that in the *Poetic Edda*.

The *Heimskringla* is an account in prose of the kings of Norway. One third of it is devoted to the reign of St. Olaf, the king who introduced Christianity and was obviously admired by Snorri. *Egils saga* is the story of the adventures of Egill Skalla-Grímsson, a poet of the tenth century. His uncle was killed by Harold, king of Norway, and he conducted, with strength and cunning, a lifelong feud against Norway. He is shown as crafty and avaricious, dark in feature but brave in battle. He survives innumerable encounters with his enemies and lives to a great age. The work is written, not unnaturally, from the Icelandic point of view. As a saga it is well done, full of incident—and speeches—and presents a brilliant picture of Icelandic culture.

Skaldic Poetry

Before turning to the other, very numerous, sagas, we should mention another kind of highly technical poetry, the skaldic. This was essentially court poetry, composed and performed by professionals. A great deal of it consists of poems of formal praise of a ruler and particularly of his deeds, suitably embroidered. Occasional verse also appears and some love poetry. Dream poems and curses are frequently found. The forms of verse used were often highly complicated. The basic system of alliteration between two half lines is always present, but the number of syllables is often fixed for a particular type. Rhyme between the ends of the two half lines is also used. Some types demand a feminine ending (long followed by short syllable). The *dróttkvætt*, the most complicated type, has eight-verse (*i.e.* four full-line) stanzas. Such sophisticated forms naturally encouraged the skalds to show their skill by producing intricate variations of rhyme and alliteration. In language and style, too, great skill was shown.

Kennings were, of course, frequent, and also the *heiti*, a poetical substitute for a prose word, such as "brand" for "sword," and complicated adjectival epithets abound.

The first important skaldic poet was Egill Skalla-Grímsson (c. 910–90), already mentioned. Part of his stirring career was the making of skaldic verse, some fifty stanzas of which are preserved in the *Egils saga*. The most famous poem is the *Höfuthlausn* ("Head Ransom"), a poem in praise of King Eiríkr, which apparently did save his head when he was captured. Others are laments for two dead sons (*Sonatorrek*, c. 961) and a poem in honor of a friend, *Arinbjarnarkvitha*. All show the skill and vigor we would expect from the hero of the saga.

Other poets worth mentioning are Kormákr Ögmundarson, (tenth century) a love poet; Hallfrethr Óttarsson (c. 965–1010), a heathen who became the close friend of King Olaf, sang his praises, and ultimately became a Christian himself; and most important, Sighvatr Thórtharson (c. 995–1045). The last poet was also a close friend of King Olaf, many of whose deeds he celebrated and for whom he executed diplomatic missions. He was away when the king was killed. His *Austrfararvísur* is a poem on a journey to the east (Sweden), describing incidents in his travels. His best poem is the *Bergsöglisvísur*, a poem of advice addressed to Olaf's son Magnus in 1038. The pre-Christian period of skaldic poetry had been, perhaps intentionally, heavily mythological. The twelfth and thirteenth centuries, by contrast, constitute a classical period when high style rather than mythological content was appreciated. The best practitioner of the art, himself a Christian, was Einar Skúlason, the seventy-one stanzas of whose poem *Geisli* ("Sun Ray"; 1153), in praise of Saint and King Olaf, are extant. The thirteenth century saw the decline of skaldic court poetry. Influences from other countries made it seem archaic and outmoded, but its influence persisted for centuries, largely because of the work of Snorri Sturluson.

Christian Poetry

The coming of Christianity inevitably meant that Christian poetry would be written. In Iceland, as earlier in Germany, poets continued to use the old meters and stylistic forms. Gamli Kanoki wrote the poem *Harmsól* ("Sun of Sorrow"), about Christ and the Day of Judgment. *Plácítusdrápa* is a martyr poem of the trial and death of a faithful Christian and his family. There are some translations of hymns and even of the Merlin prophecies of Geoffrey of Monmouth, but the two best sacred poems are the *Sólarljóth* ("Song of the Sun") of about 1200 and the *Lilja* ("Lily"), composed 1343–4 by Eysteinn Ásgrímsson. The *Sólarljóth* is put in the mouth of a father returned from death. It is therefore a vision poem, of life to death, of the sinking sun, of the flight of the soul and its perils, and of Heaven and Hell. Although clearly didactic in purpose the work derives its value from its brilliant imagery.

Eysteinn was a monk, apparently of somewhat violent character, who divided his life between Iceland and Norway. His poem *Lilja*, of one hundred stanzas, is of a type common in other countries—a brief history of the course of Salvation from Creation to Last Judgment. There is considerable mention of the Virgin (the Lily), and the last part of the poem is praise of her and a prayer for her help. Eysteinn writes in simpler language than his predecessors, abandoning the kenning, but still keeps a dignified style. A considerable amount of sacred poetry, much of it anonymous, continued to be written in the fourteenth and fifteenth centuries.

There were other types of poetry in Iceland from the twelfth century on. The *danz* was a *carole*-type poem imported, in form at least, from France. The rhyme schemes and metrical forms so used were later employed in metrical romances and ballads, but they were combined with the use of kennings and other characteristics of skaldic poetry. One interesting variant in this group in the *Skítharíma,* a parody in which a man dreams he was entertained by the old gods, falls out with them, and fights them. The ballads often have foreign settings, *e.g.* Denmark—or their characters travel in the other world or meet supernatural characters.

The best and most characteristic of Norse poetry was the Eddic and skaldic. We must now turn to the other famous branch of Icelandic literary production, the sagas.

Prose Sagas

Iceland is unique in medieval Europe—with the possible exception of Ireland—in having some of its most important literature in prose. The kings' sagas are, as might be expected, prose accounts of great rulers. The first extant saga, and that only in fragments, is the oldest *Ólafs saga helga*, from which Styrmir Kárason made up his *Ólafs saga helga* about 1207 and from which the long thirteenth-century legendary *Ólafs saga helga* is derived. *Sverris saga*, by the abbot Karl Jonsson, is the life of a king contemporary with the author and partially dictated to him by his subject between 1185 and 1188. A survey of Norwegian history appears in *Noregs Konungasögur* about 1220.

After 1200, isolated sagas were combined into long histories, such as *Morkinskinna* (c. 1220), which covers the period 1035–1177, intermingling chronicle with anecdote; *Fagrskinna*, again on Norwegian history of about the same period; and the *Heimskringla* of Snorri, already discussed. There are also histories of the rulers of Denmark and the Orkney Islands. The period of kings' sagas comes to an end with Sturla Thórtharson's story of King Hákon. Born in 1214, Sturla was Snorri Sturluson's nephew. He wrote his saga at the request of Magnus, his successor, and after completing it, he stayed in Norway to draft laws for Iceland. Later he wrote the (lost) saga of his patron Magnus.

The kings' sagas are the vernacular equivalent of Latin chronicles, by which they were greatly influenced. They are historical within the limits of possibility, for too great frankness even about a dead ruler could cause trouble. It is interesting to note that they often include fragments of skaldic poetry to support their authenticity.

The other types of sagas have much less claim to consideration as history but much more to literary merit. The *fornaldar sagas*, dealing with heroic, even mythological heroes, are the oldest, followed by the kings' sagas already treated, and the family sagas. It should be realized that any account of events is technically a saga, even if it is a translation of a fictional poem, such as an Arthurian romance. There has been much dispute about the composition of the sagas, especially the family sagas. Some critics argue for a long oral tradition, others for an early written form. Recently the historicity of the family sagas has been questioned and the theory advanced that they were largely fictional and do not, in spite of their genealogies and profusion of place names, describe the actual history of Icelandic families. Whatever the truth of this, many sagas are brilliant works of art. Their style is unpoetical and plain, although skaldic verses are often quoted, but pungent and direct. Their code of morality is clear and their purpose is to show their heroes gaining honor and dying nobly. These heroes are surrounded by equally brave wives and retainers. There is a great deal of fighting and bloodshed and revenge for loss of honor and—what amounts to the same thing—loss of kinsmen, which is a very common motif. The stage is crowded with characters and the relationships are always told in full. Fictional or not, these are works dedicated to a people proud of its ancestry and its society.

The *fornaldar sagas* take most of their subject matter from the heroic past common to Scandinavia and the other Germanic countries, or from the wanderings of the Viking raiders. One of the latter tells of the exploits of Hrolf, a fifth-century Danish king, another those of King Hálfr of Norway, but best known is the saga of *Ragnar lothbók*, a Dane of the ninth century whose laughing defiance of death is characteristic of the saga hero. Of the heroic sagas of the distant past, by far the most important is the *Völsunga saga*. This work has obviously drawn on the Eddic poems for a great deal of its subject matter, but some of the incidents have no parallel there or in the work of Snorri Sturluson. A brief account is given here of its contents, since it is the clearest account of the Scandinavian version of the story of Sigurd, Brynhildr, and Guthrún. We are told how Sigmund, the son of Volsung, escaped when his father and brothers died at the hands of Siggeir, who had married Sigmund's sister Signy. Sigmund lived in the woods, and Signy sent her two children in turn to be tested by him for bravery. Both failed and were killed. Then Signy herself came to him in disguise and had by him a child, Sinfjötli, who was brave and strong. The three took revenge on Siggeir, and Sigmund recovered his kingdom. Adventures of his son Helgi by Borghild and of Sinfjötli are recounted. Then we are told of his marriage with Hjordis, daughter of Eylimi. Another suitor, Lyngi, brings an army against him. Sigmund is killed because of the intervention of Odin, who shatters his sword. Hjordis takes the pieces, which her son Sigurd later forges into the sword Gram. Sigurd has been instructed by Regin, a dwarf, who teaches him the trade of smith—for his own purposes. For Regin wishes to get a gold treasure from his brother Fafnir, who guards it in the form of a dragon. The treasure was blood money provided by the gods Odin, Loki, and Hoenir for the death of the son of Hreidmar, Regin's father. The dwarf Andwari, from whom they had extorted the gold, put a curse on it. This curse is now fulfilled. Sigurd kills Fafnir but, while roasting his heart, touches some of the blood on his lips, which lets him understand the speech of birds. They tell him that Regin proposes to kill him, and Sigurd disposes of the dwarf.

After seeing flames on a hill, Sigurd rides through and awakes a valkyrie, Brynhildr, who teaches him much and to whom he plights his troth. Sigurd now comes to the court of Gjuki and, after a drink of forgetfulness, marries Guthrún. By again riding through the flames he wins Brynhildr for Gunnar, Guthrún's brother. Later a quarrel between the two queens brings to light Sigurd's winning of Brynhild. She demands revenge, and Sigurd is treacherously killed by Guthorm, Gunnar's brother.

In spite of her sorrow, Guthrún is persuaded to marry Atli (Attila), king of the Huns. To obtain their treasure, he treacherously invites her brothers to his palace. Guthrún sends a warning, but they go. After a great fight, Gunnar and Högni are captured. Both show laughing defiance of death. Gunnar even plays the harp with his toes while in a pit of adders. Guthrún revenges herself by serving Atli his sons for a meal and then killing him.

The grim horror of the story needs little comment. Revenge is the principle motif—of Brynhildr on Sigurd, of Guthrún on Atli. Blood kinship is more important than marital love, and honor more important than anything. Atli is a dark, treacherous figure, and gold is the bane of mankind, as it is in the last scene of *Beowulf*. Mythological elements are strong, but the last part of the story goes back to the historical conflict between Burgundians and Huns.

We find many of these same traits in the family sagas, the oldest of which date to about 1200–20. They are very numerous and vary greatly in length and treatment. The *Íslendinga þættir* are short stories about various Icelanders. *Egils saga* has already been mentioned. Two books important as sources should be mentioned, the *Landnámabók* of Styrmir fróthi and the work of the same name by Sturla Thórtharson, dated respectively 1222 and about 1270. A few of the more important family sagas are listed here. The *Laxdæla saga* (about 1230) tells of the four loves of Guthrún and of the interplay of jealousy which causes murder, revenge, and more murder.

Gísla saga is the story of two outlawed brothers. Again there is murder and revenge, but one feature is that Gísli's wife, Authr, stands by her husband and avenges him on her brother —although she arranges also to avenge the brother! There is a good deal of Christian influence in the poem. Some of the best and most famous of the sagas belong to the latter part of the thirteenth century. Of these the longest and best known is *Njáls saga* (c. 1300). The tale is very complicated, with numerous side plots and secondary characters. The first part tells, with considerable digression, how Gunnar married Hallgerd, a proud and weak woman, who attempts to stir up trouble between the friends Gunnar and Njál and with Otkel and others, who finally join against Gunnar, force him into exile, and kill him on his return. Njál is out of Iceland for a time in the second part. His sons are falsely implicated in the misdeeds of Thrain and Hrappr. Their demands for redress are scorned, and they kill their adversaries. Njál adopts Hoskuld, Thrain's son, as part reparation, but this leads only to jealousy when Hoskuld reaches high office, and he is killed by Njál's other sons. Revenge follows, culminating in the death of Njál and his wife and sons.

Kári, Njál's friend, brings a suit before the assembly, but this degenerates into a battle. A settlement is accepted by all except Kári, who carries out acts of revenge until finally reconciled with Hoskuld's family.

This brief summary does no justice to the complexity and intricate structure of the work, nor the pageantry with which the life of the heroic tenth century is described, both in peace and war. So realistic and convincing is the storytelling that it is easy to believe that it is a description of actual events. Unlike many saga writers, the author has a keen eye for variations of character, from the vicious to the heroic, the holy to the grotesque.

Gunnlaugs saga is much simpler and has fewer characters. It tells the deeds of the viking Gunnlaug Snakestongue and his fights for his love Helga, a woman more like a heroine of romance than of saga. *Hrafnkels saga* (c. 1300) is also brief but not romantic. Rather it is didactic, showing its hero learning from experience. *Grettis saga* (c. 1320) is a composite of incidents found as far apart as *Beowulf* and *Tristan*. But again the hero, although he struggles bravely, is the victim of fate.

It will be seen that there is considerable variation in the family sagas. Yet many things remain constant—the narrative style, the code of honor and, most of all, the essentially tragic ending. Greatness consists in glorious failure, not success.

The *Sturlunga saga* is a great compilation, composed about 1300, of sagas dealing with characters of the previous two hundred years of Icelandic history. Besides the *Sturlusaga,* about the father of Snorri, the most important part of the work is the *Islendinga saga* of Sturla Thórtharson. It is a history of Iceland from 1184 to 1249, with one or two short gaps. Probably it was left unfinished by Sturla, who died in 1284. By this time Icelandic culture was declining and independence was gone.

Only one type of saga remains for discussion, that which was based on foreign models. These were mostly written in Norway at the behest of King Hákon Hákonarson. Since their originals are treated elsewhere in this book, it will be sufficient to list them. The *Tristan and Isolt* of Thomas of Britain was translated by Brother Robert in 1226. The work is important because a large part of the original is lost. The romances of Chrétien de Troyes were also translated, as were the *chansons de geste* (*Karlamagnussaga*). The romances of classical antiquity appeared about the middle of the thirteenth century as *Trójumanna saga, Rómverja saga* and *Alexanders saga.* Even *Barlaam and Josaphat* and *Floris and Blancheflur* were not excepted. Iceland also produced some romances of its own, sagas often based on French material but not translations. They are romantic and often crude stories of adventure, usually far removed from the realism of the sagas.

The flourishing literature of Iceland in the Middle Ages is a remarkable phenomenon. With relatively little influence from non-Scandinavian countries, at least in the early stages, works of great skill and power were produced. But it will have been observed that the main strength is in narrative. There is a remarkable absence of true love poetry, of contemplative works, and of drama. Within this relatively limited scope, however, the achievement was considerable.

Medieval Latin Literature

GENERAL

LITERATURE IN LATIN was written in all the countries of western Europe, and in the majority of cases it is possible to determine in what country a particular work was written. Some Latin works have been mentioned in connection with vernacular literature, but often, particularly in the case of the lyric, the work is so international in character that it seems desirable to devote a separate chapter to important works of literature written in Latin. It should be stressed that these are works of literature in the modern sense. No reference will be made to material which is theological or philosophical in nature or to the enormous number of works on the other arts and sciences, which constitute the bulk of medieval Latin writing. We shall, as in vernacular literature, divide up the works into verse—narrative, lyric, didactic—and prose. Drama will be treated in the separate chapter devoted to that topic.

NARRATIVE VERSE

The early centuries of medieval Latin literature saw little effort to write secular narrative poetry. The poets regarded it as more important to write the lives of saints, martyrs, and apostles in verse, and of these there exists a very large number. One work, however, deserves to be mentioned not because of any intrinsic value, but because it is the first known medieval Latin version of an extremely popular and influential story. *Apollonius of Tyre* appears to have been written in Latin in the fifth or sixth century, probably based on a Greek original. There are numerous manuscripts of the Latin prose version from the ninth century on, and fragments of an Anglo-Saxon version are extant. The story follows a typical Greek romance pattern. The hero, fleeing the wrath of a king whose incestuous union he has discovered, is shipwrecked but appeals so much to the king on whose shores he lands that he is given the king's daughter in marriage. However, their happiness is of short duration. The princess apparently dies aboard ship when Apollonius is returning to Tyre. Her body is sealed in a coffin and washed ashore. There she recovers. The daughter born to her is brought up by strangers.

51

Both she and her mother go through many hair-raising adventures, but in the end the family is united.

The interesting thing about this story is that the hero is not a warrior but a skilled artist. Hence many stories, including that of Tristan, borrow from the tale. The versification of it was made in the tenth century by an unknown cleric. There survive only 792 lines of leonine hexameter (a line like that of Vergil with rhyming words in the middle and at the end of each line). Prose versions were made in the later Middle Ages in practically all the western European languages.

During the tenth and eleventh centuries several important narrative poems were written. One of the best of these, *Waltharius*, will be discussed under German literature because of the close affinity of its subject matter with Germanic legend. We shall concern ourselves here with the *Ruodlieb* and two versions of the beast epic.

The *Ruodlieb* was written about the middle of the eleventh century in Germany, possibly at the court of the emperor Henry III. The text as we have it is much damaged, and the poem is not complete, but it is easy to see what kind of a work was intended. Many of the situations were to become commonplace in later romances, and the *Ruodlieb* may well reflect oral vernacular works which remained unwritten, although no one would claim that it is based directly on such a work. A young man of noble birth, unable to make his way, leaves home and, in a different country, meets a king's hunter who takes him to the ruler. Ruodlieb soon ensures his position by demonstrating his skill in hunting. After some time the kingdom is invaded by a margrave whom Ruodlieb, now a general, defeats and spares. His own ruler sends him as emissary to the king whose men had invaded the country, and since this king is as kind as Ruodlieb's master, there is no difficulty in arranging peace.

Now the hero is asked to come home. The king asks him whether he prefers wealth or wisdom. Ruodlieb of course chooses the latter and receives twelve pieces of advice, of which three are exemplified on the way home. He receives wealth too—treasures enclosed in two loaves. On the way home Ruodlieb meets a nephew. While staying at a castle they are able to see many tricks, and the hero shows off his own skill. The nephew marries the daughter of their widow host at the castle, but Ruodlieb exposes the deceitfulness of a girl proposed for him. Just before the poem breaks off Ruodlieb is about to gain a great treasure which will allow him to marry a king's daughter.

In this work of 2,308 leonine hexameters there are many familiar motifs—the man in a far country, the hunter, the wisdom-wealth opposition, the young wife-old husband situation. These have been brought together for didactic purposes, for there can be no doubt that the poem was intended to be the story of a successful knight, progressing not only because of his skill and talents but because of his virtue. His readiness to take wisdom instead of wealth and the contrast between him and other characters show this clearly. The morality is, however, formal and worldly. There is little pursuit of virtue for its own sake and none of the moral problems we find in the great romances. The emphasis is on worldly success achieved in the right way. The poem contains a great deal of popular wisdom besides formal moralizing. It may be regarded as an early forerunner of the courtly romance.

Beast Epics

Two works separated by two hundred years will next be considered because they both represent versions of a type very common in the Low Countries, northwestern France, and northwestern Germany but hardly found elsewhere: the beast epic. The beast epic is quite different from the fable, although it shares with the latter the convention that beasts talk and have institutions like human beings. In the epic form the basic struggle is between the cunning Renard the fox and the cruel and stupid Isengrim the wolf. The oldest incident in this struggle is to be found in one of the fables of Aesop, which did not, however, appear in the so-called Romulus version of the fables known in the Middle Ages. The first medieval story is to be found in a short poem of Paulus Diaconus (early ninth century) in which a bear (not a wolf) is made to give up his skin because Renard says that King Lion can cure his sickness by wrapping himself in it. This is the same story as that in the fable except for the substitution of the bear for the wolf, and it seems likely that its author had access to some version of Aesop's fables of which we have no knowledge.

The incident of the curing of the sick lion is central in all the Latin and French versions of what came to be called the

Roman de Renart. It appears next in a Latin allegorical poem called *Ecbasis captivi*, written about 940 (some say earlier) by a German monk in Toul. Its 1,228 lines frame one story within another. A calf escapes from the farm and is captured by a wolf. While it is in the wolf's lair, the other farm animals trace it. They make plans to get in, and during this interval the wolf regales his friends the otter and hedgehog with the story of how Renard cured King Lion with a wolf's skin. Hence he is terribly afraid of the fox. And with good reason, for the fox does tempt him outside, where he is killed by the bull. The calf returns to its mother.

The allegory is that of a monk who leaves his cloister and is seized by the devil, from whom he must be rescued. (The title means "Escape of the Captive.") The interest, however, lies chiefly in the sick-lion episode, which is told very largely through dialogue. The poem is clumsily constructed and hard to follow, and many of its lines are borrowed from other authors, particularly Horace. It is, however, the first long poem in which the enmity of the fox and wolf is developed.

There can be no doubt that in the two hundred years between these two Latin beast epics the story of Renard had become popular, and that a large number of different oral versions of stories about the rivalry between fox and wolf had come into existence. Some were very old, but there is no reason to think that new ones were not invented also. The author of the *Ysengrimus*, who is usually called Master Nivardus of Ghent, clearly selected the stories he used from the available material, and from them he constructed a genuine epic in classical form which could easily be called the "Decline and Fall of Isengrim the Wolf." We know nothing of the author except what we can learn from his work, but he was certainly a well-traveled and very learned man whose mastery of Latin equaled that of any medieval writer. According to some of the allusions to events in the Low Countries, the poem must have been written about 1150.

Like any good epic poet, Nivardus begins in the middle of his story. Renard is in trouble with the wolf because of earlier tricks. He steals a ham for both but gets only a bone. The next time he persuades Isengrim to go fishing through the ice with his tail and when he is well frozen in, leads a band of peasants his way so that they will beat him. Later Isengrim is persuaded to act as referee in a land dispute between four rams. He receives all four of their heads at once as they charge him—he had asked for their fleeces in payment! Then follows the sick-lion episode, brilliantly handled with full attention to the way in which all animals are turned against Isengrim before Renard proposes to use his skin. Renard's brilliant success leads to a poem in his honor by the bear, recited by the wild boar.

It tells of the pilgrimage of the animals, in which Renard saves them from wolves, of how Isengrim was persuaded to enter a monastery (by the prospect of good food!) and how he was tonsured. Too stupid to learn, he is beaten and thrown out. When he returns, he finds that Renard has raped his wife. This brings us to the beginning of the story. Further incidents follow, in all of which Renard persuades the wolf to do something which will lead to his being beaten by another animal. Finally, wounded in one leg, Isengrim is torn to pieces by swine. Renard pronounces a mock oration over his body.

It will be seen that the situation of the wolf declines constantly. He is successful only in the first scene. Yet he has only himself to blame. He is greedy, cruel, hated by the other animals, and, worst of all, stupid. None of the characters is pleasant. The lion is selfish, using his power for his own ends. There is servile flattery at court. Renard succeeds because he is utterly amoral. Yet the worst criticism is directed, by implication, at the clergy. Isengrim is a monk for part of the story, and there are constant allusions to his stay in the monastery. The confusion of monks with wolves is inevitable. The author also makes clever use of legalistic formulae to make his points. Dialogue is brilliantly treated and is carefully constructed to fit both the characters and the situations.

The animals have, of course, their "world order," but it is certainly not one controlled by virtue. The best goes to the strongest and most cunning. Isengrim is the principal menace to the kingdom because of the fact that he, even more than the others, is dominated by the lusts of the flesh, especially his belly. With all this he is hypocritical, which the fox is not. The thought of a human world run like this animal world is terrifying. Master Nivardus clearly intended his brilliant work to be both a warning and a satire. Certainly he saw much in the world of men, and particularly of clerics, which he depicted in his world of beasts.

From the purely literary point of view, the *Ysengrimus* is

far superior to any of the other beast epics in any language. It is well constructed and brilliant in its handling of character and dialogue, it makes full use of the best rhetorical traditions, and it is witty and pungent. Yet its influence appears to have been small. None of the other beast epics is modeled on it, and it is not mentioned by other authors. Nor, for that matter, is it as well known now as the later versions in French and German.

Classical and Historical Epics

We may now turn to some of the verse forms of older material which were produced in the twelfth century. Simon Aurea Capra (Chèvre d'or) wrote a short verse work which tells the origins of the Trojan War and the destruction of the city in its first book and the flight of Aeneas and his coming to Italy in the second. The first part is based on the standard medieval source for the Trojan War, the brief prose account of events called the *Ephemerides* of Dares Phrygius. This fourth-century work, of absolutely no literary value, claimed to be an eyewitness account by a supporter of the Trojans. The second part of Simon's work is based on Vergil's *Aeneid*. It has very little merit.

Much better was the *De Bello Troiano* ("On the Trojan War") of Joseph of Exeter. Written about 1191 and based on the same source as Simon's, the work is rhetorical in the best sense. It uses all the resources of language to make its narrative move and its characters live. Like his source, he begins with the story of Jason and the Golden Fleece and the first quarrel between Greeks and Trojans. Then he tells how Hesione was seized at Troy and about Paris' rape of Helen. There is a long list of personalities, not always the same as those of Dares, and then the events of the war, including Achilles' love for Polyxena and finally the destruction of Troy and the various homecomings of the Greeks. He uses many other sources beside Dares. The work is long, eight books of epic length. Like most writers on Troy, Joseph is prone to moralizing asides, but in spite of this fact and a certain slowness in action, his is the most successful Latin Troy story.

Another successful poem on a subject from antiquity was the *Alexandreis* of Gautier de Châtillon, who lived in the second half of the twelfth century and who is now better known for his satirical verse. In his day the *Alexandreis* was regarded as his masterpiece. It is an epic in ten books and of about 5,500 lines. This work is not, like most vernacular poems on the subject, full of fantasy and romance. It follows reasonably closely Alexander's youth, his expeditions against the Persians (not forgetting his visit to Jerusalem), his visits to Egypt, the campaigns ending with the capture of Babylon, the expeditions to the East, and his death through poison. Alexander is shown as a true hero whose course is divinely guided. There is no trace of the portrayal of him as a worldly success but spiritual failure. Gautier loses no opportunity in his poem to describe such things as Babylon or Alexander's tomb. His poem, written in classical hexameters, is one of the most successful medieval attempts to recreate the classical epic.

A number of longer poems were written on contemporary events, none of which has the stature of those just discussed. We may mention the *In Honor of Louis* (c. 830–40) of Ermoldus Nigellus, *On the Battle of Hastings* (about 1070) of Gui d'Amiens, the *Song of the Saxon War* (c. 1075) about the wars of the emperor Henry IV, and the *History of Jerusalem* of Baudri de Bourgeuil, an account of the first crusade written before 1130. The deeds of Frederick Barbarossa were celebrated in the *Deeds of Frederick the First in Verse*, a long poem written about 1160. Deeds in England and France were also celebrated.

The twelfth century saw the last of the attempts before the Renaissance to write Latin epic. The vernacular, with its wider appeal, was used more and more for such attempts, and we find nothing in the thirteenth century to engage our attention.

LYRIC POETRY

Early Quantitative Verse

There is no trouble in discovering lyric poetry written in Latin, provided that we are generous in our interpretation of the word "lyric." There is no break in the classical tradition of lyric poetry, since from the fifth century to the Renaissance poets continued to write quantitative verses which imitated the work of the classical Latin poets. Unfortunately the great bulk of this is nothing more than the production of poems according to rules. The medieval writers had no feeling for quantity (length of syllable), which was the basis of all classical Latin poetry. They knew the rules for determining quantity and were therefore able to turn out verse which was technically correct. But both in prosody and subject matter there was a lack of real feeling. Many of the subjects most important to classical Latin writers were barred to medieval clerics, who constituted the great majority of those who wrote. They could not write of sexual love, politics was a difficult subject, and mythology was, at least in the earlier centuries, suspect. Thus we find that they were thrown back on commonplaces. They would write in formal praise of persons or cities, they could describe their favorite garden, they could lament the passing of youth, poverty, old age, lack of books. Description was the easiest and safest course to pursue, and much medieval Latin poetry is confined to describing. All of which does not mean that there was not beautiful and sensitive poetry written. But until the eleventh century there is no true originality or power in the work. We shall mention here just a few of the most famous of the writers of lyric or occasional verse whose work has some claim to distinction.

Venantius Fortunatus (c. 535–600) is very typical of the trends mentioned. He was born in Italy but spent most of his life in Poitiers, of which he later became bishop, on terms of close friendship with St. Radegunda and her daughter Agnes. He wrote a verse life of St. Martin and one in prose of Radegunda, but the bulk of his work is eleven books of *Miscellanea*, occasional verse, much of it verse epistles. He is full of reminiscences of classical poets, and most of the subjects are trivial in the extreme. His greatest works are the two beautiful hymns *Pange lingua* ("Tell, my tongue, the battle of the glorious strife") and *Vexilla regis prodeunt* ("The banners of the king advance").

The work of Alcuin (735–804) is very similar. In his prose works he was a compiler rather than an originator, and the same is true of his verse. His best work is his verse history of York, in almost 2,000 lines, and a lament on the destruction of the abbey of Lindisfarne.

Some of the poets of the Carolingian school were a little more interesting. Anghilbert, who wrote about 790, was called Homer by his circle and is best known for a description in verse of Charles and his court at Aachen. Theodulf, his contemporary, is best known for his religious verse, as is Paulus Diaconus. Hrabanus Maurus (780–856), a great churchman and encyclopedist, wrote a vast quantity of material, some of it poetical epistles. He is credited with writing the magnificent hymn *Come Holy Spirit*. Of all the poets of this period, the most sincere and original is Gottschalk (810–69). A pupil of Hrabanus, he fell foul of the church because of his predestination heresies and suffered severe punishment. In his poetry he also shows originality, for he is one of the few to use rhyme. His poetry, as might be expected, shows true feeling and, at times, deep melancholy. Walafrid Strabo (809–49) is the last of this school. He was a friend of Gottschalk's but soon became tutor to the emperor's son and ultimately abbot of Reichenau. His work is of the descriptive kind, but pleasantly done, particularly his *Hortulus* ("Little Garden").

The Development of Rhythmic Verse

Up to this point most verse had been written in the Latin quantitative meters. There are, however, a few examples of a completely different type of prosody, based not on length of syllable but on stress. It is far from clear when this poetry began to develop. The Ambrosian hymns have been claimed as the first examples of this rhythmic verse, but they can be scanned as quantitative also. In fact it seems probable that as feeling for stress became more natural than feeling for length of syllable, poets tried to make what would be a long syllable in a foot correspond with a word stress. This was relatively easy to do in the iambic and trochaic verse in which many hymns were written, particularly if the last word in the line had three syllables, as is in fact the case in a great many lines. Whatever the reason for the development of stressed verse, it became more and more popular in hymn writing. The number of syllables in a line was fixed for any particular meter, and so was the position of the stress in the foot before the caesura (or main break in the line) and in the cadence or line ending. Elsewhere the position of the stress could vary, although it became more and more common to have strict alternation of stressed and unstressed syllables.

The development of rhythmic verse forms was paralleled by the introduction of rhyme. Here again there is a question. Latin poetry in classical times did not consciously use rhyme, but it is easy to see how accidental rhyme could appear because of the numerous similar endings of words. Quite probably this similarity was exploited by poets, but some critics have claimed that Hebrew poetry influenced Latin hymns and produced rhyme. Certainly its introduction was gradual, for the first attempts at rhyme are mere vocalic assonance. Then comes rhyme of vowel and one consonant, then the "full" rhyme of vowel/consonant/vowel. By the twelfth century rhyme schemes had become very elaborate and the poets very skillful.

Rhythmic poetry reached its highest development in the twelfth century. By that time strophic forms of great complexity with varying lengths of line and complicated rhyme schemes had been worked out. One type of line deserves special mention because of its frequency and use in many famous poems. It is the line used in *Gaudeamus igitur* and is as follows.

Gaudeamus igitur iuvenes dum sumus
/ x / x / x / || / x / x / x

Lines of this length were grouped into strophes and held together by end rhyme. The rhythmic lyric poetry written in these meters is probably the best literary product of the Latin Middle Ages.

We should also mention a special type of verse which developed from church music. There is good evidence that the last note of the Alleluja was prolonged with a melisma, that is, a series of notes. These became highly complicated, and words (*prosa*) were fitted to them to assist in remembering them. Then followed verses and ultimately a verse form called a sequence. This consisted of a single strophe followed by one or more pairs of strophes. The members of each pair had exactly the same metric form as one another but not necessarily as that of the other pairs. A single strophe of exactly the same form as the first ended the poem. There are some secular sequences but many more religious ones.

The poetry of the tenth century on is a mixture of the old and new. It is a curious fact that the older, classical forms were written mostly by clerics whose names we know, whereas the rhythmic poetry is largely anonymous. For this reason there arose the legend that most secular rhythmic poetry was written by wandering scholars who were educated but poor vagrants. Certainly wandering scholars existed, but there is no evidence that they wrote the secular poetry. Most of it was no doubt written by respectable clerics, but since it was regarded as playful trifling they did not sign their names. It should not be forgotten that the *Chanson de Roland* and the *Nibelungenlied* are also anonymous.

One of the most famous names connected with the sequence is that of Notker of St. Gall (c. 840–912), who was once credited with inventing the type. He certainly wrote many new ones. An important manuscript of the eleventh century, called the *Cambridge Songs*, contains a very varied collection of material. Some of it is formal, moral, and religious, some versified popular stories, such as the man who went to Heaven and Hell, and the abbot who tried to live on herbs "like the prophets" but was glad to be back in his cell. There are also some love poems in rhythmic verse, one an invitation by a student to his girl, another, a very beautiful poem, of a girl contemplating the beauties of spring and her own lonely state.

The poem on the ambitious abbot was written by Fulbert of Chartres (c. 970–1028), a great churchman and head of the most celebrated of all schools in the twelfth century, that of the cathedral at Chartres. He himself was a fine poet, and his *Ode to the Nightingale* anticipates the great poetry to come. Peter Damian (1007–72), a mystic of great fame as a theologian, wrote religious poetry of great fervor and deep melancholy.

Three poets stand out in France at the beginning of the twelfth century. Hildebert of Lavardin (1056–1133), bishop of Le Mans, had a true sense of beauty. His best poetry is elegiac and classical, for example his superb elegy on the ruins of Rome, which he visited in 1100. He also wrote moving religious poetry in rhythmic verses. Marbod, bishop of Rennes (1035–1123), was more didactic by nature. His poem on precious stones and their allegorical qualities was famous in his day. He also wrote some conventional antifeminine and anticlerical satire. Baudri de Bourgeuil (1046–1130) was also both a bishop and a man of letters. He had a circle of correspondents, among them Adela of Blois. These letters gave him plenty of opportunity to display his powers of poetic rhetoric. The hymns of Abélard (1079–1142) are well known, but of the secular poetry he is said to have written, nothing remains. Serlo of Wilton (or Bayeux, c. 1160) was in his youth a great satirist and writer of antifeminist verse. In his old age he confined himself to religious poetry.

Before we discuss the great mass of twelfth-century rhythmic verse, the names of a few of the great hymn writers should be mentioned. Adam of St. Victor (c. 1110–c. 1190) was the great writer of sequences. He exploited all the allegorical imagery which had grown up over the centuries and was a master of form. Philippe de Grève (c. 1180–1236), also called Philip the Chancellor, was not only a mystical hymn writer of great tenderness but a satirist of laxness in the church. John Peckam (c. 1230–92), archbishop of Canterbury, is most famous for his poem *Nightingale*, in which a nightingale is made to sing through the hours of the Christian day until it dies at nones, just as the human soul sings to and searches for God. Jacopone da Todi (c. 1230–1306), a Franciscan who sought to follow strictly the poverty of his master, wrote a good deal of ascetic verse but is most famous for the hymn *Stabat Mater dolorosa* ("The Mother of Sorrows"). Similarly his fellow Franciscan Thomas of Celano (c. 1225) is remembered for his great poem on the Day of Judgment, *Dies irae*.

The secular lyrics of the Latin Middle Ages, like their counterparts in the vernacular, are almost all to be found in manuscript collections made many years after the poems were written. Thus the same poem often occurs in several manuscripts, sometimes in slightly differing form. No one knows why these manuscripts were put together or how. It is not likely that they were the repertoire of wandering singers, for most of the works are too sophisticated for a popular audience. Presumably there were people who appreciated having such a collection. There are manuscripts of lyric poetry at Oxford (Rawlinson), Orléans, Paris, London (British Museum), and elsewhere, but by far the largest and most famous is the collection called *Carmina Burana*, songs from Benediktbeuern, a monastery in Bavaria. Contrary to a widespread belief, a large number of the poems in this manuscript are serious, moral, or religious in nature, but many of them are light-hearted love poems, and a few tell of gambling and drinking.

Love Poetry

Latin love poetry differs markedly from the vernacular love lyric. It is very rarely personal in feeling and almost never mentions an identifiable girl. There is no question of the kind of reverence and worship which we shall find in the lyric of Provence and Germany. The poems are usually general exhortations to play the game of love in the springtime. Occasionally the poet describes briefly the wonderful girl whom he has chosen. There are also a few poems in which the author recounts a single amorous adventure, often with a peasant girl or in a brothel.

The great majority of the love poems begin with a description of an idealized, highly formalized spring landscape, and proceed to urge that man should join in the spirit of spring. The influence of rhetorical training is everywhere in evidence, in the formal spring opening, in the stylized description of the lady, and in the skillful use of rhetorical figures.

Satirical Verse

If love poetry were all that was to be found in the collections, we would be pleased but hardly overwhelmed. The mind soon becomes tired of routine calls to love, however skillfully put, and although there are some moving poems among them, especially those put in the mouths of women, they are rare. The finest flower of this rhythmic poetry lies in its satire. Learned poetry is often more successful in this type than any other, since it calls for wit rather than humor, skill rather than feeling. Wit and skill the writers of medieval Latin poetry had in abundance. They had another very powerful ally—parody. Medieval audiences, especially learned audiences, knew a few works very thoroughly indeed and especially, of course, the Bible and the Apocrypha. Any reference to these was hardly likely to pass unnoticed, and many of the best comic effects in medieval satire were obtained by using quotations and references in a context sharply contrasted with that in which they originally appeared.

The principal target of these satirical poems was the church, not its doctrines or teachings but those whose activities brought it into disrepute. There are no attacks on the Pope but many on cardinals, prelates, and indeed the whole papal curia. The attacks are not recognizably personal. They take to task the old sins—greed, simony (office selling)—which had plagued courts for centuries. The delightful feature of the poems is not what they satirize but how they do it. Parody and pun, double meaning and innuendo, classical myth and topical allusion are all made to play their part. Yet it should be recognized that this satire too was formal. It offered the author an opportunity for verbal fireworks. Gautier de Châtillon is probably the best of these satirists, and at his best he is very funny. But the funniest poem of all is not directed against anyone explicitly but against everyone by implication. It is the poem called *The Confession of Golias* by the Archipoeta, an unknown poet who apparently was in the entourage of Rainald Dassel, archbishop of Cologne. In quick tripping "Goliardic" lines (13 syllables in an iambic pattern with fixed caesura), the poet "confesses" his sins of wine, women, and gambling. But he lays it all at the door of irresistible nature and implies that others suffer from the same urges. Certainly wine is essential to him, otherwise his poetry would be completely uninspired. Every line in this poem has some reference to another work, and recognition of these references adds immeasurably to the pleasure of reading. The Archpoet has other neat and effective poems, for example one in which he rejects a request to take a week off to write a poem about the deeds of Frederick Barbarossa!

Before leaving this delightful group of poems we should mention one of the *Carmina Burana* which is found in many manuscripts and which was even known in Elizabethan England. This is a debate poem on the subject of love. Debate poems were common—Body and Soul, Beer and Wine, Winter and Summer were set to arguing their respective merits throughout the Middle Ages. The twelfth century, however, was more interested in the topic of love, and there are several poems extant, among them a debate of nuns called the *Council of Remiremont*, which take up the topic of who makes the better lover, a knight or a cleric. With the increasing education of the laity, these debate poems may reflect an actual rivalry between the clerics and the knights for influence with ladies at court. However this may be, the *Debate of Phyllis and Flora* is a charming and witty poem. Each girl is, of course, divinely beautiful, and it is spring. Not without maliciousness, each praises her lover, and it is interesting to note that it is the cleric who is well fed and clothed and able to give rich presents, while the knight is thin and starved but still sings the praises of his lady when going into battle. Obviously the poet is laughing at exaggeration on both sides. The two ladies finally mount magic steeds and are borne into the world of myth where the god of love reigns. He decides for the cleric! The work is probably the most graceful and elegant of all medieval Latin poems.

MORAL AND DIDACTIC WORKS

A considerable number of the poets already mentioned wrote didactic works of various kinds. We shall mention here a few other important poems, most of them fairly long, which fall into this category. Probably the most famous moral poem of the Middle Ages is the *Contempt of the World* of Bernard of Cluny or Morlais, who died about 1200. It is 3,000 lines long, in three books, and uses a peculiar form of hexameter with two rhyming words in the middle of the line and normal end rhyme in couplets. The lines are based on stress, not quantity, and the effect of the many rhymes and dactylic meter is one of insistent hammering. This indeed is what the author desires, for he describes in great detail the pains of Hell and the joys of the blessed. His denunciation of sin is scathing and detailed, and no class of society is spared. Like many ascetics, Bernard seems far happier describing sin and its punishment than with the joys of the blessed. He was not, of course, the only person to write such poems. An anonymous *On the Vanity of the World* of about the same time is very similar if not so realistic. There were many others.

Nigellus Wireker (c. 1130–c. 1206), an Englishman, is one of the more successful satirists of the period. He wrote a prose work, *Against Courtiers and Prelates,* but his most successful effort was the *Mirror of Fools.* Here he tells the story of foolish monks in the guise of a donkey which sets out on its travels to learn how to lengthen its tail. The story of the donkey at towns and particularly at universities gives Wireker an excellent chance to poke fun at the attempts of stupid people to become learned and at university life in general. The donkey never does learn to say anything but "Hee haw."

We shall mention the allegorical works of Alain de Lille and Bernard of Tours (Silvestris) in connection with French literature. An anonymous work of about 1184, the *Archweeper,* covers much the same ground as they do but with less skill. It is an allegory of a man who laments his lack of will and who passes through all the vices of the flesh until Nature finds him a wife, Temperance. Needless to say the poem is not sparing in its attacks on these vices and those who practice them, lay or cleric. Further attacks on the clergy are to be found in the *Overabundance of Clerics,* written in 277 four-line Goliardic strophes, apparently by a member of the lower clergy, since he attacks the upper ranks. More general in its comments and with a good deal of classical background is the *Changes of Fortune and Consolation of Philosophy* (1194) of Henri de Settimello.

To end this section we should say a word about a few of

the more technical poems. There had appeared very early in Europe a Latin version, called *Physiologus*, of a Greek work which attributed allegorical characteristics to real and mythical animals. It was known to and used by such persons as Isidore and Bede. In about 1100 there appeared a verse form of this work which became very popular and of which numerous versions with commentary appeared throughout the Middle Ages. It had a dozen sections of twenty-five lines or so each. The author was a certain master Thibaut.

The *Distichs of Cato*, a set of didactic proverbs and sayings which had nothing to do with Cato, appeared in various Latin versions. Ovid also appeared in "moralized," that is, allegorized, forms. The most celebrated of these was that of John of Garland (1180–after 1252). He was a highly cultivated man who worked on grammars and other technical schoolbooks. His *Coverings of Ovid* and *Allegories of Ovid's Metamorphoses* are attempts to interpret the author in a Christian sense by an elaborate system of symbols.

The twelfth and early thirteenth centuries produced several "arts of poetry," works which gave instruction on types of poetry and in particular on how certain types of description should be handled. They are also important in showing us what branches of rhetoric, and especially figures in rhetoric, were popular at this time. The best known, probably, is Matthieu de Vendôme's *Art of Versifying* (c. 1175). It gives carefully constructed examples of how poetry should be written. Even more popular was Geoffroi de Vinsauf's *New Poetry* (c. 1210). It is more than 2,000 lines long. A shorter, more technical work was the *Colors of Rhetoric*, again with examples. Evrard the German wrote his *Labyrinth* after the other two, whose work he quotes. He covers a wider range of subjects.

PROSE WORKS

Very little of the enormous mass of medieval Latin prose can be properly termed literature. Most of it consists of theological commentary, works on the subjects of the trivium and quadrivium, chronicle history, and lives of saints. We shall mention here only a few works of special interest to students of literature.

The life of Charlemagne by his minister Einhard (770–840) is one of the great biographies of the medieval period.

The author knew Charles personally, but his object in writing his life was to equate his hero with the great emperors of Rome as depicted by Suetonius, whose *Lives of the Caesars* was preserved at Fulda, Einhard's birthplace. He does not hesitate to make wholesale borrowings from his model, but the biography is an independent work. It tells of Charles' deeds, including the defeat of Roland at Roncevaux by the Gascons, but the second part is devoted to an account of Charlemagne's person and family life. Naturally it is complimentary, but is not without its touches of humor. Einhard glosses over many of Charlemagne's weaknesses, but his portrait was in general accurate. To see how good it is we need only compare it with the legendary stories about Charlemagne by the Monk of St. Gall (late ninth century) or the rather feeble biography of Alfred of England by Asser (850–909).

The only other medieval biography worthy of comparison with Einhard's is that of Frederick Barbarossa by Otto of Freising (c. 1112–57). Otto was a man of real distinction. He became bishop of Freising when only twenty-six and immediately instituted wide reforms in education. He wrote a *Chronicle* in eight books which is deeply influenced by St. Augustine but sees the City of God realized on earth by the perfect harmony of church and empire. Otto's biography of Frederick gains a great deal by his detailed knowledge of persons (he was the emperor's uncle).

A historical writer of a different period should be mentioned for the originality of his work. Liudprand, bishop of Cremona (920–72), was a statesman of fire and temper. He was sent on an embassy to Byzantium in 949—at his stepfather's expense—and was angry at the way in which Berengar, king of Italy, had failed to provide him with suitable presents for the emperor. He broke with Berengar on his return and for the rest of his life was a faithful servant of Otto I of Germany, for whom he also untertook an embassy to the East. Liudprand's work is full of denunciations couched in the bitterest language, of which Liudprand was a master. His observation of courts and princes, if prejudiced, is brilliantly amusing, but best of all is the account he gives of Byzantium in his *Antopodosis* ("Tit for Tat"; 958–62) and his *Embassy* (c. 970). He hated and despised the ceremonial and rigid ordered life of the Byzantine court and thought its people mean, degenerate, conceited, and extravagant by turns. He provides the best account of the Eastern Empire through Western eyes in the period before the crusades.

William of Malmesbury (c. 1095–1143) and Geoffrey of Monmouth (c. 1100–1154) both wrote histories of the kings of Britain which are important for the light they throw on material used in romance. The same may be said of Saxo Grammaticus (late twelfth century), whose *Deeds of the Danes* is a very good source for Germanic mythology and early history. Giraldus Cambrensis (1147–1223) performed a like service for Wales in his *Annals of Cambria*, and his *Topography of Ireland* is a careful look at the Ireland of his day. Two works of English history are recognized as providing important material, the *Ecclesiastical History* of Bede (673–735)—whose other works cover much of the knowledge of his day—and the *Greater Chronicle* of Matthew Paris (c. 1190–1259), who provides an interesting account from the conquest to 1259.

John of Salisbury (c. 1110–80) was the most learned man of his day. Educated at Chartres, he became secretary to Thomas à Becket, archbishop of Canterbury, and devoted to him his best-known work, the *Policraticus* ("Statesman"). In this he is mainly concerned to outline the duties of the prince and his servants. He does not discuss the form of government, which to him was fixed, but how its members should behave. He has little time for courtiers and takes care to emphasize the superiority of churchmen. His knowledge of the classics is evident on every page. His other works, the *Metalogicon* and *Entheticus*, are philosophical. He left numerous letters.

The subtitle of the *Policraticus* is *On Courtier's Trifles*. This same title was used by Walter Map (c. 1137–c. 1209) for a collection of tales which really deserve the title. It is a disorderly collection of tales from all kinds of sources, many of them parallels of verse works, many others illustrating folk customs of the various parts of the British Isles. One of the most famous parts of the work is the letter to a friend advising him not to marry.

A more famous work on men and women was the *De amore* ("On Love") of Andreas Capellanus (c. 1170–80), often called *The Art of Courtly Love*. It purports to be written at the request of a certain Walter and talks of the women one should love and how men of various social classes (noble, honorable, bourgeois) should approach women in these various classes. The first book is really a series of model speeches for lovers. The second is devoted largely to examples and judgments allegedly delivered by Marie de Champagne at her court, where Andreas obviously spent much time. The third book is a complete retraction. It urges Walter to avoid women, be honorable, and not dabble in love. Critics are not agreed on which parts are really sincere. The book has too often been regarded as a kind of manual whose precepts can be applied to the romance and lyric, whereas it is actually more of an indication of the kind of discussions which went on in the circles at court.

The love affair of Abélard and Héloise was certainly matched in the Middle Ages only by the fictional one of Tristan and Isolde. Abélard (1079–1142) was a brilliant cleric and lecturer in Paris. Engaged as tutor to Héloise, he soon fell in love with her and she with him. A son was born and Abélard insisted on marriage. Later Héloise's vengeful uncle had him emasculated. All this he tells in the *History of Misfortunes*, a letter sent to Héloise when she was abbess of the nunnery of the Paraclete. Abélard had continued his career as a theologian, but his views were too radical for most churchmen, and he was a disappointed and embittered man. Héloise, still apparently in love with him, continued to write and he to reply, but only as spiritual adviser. The letters from both are beautifully written. Abélard's main work was, of course, his theological writing, which, although in part condemned by the church, did begin a new method of critical interpretation.

Much of the prose work from the thirteenth century on consists of collections of stories which could be used as examples in sermons. The orders of friars, who revived the custom of frequent preaching to the laity, are probably largely responsible for the assembling of these collections, of which the best known are the *Gesta Romanorum* ("Deeds of the Romans"), which has little to do with the Romans, and the *Golden Legend* of Jacob de Vitry. The stories are always moralized, that is, given a Christian interpretation. A similar work is the *Dialogue of Miracles* of Caesarius of Heisterbach (c. 1180–c. 1245), a collection of moral but often amusing stories of the ways in which people can be tempted. Vincent of Beauvais (c. 1190–c. 1264) combined all the knowledge of his day into a vast encyclopedia, the *Speculum Maius*.

The greatest of the writers of medieval Latin was Dante Alighieri (1265–1321), although it is not primarily on his Latin works that his fame rests. (He is said to have seriously considered writing the *Divine Comedy* in Latin.) His two most important Latin works are *On Monarchy* and *On the Vernacular*. The former is largely political in intention. It is a carefully reasoned defense of the proposition that the empire was an institution founded by God as independent here on earth and not subservient to the church. The papacy's claims to control the emperor are refuted, and much attention is paid to the historical independence of the Romans and to showing that Constantine had no authority to hand over that power to the Pope. The work *On the Vernacular*, which is incomplete, was intended to show which types of literary work could best be written in the vernacular languages. After a brief account of the "development" of the languages, especially Italian, Dante discusses the composition of the highest form of vernacular poetry, the *canzone* or formal love lyric. His remarks throw a good deal of light on the poetic theory of the day.

We have seen that the purely literary material in medieval Latin is only a small part of its bulk. And of the literature, by far the most original and successful type was the rhythmic, rhymed song, particularly in satire and love poetry.

French Literature

GENERAL

IT HAS ALREADY been pointed out that there were two literatures in France for a considerable part of the Middle Ages: that of northern and central France (*langue d'oïl*) and that of southern France (*langue d'oc*). These two divisions excelled in different literary forms, as will be seen.

Vernacular literature was relatively slow in developing, partly, no doubt, because the languages were Latin in origin, and it was some time before it became clear that formal Latin was no longer comprehensible to the bulk of the people. Whatever the reason, the first piece of literature written in French did not appear until about 1040. Yet there was already a long tradition of literature in France, for important writers of Latin verse had lived there ever since the time of the Roman empire—Fortunatus (c. 535–600), an Italian, lived at Tours for most of his adult life and wrote religious and occasional poetry in Latin verses of considerable skill. But it was the phenomenon of the "Carolingian renaissance" which had most influence on later poets.

Charlemagne (742–814) was, of course, as much an emperor of the Germans as of the French, and his chief educational adviser, Alcuin, was an English monk. The great importance of the activity in his court lies not so much in the literature it produced, which was largely pedantic and imitative, as in the new intellectual climate. The emperor himself had little formal education, but he appreciated its value both for the individual and the state. He therefore encouraged schools, and Alcuin, more industrious than original, saw in the Latin authors the ideal means of inculcating moral training. In the process he revived interest in classical poetry, in accurate Latin, and in the transmission of the texts of Latin authors. Rhetoric and good style were cultivated, and the tradition survived the confusion of the reigns of Charlemagne's successors. Alcuin's own work is indicative of the spirit of the age—several school manuals, saints' lives, numerous letters, occasional poetry, fables, and some neat descriptive pieces. Anghilbert (died 814) has a little more poetic spirit, Theodolphus (died 821) at times a lighter touch, but their range is limited. Not surprisingly, the most important writer of the period was the historian, Einhard (see chapter on medieval Latin literature).

The Carolingian renaissance rescued a great deal of the literature, language, and style of classical antiquity, but it did not create any new forms. The following century saw little of importance written in Latin either in poetry or prose. There was a strong concentration of effort on history and didactic material. Yet below the surface new developments were taking place. The old quantitative verse of the Latin classics, so rigidly imitated by the Carolingians, was being replaced by lyric forms based on rhythm and rhyme. We shall discuss these later. The experiments also extended to vernacular poetry—for when it appears in the eleventh century, rhyme has already evolved and lines of fixed numbers of syllables are standard. Our knowledge of the early stages of these developments is too slight to warrant serious discussion. We can only assume from the results that there must have been a gradual development.

Before proceeding to the actual works produced in French, we should note one other important phenomenon. After the end of the invasions of the Norsemen in the tenth century, France enjoyed a long period of comparative peace. There was opportunity for a settled life, for cultural amenities—in short, for leisure. This seems to have been especially true of southern France, where several courts could boast a number of cultured laymen. The effect was profound, for it made patronage possible, raised the status of secular letters, encouraged the rise of professional writers, and made poetry a respectable occupation for a gentleman. The crusades did not shatter this culture, as might have been expected. On the contrary, intelligent women were given a more important role to play because of the absence of their lords, and there was revealed to the crusaders themselves a culture much higher in many respects than their own—that of the Saracens. There can be no doubt that much of the success of secular letters in the twelfth century was due to opportunities which had not existed before for the exercise of patronage by the nobility. Not unnaturally, it was literature in the vernacular which appealed to these courtly circles.

The first poem in French, not surprisingly, was a saint's life, *Chanson de St. Alexis* (c. 1050). It has 125 strophes of five assonanced lines, each of ten syllables, and tells the story of the saint who gave up all his wealth and family to be a beggar. A *Chanson de Ste. Foy* (c. 1060) is also a versified saint's life of martyrdom and salvation, showing great literary sophistication, including careful rhymes.

These two poems are interesting primarily because they are early works in the vernacular. What is astounding is the fact that only sixty years at most separates the earliest French poem from that which many would consider the greatest poem of the French Middle Ages—the *Chanson de Roland*.

CHANSONS DE GESTE

The term *chanson de geste* is applied by French critics to epic poems whose action takes place at some period in French history, usually during the reign of Charlemagne and his immediate successors. The poems are thus "historical," although they contain a great deal which is apocryphal, legendary, or pure invention. In spite of many variations in detail, they have a common theme—the relation of a ruler to his knights. Sometimes this is generally close and friendly, as in the *Chanson de Roland*, sometimes outright hostile, as in some parts of the *Chanson de Guillaume*. Thus one of the principal motifs is loyalty and hence conflict of loyalties.

There can be little reasonable doubt that the stories, or parts of them, were made up and circulated orally for a considerable time before they were put into their present form. Often versions exist which are partially contradictory. Although some of the elements in these stories were historical, still more were tales of adventure, magic, and even jest which can be found in the folklore of many nations. Nevertheless it should be kept in mind that the poems were felt by writer and audience alike to be historical in the sense that they were connected with the past of the French nation.

Some of the moral imperatives of the poems are Germanic in origin, or at least are similar to those found in Germanic poetry. But it would probably be wrong to see too much Germanic influence. Christianity and the conflict between Christian and pagan are also very important, and this led the French critic Bédier to believe that the clergy had played an important role in fashioning the *chanson de geste*, the *Chanson de Roland* in particular.

Chanson de Roland

There can be no doubt that the basic story of the epic goes back to a historical event of the year 778, the defeat of Hruoland, count of Brittany, by Basque mountaineers, when he was in command of the rear guard of Charlemagne's army returning from Spain. This much we know from the life of the emperor by Einhard, who was virtually a contemporary. The reason for writing an epic poem about a defeat is less obvious, although defeats are frequently the subject of early epics. If, however, we assume that the main purpose of the poem is to glorify Charlemagne as the Christian emperor, we can see a purpose. For Roland dies repentant, a martyr, and Charlemagne exacts vengeance not only on his conquerors but on the much greater host of the pagan Baligant. And vengeance on Ganelon comes about as the direct result of divine intervention in trial by combat.

Bédier noted that many of the places mentioned in the poem were on the pilgrimage route to the famous shrine of St. James of Compostella, in northern Spain, and he evolved the very plausible theory that early stories about the defeat of Roland were worked into a fundamentally Christian epic by clerics on the pilgrimage route. Thus the poem would be a Christian adaptation of stories based on historical events.

The poem has come down to us in several redactions, of which by far the most important and the only one to be considered here is the one contained in the Digby MS at Oxford. It is written in a Norman dialect and is certainly not the original form of the poem. Its author is unknown. A certain Turoldus names himself at the end as the maker, but he may be only a copyist and is in any case unknown. The Oxford version contains about 4,000 ten-syllable lines divided into *laisses* or poetic paragraphs. The date of the manuscript is about 1175, but the poem was written down much earlier, almost certainly between 1090 and 1105. Its obvious crusading spirit is perhaps the best argument for placing it after the first crusade. The story runs briefly as follows. Charlemagne's forces in Spain have conquered everything but the city of Saragossa. The others wish to negotiate but Roland in his pride is for using force. He succeeds in getting his stepfather Ganelon sent to treat with Marsile, chief of the Moslems, who is feigning willingness to surrender. While conducting these negotiations, Ganelon and Marsile work out a plot to feign submission to Charlemagne and then attack Roland, whom Ganelon says he will have put in command of the rear guard. And so it is arranged. Both Charlemagne and Roland are suspicious, but nothing can, in honor, be done. Roland and his friend Oliver and all their men are attacked by overwhelming numbers. Oliver, wise as well as brave, bids Roland sound his horn for help but is refused. After hordes of the enemy have been slain, everyone but Roland is either dead or gravely wounded. Oliver reproaches Roland for his pride. Roland, full of pity for his dying friend, attempts to comfort him and sounds his horn, bursting his temples with the effort. Charlemagne hears it, recognizes the treachery, puts Ganelon in irons, and hastens back, only to find Roland and all his men dead.

God makes the sun stand still as Charlemagne pursues and smashes the pagan host. The emperor laments the death of his brave men and Roland especially. But an even mightier host of Moslems, under Baligant, is approaching. The emperor's army is passed in review, before the reader's eye, then that of Baligant. A tremendous fight follows, culminating in single combat between the two leaders, a combat which Charlemagne wins only through the direct intervention of the angel Gabriel.

It now remains only to try Ganelon, but here there is a startling development. He pleads that his actions were part of a private quarrel with Roland and hence not subject to prosecution for treason. The peers are inclined to agree, and only Thierry, a relatively weak man, is prepared to defend Charlemagne's cause against Pinabel, a powerful warrior. Thierry's victory makes Ganelon's guilt certain, and he is torn to pieces by wild horses.

Obviously the poem has clear divisions: Roland's pride, defeat, repentance, and reception into Heaven, and Charlemagne's defeat of the pagans. Or the poem can be seen in three parts—treason, death, and vengeance. Only one part is in any case a true *Chanson de Roland*, and some critics see the Baligant episode as a later addition. If it is assumed, however, that the poem is a Christian epic, it is well balanced. The first part is about Roland the individual, the pride which leads to destruction and later self-knowledge. Oliver, never proud, always brave, is a foil to Roland but not so interesting, for he suffers no crisis. Bishop Turpin, mindful of his fellow men even in death, is another moving character. In this first part Charlemagne is a shadowy figure, an emperor fitted out with all the traditional appurtenances of greatness, yet weak and slow in decision. In the second part he comes into his own but more like a biblical patriarch. He dreams dreams and is directly assisted by God.

The style of the *Roland* is simple and unadorned. Its stylistic devices are the relatively primitive ones of repetition, rhetorical question, and apostrophe. Yet it is immensely effective, particularly in descriptive passages.

The virtues of loyalty and bravery are present in the poem, but they are assumed rather than stressed. Its heroes do not die defying fate but rather as humble and repentant Christians. It is the Christian virtues of humility, faith, courage, hope, and charity which are valued, while pride, greed, and treachery are condemned. The pagans exhibit these latter vices, and their characterization is clear evidence of how strongly the author was influenced by the crusading spirit. There are no good pagans. One or two might have been good—if they had been Christians—but all, finally, are destined for Hell. They do not fight for their faith, as Christians do, but for gain or at best earthly honor.

The poem shows no spirit of tolerance nor indeed much concern with the niceties of social life or morals. The organization of Charlemagne's court is still relatively primitive. The emperor's word is law, but the powerful peers believe in having their say. Only great nobles are of any importance. Of the other members of the army we hear little—and of women next to nothing.

The poem shows the tendency of the primitive epic toward episodic structure. Brilliant pictures pass before our eyes, one after another. There is little comment, little intrusion by the author. But the total effect is one of great power and dignity. We may add that although Charlemagne was a German, the *Chanson de Roland* is a French poem, of deep patriotism and certain conviction.

No other representative of this very numerous type can compare with the *Roland* as a work of literature. Partly, perhaps, because of its success and popularity, other works followed in great profusion in the twelfth and thirteenth centuries. They have been classified into cycles, some of the most important of which are here listed.

The Cycle of William of Orange

A number of poems, of different and uncertain dates, are included in this cycle. The earliest was the Norman *Chançun de Willame* (early twelfth century). There followed, possibly in this order, *Crowning of Louis* (c. 1130–60), *Cart of Nîmes* (c. 1130–60), *Capture of Orange* (c. 1150), and *William as Monk* (uncertain, may be later or earlier than the others). These poems, which are supplemented by the *Battle of Aliscans* (c. 1180), telling almost the same story as the *Chançun de Willame*, and a continuation, the *Chivalry of Vivien*, together constitute a biography of the hero, William of Orange. In his youth he quarrels with Louis, Charlemagne's feeble successor, not because of disrespect for the crown but because of Louis' unworthiness. He captures himself a fief at Nîmes by cleverly entering the city in a cart, wins a Saracen bride, Orable (in the *Capture of Orange*), and finds in her —renamed Guibourg—the most faithful of wives. In the *Chançun de Willame* and *Aliscans* the tide turns against him. He loses his noble nephew Vivien and his whole army in combat and is reduced to dire straits before final victory, largely gained by the club-wielding, comic giant Rainouart.

The William of Orange cycle is a loose agglomeration of adventure stories. Its hero is a rough-and-ready warrior, who is a Christian largely because it gives him the chance to fight pagans. There is little or nothing of the loftiness of the *Roland* here. Only two characters stand out—the brave and innocent nephew Vivien and the faithful, strong-minded Guibourg. William is loyal to his lord, but that lord is unworthy of his loyalty. We see here the reverse of the Charlemagne-Roland relationship.

When a particular character became popular, it was necessary to provide him with a lineage. There was a Count William of Toulouse about the year 790 who became a monk in 806 and one of whose wives was called Guibourg. But the ancestry provided in the cycle has nothing to do with this man. Poems grew up about a father called Aymeri of Narbonne, his mother, Hermerjart, and his brother. One poem tells of Aymeri's capture of Narbonne, another of William's own youth, and others about the various exploits of the brothers. They are conventional adventure stories of the brave Frenchman and wicked Saracens, written at the end of the twelfth century and beginning of the thirteenth century. The ultimate in derivative story was reached in the mid-thirteenth-century epic about William's great-grandfather, Garin de Montglane.

The Revolted Barons

This so-called cycle is really a series of distinct poems of adventure whose bond lies in a common theme. They all tell of feudal subjects who revolted against the emperor, usually Louis. There are no really good poems in the cycle, but the best are probably the following. *Chevalerie Ogier de Danemarche* tells of the exploits of a historical personage who actually fled to Italy because of a quarrel with Charlemagne. In the poem the trouble arises because Charlot, Charles' son, has killed Ogier's nephew. Ogier's desire for revenge leads to his banishment, but pressure from the army finally brings him back to fight the Saracens. *Girart de Roussillon* tells how Girart and his wife Berthe were exiled by Charles Martel because the emperor wished to prevent Berthe's younger and more beautiful sister from marrying Girart. In a similar situation in *Girart de Viane*, it is the hero who rejects the lady desired by Charlemagne and she who, when married to the emperor, pursues him with her vengeance. Many well-known characters, such as Roland and Oliver, appear in the numerous battles.

Raoul de Cambrai (end of the twelfth century) is in many respects the best poem of the cycle. It tells of the wild conduct of Raoul, his sacrilege and blasphemy and eventual death at the hands of Bernier, once his friend. Bernier is remorseful. Later in life he is forced to fight Gautier, Raoul's nephew, and both are gravely wounded. Ultimately an abbot reconciles them, and it becomes clear that the whole quarrel had been fomented by the weak king Louis and Raoul's uncle Guerri. In the second part of the poem this same Guerri treacherously murders Bernier. The whole poem follows the common adventure tradition, but has a good deal of vigor, not to say crudity, in its composition.

The Cycle of the King

This group consists of those epics in which Charlemagne himself is a principal figure. The cycle is thus a very loose affair. It includes the *Pilgrimage of Charlemagne* (to Jerusalem), an epic of comic drinking and boasting far removed from the *Roland*, written early in the twelfth century in twelve-syllable alexandrine lines instead of the usual deca-syllables. The *Chanson d'Aspremont* (late twelfth century) shows us some exploits of Roland's youth, when he saves Charlemagne's life and kills a young Saracen hero, Eaumont, son of the heathen king Agolant. From Eaumont Roland obtains the famous sword Durendal.

Another poem involving Roland is the *Fierbras* (late twelfth century). This tells of Charlemagne's determination to recover holy relics captured by the Saracen Laban when he took Rome, an event described in the *Destruction of Rome*, a mid-thirteenth-century work. Fierbras, Laban's son, challenges any six of Charlemagne's knights. Roland, angry about a remark of the emperor, refuses to fight, and the battle is between Oliver and Fierbras. The heathen, gravely wounded, asks for baptism and is christened Florien.

Two works which are not strictly *chansons de geste* should be mentioned here. One is the *Chanson des Saisnes* ("Song of the Saxons") of Jean Bodel, who lived in Arras at the beginning of the thirteenth century. He tells of Charlemagne's war against the invading Saxon king Quiteclin and the final single combat between the two kings. A strange and almost ironical element is introduced, however, by the action of Queen Sibille, who induces many wives of barons to follow her example and betray their husbands.

More important is a Latin prose book, the *Chronicle of Turpin* (mid-twelfth century). This work is purported to have been written by the Bishop Turpin, who died with Roland. Needless to say, he is here shown as surviving, and he gives an account of the fourteen-year campaign in Spain. The epi-sode about Agolant already mentioned is described and also the fierce fight between Roland and the giant Ferracutus. Both these episodes enjoyed considerable popularity outside France. The whole work is pious in nature—it was part of the *Book of St. James* and the demonstration of the superiority of Christianity was its main aim.

There are a few other works with some slight narrative connections with *The Cycle of the King*, including *Renaut de Montauban*, *Aye d'Avignon*, *Guy de Nanteuil*, *Parise la duchesse*, *Doon de Nanteuil*, and *Garin le Lorrain*, all of about 1200.

Independent *Chansons de Geste*

There are a few works which do not fall into any cycle. *Aiol* is the story of a simple boy, at first mocked, who, like the hero of Chrétien's *Perceval,* receives high honors in the end. *Amis et Amile* is one of the very numerous versions of a friendship story. Two young men, born on the same day and undistinguishable in appearance, go to court. One marries and leaves the court; the other is loved by the king's daughter, but a disgruntled ex-adviser of the king betrays them. A judicial combat is arranged and the lover, knowing he cannot win, persuades his friend to fight for him. The friend agrees, and while he wins the judicial combat, his friend sleeps with his wife, with a sword between them. However, the winner of the combat has to marry the king's daughter and thus technically commits bigamy, even though each returns to his legal spouse as soon as possible. For this crime he is punished with leprosy. The only cure is the blood of innocent children, and the friend for whom he had fought now sorrowfully agrees to sacrifice the two boys born to him. The leprosy vanishes, and the two children are miraculously restored.

This story of faithful friends is found in several Latin versions, of which the best known are that of Radulphus Tortarius (second half of the eleventh century) and the *Vita Amici et Amelii* of roughly the same date. The latter has strong religious overtones. Basically the story is the very common one of faithful friends. The interest lies in the miraculous leprosy cure and the combat theme. The women in the poem are of little importance—one is sensual, the other cruel—and it is this fact and the stress on loyalty which lead critics to regard *Vita Amis et Amile* as an epic rather than a romance.

Conclusions

It is clear that the popularity of the *chanson de geste* was at its height in the twelfth century. The *Chanson de Roland* was by far the greatest of these works, and it caused numerous imitations. All have some historical basis, however thin, all are concerned chiefly with men's deeds in support of or against a ruling monarch. Bravery and loyalty are the main virtues. Religion is largely hatred of the infidel. None of them is marked by subtlety in style, characterization, or morality. The world they show is a man's world of fighting, feasting, politics, and sometimes privation. Except in a very few instances, women play a subordinate role. There was little room for development in such a type, and it is small wonder that by the early thirteenth century it had already degenerated. Yet its influence in other countries was considerable, as will be seen.

THE ROMANCE

General

It is not easy to define the medieval romance exactly, particularly since critics of different nationalities use different words for it. The French often use the expression *roman courtois* ("courtly romance"), the Germans *höfisches Epos* ("courtly epic"). It is always a long narrative work, usually in verse (but Malory's *Morte d'Arthur* is in prose). The subject, although apparently historical, always has large elements of fiction. Neither the poet nor his audience felt that the characters belonged to the past of their own country. The primary purpose was entertainment and furthermore, entertainment for a relatively sophisticated and cultured audience. The didactic elements are not obvious, although many romances have important moral overtones. The principal activities of the characters are adventures of a relatively lighthearted sort and the pursuit of love, both of which activities are governed by complex conventions. The earliest extant romances are French, and we find established as early as Jean Bodel a division of subject matter—or *matière*. The *matière de France* provides stories for the cycles of *chansons de geste*. In the romance the stories are drawn from the *matière de Rome*—which includes romances about Alexander the Great and Troy—and the *matière de Bretagne*, matter of Britain. The last of these is by far the most important, for it is the subject matter of the Arthurian romances.

Before speaking of individual works, it may be well to outline certain features which are common to all. Whether the subject is drawn from the classical or the Arthurian world, a highly developed code of manners is assumed. Bravery is still important, of course, but since the combats are usually between social equals, chivalry and mercy to a beaten foe are essential. Only a recreant knight who has already put himself beyond the pale is killed. Courtesy and good manners, skill in arts, and the ability to please are as important as skill in arms. Moderation is the greatest of all virtues. Although loyalty is still stressed, it is not uncompromising loyalty to a liege lord but very often loyalty to a friend or lady.

All the romances stress the importance of women in society. They must be served without stint, protected, even worshiped. In return they should grant their love to their chosen knight. It is by no means always true in the romances that love is adulterous. Against the affairs of Tristan and Isolde, Lancelot and Guinevere, we can set the successful marriages of Erec and Enid, Parzival and Condwiramurs. Nevertheless it is the pursuit of love and service to the lady which are important. Gawain, the typical knight, is essentially a bachelor but has many loves. Although physical passion is recognized, true love is thought of as an ennobling experience. The ladies are women of culture and dignity, worthy of the service of knights, although there are female characters also who fall short. This development of great respect for women is remarkable. Classical antiquity had shown love as at best a fiery passion, at worst mere sensuality. The church tended to regard women as the daughters of Eve, who tempted men to sin. Yet in the romance (and, as we shall see, in some lyric poetry), woman is idealized. Of the many attempts which have been made to account for the phenomenon, that which points to the amount of patronage in the hands of women at court and the increasing number of women interested in literature has probably most force.

Both in love-making and adventure the great motivating force was honor. Usually this meant having a good reputation among one's peers rather than any internal sense of honor. Isolde can still speak of preserving her honor after her adultery with Tristan. In the romance this code of honor tends to replace the force of religion. Except in stories of the Grail, Christianity plays a small part and is a matter of convention rather than feeling.

The world of the romance is thus one of formalized combat and formalized love service, all taking place in a timeless never-never land. Yet in the greatest romances these conditions produced works of outstanding merit showing great literary sophistication and deep moral understanding. This is especially true of the Arthurian romances.

Arthurian Romance

In Arthurian romance it would seem that the most important figure should be that of King Arthur. Yet in the great works of the twelfth and thirteenth century this is never so. The Arthurian court and the virtues it stands for are very important indeed, but the figure of the king himself has receded into the background. Only in later and lesser works and in Malory does he again become a major figure. Clearly this phenomenon indicates a number of early romances or narratives in which the character of the Arthurian court was established and through which the traditions of the Arthurian romance became widely accepted. For the court, in every romance, is accepted as the center of civilization. Acceptance there is happiness, banishment is misery. Adventures take place in an outer world, but true happiness consists in return. We may now briefly state what knowledge we have of Arthur and his court from works which antedate the earliest extant romances, those of Chrétien de Troyes.

THE BACKGROUND OF ARTHURIAN ROMANCE

That Arthur and most of his knights were originally Celtic heroes and that many of the stories attached to them can be found in Celtic legend is now beyond reasonable doubt. The admission of this fact does not mean that the authors of the romances were aware of it, or that it affected their literary use of the material.

The first known mention of Arthur is in a Welsh poem, *Gododdin*, of about 600, whose hero is said to be second only to Arthur. In the *History of the Britons* ascribed to Nennius (c. 800) his victories are listed. In *Kulhwch and Olwen*, a Welsh prose work of about 1100, several knights appear who are common in the romances, but in this same work there is also evidence of influence from two sources, French poetry and Irish saga. The latter influences can be seen by comparing the deeds of such Irish saga characters as Bran, Cuchulain, and Finn with those of Arthurian characters. The Irish Book of the Dun Cow (c. 1100) and the Book of Leinster (c. 1150) give us evidence for this. It has been shown that many of the incidents in the Arthurian romance at all periods can be paralleled from these Irish sources. Since motifs of a general sort can be found in the folklore of many peoples, it is important to notice here that certain details and the names of characters very often correspond.

Our next evidence comes from two British writers, William of Malmesbury in the *Deeds of the Kings of Britain* (1125) and Geoffrey of Monmouth in the *History of the Kings of Britain* (1130). It may be thought that such evidence proves that the romances developed in the British Isles. But there is considerable scattered evidence that stories about Arthur were known on the Continent before this and that Bretons who migrated to Brittany in the sixth and seventh centuries had brought them. Many Breton singers performed at French courts and may well have told tales of Arthur. Such minstrels are mentioned by William of Malmesbury.

Geoffrey's history devotes a quite disproportionate amount of its text to Arthur; indeed it sometimes seems that the rest of the work was written as a frame. Arthur is a great king, the most civilized of his day, holding at bay Roman and barbarian alike. He has a splendid court and is surrounded by great knights. His downfall is brought about by the treachery of his nephew Modred, who commits adultery with Guinevere and, though defeated in battle, causes Arthur's departure to Avalon "to heal his wounds." Geoffrey may have intended Arthur as an anti-Charlemagne. He certainly increased the king's reputation.

Wace, an Anglo-Norman poet, worked much of Geoffrey's history into his poem *Brut* (1155), and it is here that we first hear of the Round Table. By this date there must have been numerous romances in existence. We hear mention of works on Tristan, and the highly organized structure of the extant works argues strongly for earlier forms. Nevertheless, the earliest works we still possess on Arthurian themes are those of one of the greatest writers of the Middle Ages, Chrétien de Troyes.

CHRÉTIEN DE TROYES

In spite of a great deal of research and pure conjecture, we still know nothing about Chrétien which he does not tell us himself. He may have been born at Troyes or lived there, he may be the "Christianus, canon St. Loup" mentioned in a document of 1173. But all we really know is that he wrote some adaptations of Ovid and a story of Mark and Iseult the Fair as well as *Erec* before writing *Cligès*. He lists these works in his prologue to *Cligès*. After these he wrote the *Chevalier de la Charette*, a Lancelot story, at the request of Marie de Champagne but did not finish it. (The work was completed by Godefroy de Lagny.) There followed *Yvain: The Knight with the Lion*; a non-Arthurian poem, *William of England*; and the unfinished *Li Contes del Graal* ("Story of the Grail"), better known as *Perceval*. The dates of these works are quite uncertain. All we can say is that they were written between 1155 and 1185. The latter date is fixed by the death of Count Philip of Flanders, to whom the work is dedicated. It is interesting to note that *Erec*, *Yvain*, and *Perceval* were all used as models by German poets; Hartman von Aue wrote poems closely modeled on the first two and Wolfram von Eschenbach used *Perceval* as the basis for his *Parzival*.

Erec and *Yvain* are similar and in some ways complementary poems. Both have as general theme the loss and recovery of the virtue of moderation. It will be convenient to summarize each briefly and compare them.

Erec is accompanying Queen Guinevere on a hunt when one of her ladies is slapped by a dwarf. Erec's attempts to interfere are treated the same way, for he is unarmed. Without arming himself, he goes in pursuit and arrives in a town where a tournament is to take place. Finding no accommodation there, he is well received by a poor knight, Coralus, and his beautiful daughter, Enid. He borrows arms from Coralus and takes part in the tournament, where he wins the silver sparrow hawk for Enid and defeats Yder, the knight whom he had pursued. Enid is kindly received at court, where she is judged the most beautiful woman. But after marrying Enid, Erec retires to his lands and seems to have no interest in adventure. His men criticize him, and Enid is worried. One night she is repeating this criticism to herself when she is overheard by Erec. He misinterprets it as *her* criticism, brusquely bids her precede him and keep absolute silence. Over and over again she breaks his command to warn him of danger. Her only reward is abuse. Finally Erec is so badly wounded in a fight with two robbers that he seems dead. Enid, lamenting, is taken by the count of Limors, with Erec's body, to a nearby castle. Here he attempts to force her to marry him. Erec is aroused, kills the count, and the pair are reconciled. One more big adventure awaits them. At the castle of Brandigan they are well received but find there the widows of eighty knights slain by a champion in a nearby enclosed garden. In spite of warnings, Erec decides to challenge the knight, whose name is Mabonograin, and defeats him. As it turns out, the knight is happy to be defeated. He has promised his lady, who proves to be a relative of Enid, that he would not leave the garden until defeated in her sight. The poem ends with a happy return to Arthur's court.

It is clear from the above summary that the work is concerned with excess of love and also with love of the wrong kind. For real love would not be mere uxoriousness but combined with the desire for adventure.

Yvain handles the same problem but in a different way. At Arthur's court Yvain hears his cousin Calogrenant tell of a disgrace he has suffered. In search of adventure, he was directed to a fountain. When water was poured on a stone, there was a great storm, and when it cleared, a black-armed knight appeared who unhorsed Calogrenant. Sir Keu (Kay) heaps abuse on Calogrenant for his disgrace, and Arthur promises to undertake the same adventure with his court. But Yvain anticipates him, wounds the black knight, pursues him and is trapped in his castle. Fortunately he is discovered by a maid, Lunete, whom he had once befriended at Arthur's court, and she gives him a ring to make him invisible. While trapped, he sees the lady of the castle, Laudine, and promptly falls in love with her. Her husband, the black knight, has died, and after some clever arguments by Lunete she is persuaded to accept Yvain as her husband.

When Arthur's court comes, it is Yvain who defends the fountain and defeats Sir Keu. Gawain warns Yvain not to be like Erec but to undertake adventures. Therefore Yvain takes leave for a year and a day, overstays it, is rejected by Laudine, and runs mad. He is restored by a lady whom he afterward assists against her enemies, joined by a lion whom he had helped kill a snake, and undertakes a series of adventures in all of which he helps ladies against some form of oppression. The most important is his championing of Lunete, who is to be burned for her part in the marriage. He reconciles her with Laudine, who fails to recognize him. His last adventure is a fight near the fountain with Gawain when they represent the interests of two quarreling sisters. Neither wins, since they recognize each other and stop fighting. Meanwhile Lunete recommends the Knight of the Lion as the fountain's new defender; he is accepted, reveals himself to Laudine, and there is mutual reconciliation.

Although *Yvain* is better organized than *Erec* there is remarkable similarity of structure. Each begins with an incident at court. Each expands this to the deeds leading up to the acquisition of a beautiful wife. The apparent happy ending of each is shattered by the failure of the knight to observe balance or to understand the true nature of love, so that a longer and much more difficult "rewinning" of the bride is necessary. The adventures entailed almost all involve service to ladies in some way, a kind of penance. Both knights suffer a kind of death or departure from the world, Erec when he lies in the castle of the count of Limors, Yvain when he goes mad. Both are different men when restored. For each the indecisive combat with Gawain is the proof of their restoration to knightly status.

It is easy to trace in both stories the influence of primitive religion and folklore. The lady of the fountain was once a nymph-goddess of the water, whose mate was chosen by defeating the previous incumbent. It is hard to rework such material in a courtly sense, for it would be impossible for Chrétien to show Laudine as automatically the property of the victor. The Mabonograin scene is a modification of the common Celtic story of the penetration of the hero into the isle of the dead, although here it is used to show Erec putting right a love situation where the mistress holds her lover back from adventure.

In both works Kay is the loudmouthed grumbler who is later chastised, Gawain the perfect bachelor knight. Arthur's court is the ideal locale, Arthur himself the wise but relatively inactive king. *Yvain* is probably the best of all French Arthurian romances. It is well constructed, full of bright adventure, light in tone, not without humor (especially in the scenes with the lion), yet morally serious.

The subject of *Lancelot* was clearly distasteful to Chrétien. He was here asked to depict a situation very different from that in *Erec* and *Yvain*. Again the poem opens at court with a familiar motif—a challenge from a strange knight. This time one knight is to be allowed to accompany Guinevere to the woods. If the stranger defeats him, he will keep Guinevere. Otherwise he will give back some eighty captive knights. Kay demands the task and in spite of entreaties rides off with the queen. On Gawain's advice, Arthur follows, and it soon appears that Kay is beaten and the queen abducted. Gawain lends a horse to a strange knight (Lancelot) and later meets him walking behind a cart, driven by a dwarf. Told that he must ride in this shameful vehicle like a criminal if he wants news of the queen, Lancelot hesitates two steps before jumping in. Gawain rides behind and after a perilous night in a castle, they are told that Meleagant was the queen's abductor. Two passages lead to the island kingdom of Baudemagus, one a sword bridge, the other a bridge under water. Lancelot takes the road to the former and after various adventures on the way, crosses the bridge and defeats Meleagant, who insists on fighting despite the pleas of his courteous father, Baudemagus. Instead of a joyful welcome, Lancelot is coolly received by the queen, who knows of his hesitation in entering the cart. He goes off and is treacherously attacked. Both Guinevere and Lancelot hear false news of the other's death, and when the truth is established, Lancelot visits the queen in a room where Kay is lying wounded. Lancelot has cut his fingers entering the window, and the bloodstains on the bed cause Meleagant to accuse Kay of being the queen's lover. Both deny it. Lancelot fights Meleagant again to prove Kay's innocence and wins.

After pulling Gawain out of the water where he has attempted the underwater crossing, Lancelot is deceived by a dwarf and captured. The others return to Arthur's court. He persuades the wife of his jailer to let him take part in a tournament at Noauz, where Guinevere is in the audience. Although victorious at first, he allows his success or failure to depend entirely on the queen's whim. After final victory he returns to prison but is released by Meleagant's sister. Gawain is all prepared to take his place in a third combat with Meleagant, but Lancelot arrives in time and kills his opponent amid great rejoicing.

Chrétien's other romance, *Perceval*, could very easily have been his most important, but death apparently prevented him from finishing it. Since Wolfram von Eschenbach followed Chrétien fairly closely, it will be easiest to summarize the story fully when writing of Wolfram, where the important differences between the two works will be noted (see pp. 129f.). Essentially the story is that of an innocent young man setting out into an unfamiliar world. He is seeking Arthur's court to become a knight but has no idea what is involved in this. By accident he stumbles on the Castle of the Holy Grail, an event which changes his whole orientation. Since the work was not finished, we do not know what Chrétien intended his hero to do, but it seems likely that he would have become chief of the band who guard the sacred Grail and hence a knight with a religious purpose, as opposed to the secular-minded Gawain, whose adventures are made to contrast with his. Several authors wrote continuations of Chrétien's work.

Here a few words should be said about the Holy Grail, which figures so prominently in a great deal of Arthurian romance. The exact significance of the word is obscure, but it seems to mean a dish, not a cup. Many authorities find evidence for a Celtic origin of the vessel, one of whose properties was the ability to provide food and drink at will. Even if this was so, it was confused very early with another sacred vessel, the dish of the Last Supper. The apocryphal Gospel of Nicodemus tells of how Joseph of Arimathea possessed this dish, with Christ's blood, how he was imprisoned and later released by Jesus. Many legends became attached to this story, one of the most important of which was that Joseph came west and died at Glastonbury in England. About 1200 Robert de Boron wrote a poem called *Joseph* or *L'histoire del roman del sankt Graal* ("History of the Romance of the Holy Grail"). In it he told of the early history of the Grail, of how Joseph was liberated from prison by Vespasian because of his miraculous cure, how Joseph and his brother-in-law Hebron and others formed the Grail company, how they suffered because of sinners among them, who were found out by passing before the Grail, and how Hebron, now called Bron, went westward with the Grail with his son Alain. He also wrote a *Merlin* continuing this story, but only fragments of that work remain. Both *Joseph* and *Merlin* exist in prose versions found in two manuscripts which contain the so-called *Didot Perceval*. It is possible that Robert wrote the prose versions of *Joseph* and *Merlin* and also a poem on which the *Didot Perceval* is modeled. In the prose *Perceval*, Alain le Gros, Perceval's father, sends him to Arthur's court. He learns chivalry, distinguishes himself in a tournament, but dares to sit at the permanently vacant thirteenth place at the Round Table. The seat splits, and a voice announces that desolation will fall on Britain which will be relieved only when one outstanding knight finds Bron, the Fisher King, Perceval's grandfather, in the Grail castle and asks about the Grail. All set out. Many of the adventures are similar to those in Chrétien's work, though there are some major differences. As in Chrétien, the first visit to the castle is unsuccessful. After meeting Merlin, however, Perceval asks the right questions. Bron is cured but dies three days after entrusting the Grail and its secrets to Perceval. The seat at the Round Table is rejoined, the enchantments cease. The remainder of the work tells of Arthur's campaigns against the Romans and the final battle against Modred. The work is interesting only as showing a Christian and apparently very popular view of the Grail and its importance for Arthur's court.

The same desolation of Britain appears in the prose *Perlesvaus* (1191–1212), in which several knights seek the Grail, but only Perceval finds it. The final collapse of the court is described, with Guinevere dying before Arthur, and Lancelot aiding his king.

The Grail is also very important in the Vulgate cycle (c. 1215–30), a great compilation of prose romances drawing on many known and unknown sources. It begins with material closely modeled on Robert de Boron's Grail romances, then begins to tell the story of Lancelot, how he loved Guinevere but had a son by another lady, Brisane, who tricked him into thinking she was the queen. The part known as the *Queste del Sanct Graal* tells of the failure of Lionel and Gawain to attain the Grail, of how Lancelot had a vision of it, and how Perceval, Bohort, and Galahad reached the castle Corbenic where the Grail was. Here Galahad alone sees the mystery inside the Grail vessel and dies in ecstasy; Perceval dies after a year and Bohort reports all these matters to the court. In the *Mort Artu* Lancelot saves Guinevere in judicial combat and takes her to his castle of Joyous Garde. Arthur besieges the castle, but a compromise is arranged and the queen returns to court. Lancelot leaves Britain. Arthur, encouraged by Gawain, who wishes to avenge a brother killed by Lancelot, pursues him. Arthur is twice forced to return home, once to repel an invasion of the Romans, once to fight his last battle with Modred, here shown as Arthur's son. Obviously the last scenes in all these works go back to the account in Geoffrey of Monmouth, but with considerable variations brought about by the importance given to Lancelot.

The brief summary of these works on the Grail and on Arthur's last years shows how weak they were compared with Chrétien's achievement. He was able to select and to produce, especially in *Yvain*, an integrated romance with a concentration of interest on one or two characters which yet allowed him to depict the imaginative Arthurian world in all its glory. Not the smallest reason for his achievement was his mastery of language and verse form.

Only one major Arthurian theme still awaits treatment, that of Tristan and Isolde.

TRISTAN AND ISOLDE

The Tristan story is Arthurian only by adoption. The world in which the events take place is governed by the same conventions as those of the Arthurian world, and in some, but by no means all, versions of the story Arthur or his knights appear. Once again it is possible to find parallels in Celtic sagas. Many of the incidents of the Tristan story show obvious affinities with the story of Diarmaid and Gráinne, in particular an incident in the Finn cycle (see pp. 217f.). The story is always concerned with the love affair between a nephew and his uncle's wife, but in the extant romances other elements have been added, and the treatment of the love theme varies widely from one version to another. There were undoubtedly versions of the story long before any of the extant versions were composed, because there are several references to Tristan in twelfth-century works, among them Chrétien's in the prologue to *Cligès*. A strange accident, however, prevents us from being as well informed as we could wish. Not one of the important Tristan romances has survived entire. The only complete work is the Norse translation, made in 1226, of the poem of Thomas of Britain. All other versions are in one way or another incomplete. The late prose versions, which have not yet been fully edited, vary considerably in content.

There was probably a French version, usually called the *Estoire*, about the middle of the twelfth century, but the earliest extant fragments are those of Thomas of Britain and Béroul. The fragments of the latter, two in number, are of considerable length but belong to the part of the story after the parting of Tristan and Isolde and cast relatively little light on the story. They are dated either around 1160 or 1190. They are relatively crude narrative poetry and are often said to represent the "common" or "noncourtly" version of *Tristan*, also to be seen in the version by the German Eilhart von Oberge (c. 1170–90). The work of Thomas of Britain, an author of whom nothing is known, is much more important. Only the last part survives, but we can be fairly sure of its contents, if not its style, from the Norse version already mentioned and from that of its great imitator, Gottfried von Strassburg. The version of Thomas (c. 1170–80) apparently ran as follows. Kanelangres (Riwalin in Gottfried's poem), a knight from Brittany, attracts the notice of Blensinbil (Blancheflur), daughter of King Mark of Cornwall, while taking part in a tournament. He is seriously wounded. Thinking he is sure to die, Blensinbil visits him and conceives a child. He recovers but is killed soon after and Blensinbil dies of grief after giving birth to Tristan. To save the child from the usurping Duke Morgan, the faithful Rual brings him up as his own son, devoting special attention to intellectual and artistic pursuits. The boy is kidnaped by merchants, but a storm makes them put him ashore—in Cornwall. He impresses all by his skills in hunt ceremonial and music, and Mark is delighted to learn later from Rual that the boy is his nephew. Tristan is knighted, kills Morgan, recovers his property, which he presents to Rual, and returns to Mark. Here he delivers the country from tribute by killing the giant Morholt of Ireland, but in doing so he receives a poisoned wound and leaves a piece of his sword in the dead man's skull. Only Morholt's sister, the queen of Ireland, can cure the wound. Tristan goes there as a musician, Tantris, and is cured in exchange for teaching the queen's daughter Isolde.

Returning to Cornwall cured, he finds that the barons are jealous of him. They urge Mark to marry the beautiful princess of Ireland and to send Tristan to get her. Mark reluctantly agrees. (In some versions he says he will marry only the girl a strand of whose yellow hair has just been dropped by a swallow.) When he arrives in Ireland, Tristan kills a dragon and cuts out its tongue, which poisons him and causes him to swoon. Again he is restored by the queen, but at court Isolde notes the notch in his sword blade and only with difficulty is prevented from killing him to avenge her uncle. As it happens, her hand has been promised to the man who kills the dragon. A seneschal claims that he has done so and produces the head. Tristan refutes him, puts forward his proposal for the marriage with Mark, and is accepted.

Isolde leaves for Cornwall most reluctantly, but on the way she and Tristan drink a love potion prepared by her mother for the wedding night. After this they are indissolubly bound by love. To save her mistress' honor, the lady Brangaene agrees to take her place in Mark's bed. Isolde, afraid that Brangaene will reveal her secret, attempts to have her killed but later repents. There follows a series of attempted meetings which arouse the suspicion of a steward and dwarf who try to arrange for Mark to catch the lovers together. Ultimately, Isolde is forced to submit to the ordeal of the hot iron. She arranges that Tristan shall disguise himself as a pilgrim and be at the place where she disembarks from a ship to undergo the test. She requests that she be carried ashore by the "holy man," and then tells him to fall with her to the sand so that they lie in each other's arms. She is thus able to swear "truthfully" that she has lain in the arms of no man except her husband and the pilgrim they have just seen. Thus the ultimate deception is perpetrated—on God himself. After another reconciliation with Mark, their love for one another becomes too obvious for Mark to endure, and he banishes them. For a time they lead an idyllic existence in a grotto of love far away from the court, but are later found by a hunting party. Mark sees them asleep with a sword between them (why this should be we do not discover) and he recalls them to court. But soon Tristan is permanently banished. He marries his friend Kaëdin's sister but on being reproached for not consummating the marriage, he brings Kaëdin where he can see Isolde. Kaëdin agrees with him. For a short time the lovers are reunited, but this and similar meetings are brief. Tristan has a giant whom he has defeated set up a shrine with near-human figures of Isolde and Brangaene where he can come for solace.

Finally Tristan is badly wounded. Only Isolde can cure him. Tristan waits on a cliff with his wife, Kaëdin's sister, who is to tell him if a white sail approaches, which means that Isolde is coming. She falsely reports a black sail, and Tristan expires. Isolde dies on his body. Mark, coming to tell them of his forgiveness, has them buried in a chapel, and from the tombs grow a vine and a rose, which intertwine.

Certain elements of this form of the story are to be found in all versions of the Tristan story. These are the loss of territory to Duke Morgan, the fight with Morholt, the poisoned wound, the notch in the blade, the love potion and subsequent adventures, and the second marriage. Obviously the story bears resemblances to that of Lancelot, although the borrowing is probably from the Tristan story rather than the reverse. That love is all-conquering and that it overrides all other considerations is clear, but it should not be assumed that the attitude of all the authors to the phenomenon is the same. In the early versions, represented in French by Béroul, and the later prose works, the love is frankly adulterous and Tristan is an adventurer who outsmarts Mark. The king is a jealous monster, who evokes no sympathy from the reader. The love potion is what causes the affair, and the "popular" versions delight in piling up incidents of Tristan's meetings with his love in various disguises and rescuing her from Mark's clutches. If the nature of their love is considered at all, it is regarded as an irrational passion which sweeps men and women off their feet and makes them behave immorally. Dido and Aeneas' passion was of this kind.

In Thomas' version, this love has been refined. Mark, although jealous, is not a monster—he has drunk the remains of the same love potion. The lovers are concerned with their honor, and both remain faithful even in absence. Tristan's marriage is a desperate attempt to console himself with a woman of the same name (Isolde of the White Hands), an attempt which fails. There is a complete absence of the exaggerated love-service we find in Chrétien's Lancelot, but here too love is an ennobling, not a debasing passion. The reader's sympathy is with the lovers and Mark. The outward trappings of courtly love are preserved, and fair speech and good manners are essential. Yet Tristan is not, in this version, a knight like those in Chrétien's works. His chief attainments are artistic rather than chivalrous, although he is, of course, a superb warrior. Thomas shows interest in the psychology of his characters, in their reactions to situations. He is, indeed, far more concerned with this than with mere narrative adventure. There is no attempt to hide the immorality of the love of Tristan and Isolde, but Thomas is much more concerned with the pathos of the situation and he so idealizes the affair that we are prepared to overlook the fact that it is adultery which he is describing. Love is a force greater than all other forces, and although its results may be antisocial, they enlist our sympathy. As we shall see (see pp. 127ff.), Gottfried von Strassburg developed this idea of irresistible love still further.

The other French works on Tristan fall far below that of Thomas. Two brief prose works, both called *Madness of Tristan*, deal with the episode in which the hero feigns madness to be near his love. About 1230–50 there were written down various episodes about Tristan which we call the *Prose-Tristan*, though it is actually a series of overlapping accounts in various manuscripts. It has little literary value and is crude in matter and style. The adventures related in these prose works, rather than those in the earlier romances, form the basis of Malory's account in English.

MINOR ARTHURIAN ROMANCES

Like the *chanson de geste*, the Arthurian romance was at its best in the earliest versions which have come down to us. Its popularity inspired a mass of inferior works whose only relation to the Arthurian tradition was their use of its conventions of service to the lady and series of adventures. Most are little more than names—*Fergus* (c. 1230); *Jaufré* (c. 1230), one of the few written in Provençal; *Rigomer* (thirteenth century), about Lancelot and Gawain; and *Humbaut* (thirteenth century). *The Fair Unknown* (1185/90) is the story of Guinglain, son of Gawain, who delivers a lady from reptile form with a kiss. Raoul d'Houdenc also wrote a romance about Gawain, the *Vengeance of Radiguel*, as well as *Meraugis de Portlesguez*, both early in the thirteenth century.

There are two romances about the unjustly accused wife. The *Count of Poitiers* (c. 1180) shows a man upholding the honor of his wife only to have "proofs" of her infidelity shown to him. These have been obtained by trickery, as he later discovers. In *Guillaume de Dole*, sometimes called the *Romance of the Rose* (c. 1200), the hero's sister is falsely accused by a seneschal, the proof being knowledge of a rose-colored birthmark on her leg. She refutes the accusation herself and marries the emperor Konrad. The work is remarkable for the interspersion of songs sung by the characters.

Some of the finest works in all countries were Arthurian romances. In this type authors had the opportunity to develop their subject matter and to move their figures in an ideal world. The result, in the best works, is noble idealism, a strong sense of form, great technical and, in particular, descriptive skill, and the invention of characters of credibility and interest. The problems posed, although set in an idealized frame, are those of all mankind at all times. In the Grail romances and particularly in the Vulgate cycle, the religious element becomes dominant, and the search for the Grail is the Christian's search for God. The knights are between sin and blessedness, each doing his best within the powers granted to him but often the victim of his own sins. There can be little doubt that in developing the Arthurian romance France made one of its greatest contributions to medieval literature.

Romances of Antiquity

The romances of antiquity, unlike the Arthurian, are based on known literary works, though often with considerable adaptation. Although much of the material used was historical, it was treated as fiction, and the author felt at liberty to change incidents and, in particular, to make his characters behave according to the code of manners and ethics which we call courtly. The heroes of Thebes and Troy behave like Yvain and Lancelot, which means that the main stress in these works is on love and adventure. Such a stress had been not uncommon in the romances of late antiquity, where, for instance, Achilles refuses battle not because of injured pride but because the war prevents him from marrying Polyxena of Troy.

The earliest extant romance of antiquity is the *Roman de Thèbes* (c. 1150), which is based on the *Thebaid* of the Latin poet Statius. The story of the struggle of the brothers at Thebes belongs, of course, to Greek mythology. In his more than 10,000-line poem the author attempts to depict characters with discrimination and emphasizes love themes. It is the first French poem to contain the stylized portrait-descriptions which later became so common. Obviously the poem was a success, for its methods were widely imitated and even surpassed—in the *Roman de Troie* (c. 1165) of Benoît de Ste-Maure, for instance, which is probably the most important of the romances of antiquity. In more than 30,000 lines it tells the story of the Trojan War. The source is not Homer but the late classical prose account of "Dares Phrygius," who calls himself an eyewitness of the events. This Latin work is very brief but covers the whole war, with portraits of the major characters, and differs a great deal from the better-known accounts of Homer and Ovid. Out of this bald narrative Benoît made a wide-sweeping chivalric account of the siege, stressing love affairs (Achilles and Polyxena, Achilles and

Penthesilea). The Dares work was written from the Trojan point of view, a matter of satisfaction to the many western European rulers who "traced" their descent from Troy. Perhaps the best-known part of the work was an incident which Benoît appears to have invented—the story of the Trojan Troilus' love for Briseida, and of her love for him. When she was sent back to her father, who was with the Greeks, they swore eternal troth, but Diomedes' love declaration won her over and Troilus died in despair. This pathetic tale of love was highly popular and widely used. Benoît followed the fashion set by the *Roman de Thèbes* in his use of analytical portraits, which are among the best parts of his work. About 1285 Guido delle Colonne wrote a Latin prose adaptation of the *Roman de Troie*.

Inevitably Vergil's *Aeneid* was treated as a romance. The unknown author of the *Roman d'Enée* (c. 1160) did not hesitate to put the incidents of Vergil's work in chronological order and remove the gods altogether. The love incident between Dido and Aeneas is played down as passionate and destructive love, while the affair with Lavinia is raised from being a political match to the status of a courtly love affair and the reason for the epic struggle with Turnus. The propaganda for the Empire in Vergil's poem has also vanished. It has become a story of love and war.

The most popular figure of classical antiquity, in France at least, was Alexander the Great. There was, of course, a considerable amount of material of reasonable historical accuracy available about him in works by Curtius, Nepos, and others. In Hellenistic times in the Greek-speaking world there had already been romances about him, which were, however, more concerned with the marvelous aspects of his conquests than with truth. These romances were supported by collections of "Letters," purportedly written by Alexander to his mother and to his tutor Aristotle. The Middle Ages knew such works as the *Journey of Alexander to the Earthly Paradise* and the *History of Battles*, a tenth-century translation of Greek sources. From these, French writers made up a narrative in which Alexander conducts a career of conquest in exotic lands. The stress is on the magic strangeness of his adventures rather than on any love interest. The first known work in French—of which only 105 lines survive, but of which a German translation is known—was by Alberic de Briançon

(c. 1100/20). A little more survives of a reworking of it of about 1150, which reworking was continued by Lambert de Tort and others in the twelve-syllable line we call the alexandrine. Alexander is made more and more the chivalric hero, with one adventure following another. Two independent poems were both called the *Vengeance of Alexander*, one by Jean le Venelais (before 1181), the other by Guy de Cambrai (c. 1190). A 7,000-line *Roman de toute chevalerie* of about 1250 by Thomas of Kent gives a complete story of Alexander.

The anonymous 15,000-line *Roman d'Alexandre* (mid-thirteenth century), which resulted from the compilations already noted, remained fairly close to the life of the hero, that is, it began with his childhood and his taming of the horse Bucephalus and followed his career of conquest with special stress on his campaigns in India, adding throughout the stories of marvels already mentioned. In the fourteenth century the same process took place that we have already seen in the Arthurian romance. Romances were composed with an "Alexandrian" background which had no direct connection with the king but simply set a scene at his court and then proceeded on their own way. Best known of these is the *Voeux du Paon* (1312) of Jacques de Longuyon, in which various knights take vows on a peacock. Here were introduced the nine-worthies (Joshua, David, Judas Maccabæus, Hector, Alexander, Caesar, Arthur, Charlemagne, Godefroi de Bouillon), and a fashion started of "bird vows" which was continued in the *Restor du Paon* of Brisebarre.

There were a number of romances on minor classical themes, many of them drawn from Ovid—a very well-worked *Narcissus* of the early thirteenth century and a *Pyramus and Thisbe* (late twelfth century) of charm and wit.

Narrative Works on Various Subjects

The most important narrative works of French literature in the Middle Ages can each be classified in one or other of the groups already discussed. But it must be noted that, in the late thirteenth and fourteenth centuries in particular, subjects for romances, many of them quite long, were found everywhere. Moreover by this time the distinction between romance and *chanson de geste* was obscured, and the same mixture of the romantic and fantastic is found in almost all works, whether professedly historical or not.

The crusades gave rise to several poems, some of them of considerable merit. The first crusade is celebrated in two works, the *Chanson d'Antioche* and the *Chanson de Jérusalem*, both of which are extant in reworkings by Graindor de Donai (c. 1180–1200). A Latin account of the crusade by William of Tyre (c. 1128–90) is put into French verse in the *Roman d'Eracles* ("Romance of Heraclius"; c. 1231) by an otherwise unknown Bernard de Corbie. The great hero of the first crusade, Godefroi de Bouillon, has several poems about his origins and deeds, of which the best known is the *Chevalier au Cygne* ("Swan Knight") of the late twelfth century, tracing his origin to a swan. The murderous crusade against the Albigenses of southern France produced a verse account in Provençal by Guillaume de Tudèle, the *Song of the Crusade Against the Albigensians* (c. 1219).

Wace, the author of *Brut*, was commissioned by Henry II of England to write a verse account of the Plantagenets, which he called *Roman de Rou* ("Romance of Rollo," first duke of Normandy). The 16,000 lines he had written were expanded to over 43,000 by a certain Beneit, perhaps Benoît de Ste-Maure (p. 96), about 1170.

The Byzantine period of history is represented by the *Eracle* (c. 1165) of Gautier d'Arras, a novel of a hero with power to perceive the best in precious stones, horses, and women. With this gift he finds the best of wives, Athenaïs, and so helps the emperor in war against the Persians that he is finally chosen emperor himself and recovers the relics of the Cross. *Ille et Galeron* (c. 1167) by the same author is an examination of the interaction of pity and love. Gautier d'Arras is one of the finest writers of romance.

Romances were written in France on themes familiar in Middle English literature. *Bevis of Hamptown* appears twice in French literature in the early thirteenth century. *Horn and Reniel* had appeared earlier, about 1180. One of the most attractive noncyclical romances is the *Violette* (c. 1227–9) of Gerbert de Montreuil. Romances set in the East were as always very popular, and of these the best known is *Floire et Blancheflur*, dating from about 1162. It tells of child lovers separated and reunited after innumerable adventures. The supernatural plays a strong role in some of the works, notably *Parthenopeus de Blois* (before 1188) and *Huon de Bordeaux* (c. 1220). *Guillaume de Palerme* (1205) is a story of a hero

turned werewolf, while *Robert le Diable* (c. 1195), makes use
of a well-known folk theme of the evil deeds of a child born
as the result of a prayer to the devil. Finally we may mention
a long poem (20,000 alexandrines), *La belle Hélène*, thirteenth century, which handles another favorite theme of the
later Middle Ages, the unjustly persecuted woman. Religious
and didactic in tone is the romance of *Barlaam and Josaphat*,
put into French in 1220/25 by Guy de Cambrai. It is a Christianized version of the story of Buddha.

Flamenca is an important romance of 8,087 lines written in
Provençal. The author may be the Bernadet mentioned in the
poem but is otherwise unknown. The date is equally uncertain,
perhaps about 1270. The story tells of Count Gui de Nemours
who marries his daughter Flamenca to Archambaut de Bour-
bon. The husband is mad with jealousy at the wedding feast
and makes his young wife miserable. Later a man endowed
with every virtue appears and approaches Flamenca by bribing
the priest to allow him to be his assistant at Mass. Thus, after
a time a rendezvous is arranged. The husband ceases to be
jealous when he has every reason for it, even when the young
man wins every prize at a tournament he has arranged. At
this point the poem breaks off. It is a masterpiece of wit,
irony, and above all of characterization. The author's portraits of jealous husband, sweet but inconstant wife, com-
plaisant clergy, and clever servants are unusual in medieval
literature. *Flamenca* is one of the great masterpieces of the
period.

LAIS

The term *lai* is a confusing one, since it is used for an ill-
defined type of lyric poetry as well as for the short narrative
which will be discussed here. Its origin is obscure. Apparently
short Celtic stories were turned into verse form and called
lais, a fact reflected in the term *lai breton*. Later any subject
matter could be used, but the typical form remained the short
narrative. By far the most famous writer of *lais* was Marie
de France, who, in spite of her name, seems to have been a
noblewoman who lived all her life in England. She says she
heard the stories in her youth and wished to translate them.
It is usually presumed that her source was Breton minstrels.
Her works, which seem to belong to the years between 1160

and 1190, have various subjects. One, *Chevrefeuille* ("Honey-suckle"), describes a meeting between Tristan and Isolde. The supernatural is important in *Lanval* and *Guigemar*, while in *Yonec* we have the fairy-tale motif of the lover who visits his mistress as a bird, is trapped and killed by the jealous husband and avenged by his son. *Bisclavret* is a werewolf story. Happy endings are rare in the *lais*, and the important theme in all is love—not courtly love but natural affection. Marie wrote twelve *lais*, and they mark the beginning of the popularity of this type. (She also wrote, about 1190, a French *Purgatory of St. Patrick*, in which the saint visits the other world, and a collection of fables.) Other, less famous writers continued the tradition up to about 1250 with *Melion* (like *Bisclavret*), *L'épine* ("The Thorn"), and *Tiolet*. Similar is the short poem *Papagai* ("Parrot"). Some longer works are also called *lais*, for example the *Mule sans frein* ("Mule Without Reins"), *Lai de Tidorel*, *Lai du mantel* (concerning a mantle which by failing to fit, reveals unchastity), and others which use Marie's own themes. The *lai* had a relatively short life and hardly appears after the thirteenth century. There are some short verse tales calling themselves *lais* which became quite well known—*Spotted Palfrey* of Huon le Roi, *Sparrow Hawk*, and others, all with romantic themes.

ALLEGORY

The discussion here is of allegory as a literary form, not as a method of interpretation. We saw in the introduction that allegorization, that is, the discovery of "higher" meanings in both sacred and secular texts, was a common procedure. But it was also common to write works in which the action was carried on by personified abstractions who behaved as human beings. The first known full-length work of this kind is the *Psychomachia* of Prudentius (fourth century), in which the virtues and vices battle for the human soul like the characters in a Vergilian epic. Almost all allegories adopt a "frame" within which they work—the dream, the battle, the journey, the hunt.

Prudentius' work was extremely influential in the Middle Ages, as was Martianus Capella's *Marriage of Mercury and Philology* (c. 375). Allegories of various sorts continued to be written in Latin, for example the *Fecunda ratis* ("Fertile

Ship") of Egbert of Liege (tenth century), which describes the learning stowed into an allegorical ship. But the really important Latin allegories appear in the twelfth century. Bernard Silvestris of Tours wrote between 1145 and 1153 his *De Universitate mundi* ("On the Whole World"), which presented in allegorical form his views of the creative force of nature. More important still were two works of Alain de Lille (c. 1128–1202), the *Anticlaudianus* and the *De planctu mundi* ("Complaint of Nature"). These latter were still influential at the time of Chaucer. The first and more important of them tells of the horror of Nature at the corruption of man. She resolves to make a perfect being and calls the various virtues to her glorious palace. Prudentia points out that they can do everything but provide the new being with a soul. Reason, when asked for her opinion, recommends that Prudentia be their emissary to God to ask for help. Concord urges her to go. A marvelous chariot is put together by the liberal arts and Concord, in which Prudentia ascends through the various spheres. As the help of the arts falters, their place is taken by Nous, or spirit, and finally, before the face of God, by Faith. God agrees to grant the soul. Once the new being is made the vices mount an attack and a great battle ensues. Ultimately, the virtues triumph. Clearly the *Anticlaudianus* shows a highly developed philosophical allegory by means of which the author expresses his views on a series of points, the most important of which are the place of man in creation and the function of nature in God's purpose.

This same form was to be followed, though with a different subject, by Guillaume de Loris (early thirteenth century) in the first part of the *Roman de la Rose* (c. 1230) and even more closely by Jean de Meung (c. 1260–1315) in his continuation of the work (c. 1275). Guillaume's purpose was to tell, in the form of an allegorical narrative, the progress of a courtly lover. Although adventure is absent, almost all the other trappings of the romance are present. The lover lies down to sleep, and the narrative is a dream. He enters a walled garden where he sees various forms of pleasant, though sensual love. Good manners reign everywhere. As he wanders off, thinking of love, he is shot by Cupid's dart and, seeing the reflection of a rosebud in the pool of Narcissus, falls desperately in love. He tries many means to attain the rose—influence, friends, even bribery. It is clear that only fair speech and long endurance will finally gain his goal. The poem breaks off at line 4,058 with the lover still far from the rosebud and his friend Fair Welcome in prison. All the characters except the lover are abstractions and have to be studied in the light of the code of courtly love—of withdrawal by the lady, of hope and despair by the man. The poem is extremely subtle.

Not so subtle but certainly much more ponderous and learned is its continuation. Whereas Guillaume had used the conceits and poetic fancy of the romance, Jean de Meung reverts to the philosophical learning of the Latin poets. There are numerous learned digressions in the form of long speeches, but the most important change is that the whole purpose of Guillaume's poem is reversed. Instead of regarding love as a game to be played according to courtly rules, Jean de Meung thinks of it purely as a means of repopulating the earth. He satirizes the manners and conventions which appear in the earlier poem and especially the timidity and fine feelings of the love it describes. Nevertheless, Jean maintains the original allegorical framework. He has Fair Welcome released from prison, then captured again, and a final assault made by the adherents of Venus and Cupid on the tower manned by the antilove forces.

There are two intellectual streams meeting in the *Roman de la Rose*: the secular, courtly convention of love as a game with highly wrought conventions and fine manners—a stream ultimately derived from Ovid's *Art of Love* and its French versions—and a clerical intellectual stream, represented particularly by Alain de Lille, which thought of love only as a function of Nature, who was herself the handmaiden of God.

The *Roman* was immensely popular. The first part appealed to the continuing interest in courtly love, the second to the growing intellectualism of the fourteenth century.

There had been isolated semi-allegorical poems on love before, for example, *Hueline et Eglantine*, *Fable of the God of Love*, and *Venus Goddess of Love*. But after the success of the *Roman de la Rose*, their number increases rapidly. Thibaut's *Romance of the Pear* (mid-thirteenth century) shows the lover besieged in a tower and the lady wounded by Cupid's arrow. In Nicole de Margival's *Panther of Love* (end of the thirteenth century) the beloved is shown as a panther. Love also was pursued in the form of a hunt in Jean

Aicart's *Prise amoureuse* (1332). Even chess is used as an allegorical vehicle for the game of love.

Other subjects also are discussed in allegorical form. Raoul de Houdenc represents courtly virtues in the *Romance of the Wings of Knighthood* (early thirteenth century). *Dream of Hell* by the same author is a journey to Hell and a vision of the fates of the wicked. Intellectual pursuits are allegorized —following the tradition of Martianus Capella—by Henri d'Andeli in the *Battle of the Seven Arts* (after 1236) and by Jehan le Tainturier in his *Marriage of the Seven Arts* (to the seven virtues).

In discussing allegory, the large and influential body of works which consisted of *allegorized* material should not be neglected. Perhaps the best known is the allegorization of the characters of birds and beasts in the *Physiologus*. This list of creatures, some mythological, with their "significances" appeared in Latin in the fourth and fifth centuries. The earliest French version is that of Philipp de Thaon (c. 1125). Better known is the *Béstiaire divin* of Guillaume le Clerc (1211), a poem of about 4,200 lines. Gervaise, also a Norman, produced a shorter bestiary a little later. There are also numerous lapidaries, descriptions of the powers of precious stones.

LYRIC POETRY

General

The tradition of lyric poetry continues unbroken from classical antiquity to medieval Europe, but this continuity applies, of course, only to poetry written in Latin. The poets of all periods continued to write learned formal poetry in the quantitative meters and strophic forms used by the Latin poets. Their efforts were often of considerable stylistic elegance but showed no originality in subject matter. Most of their work was either religious or, if secular, purely descriptive and impersonal, although, on occasion, close bonds of personal friendship did bring a little life to their works. Nevertheless these poets did considerable service to the development of the vernacular lyric, for they kept alive the traditions of language and rhetoric which were essential if the new vernaculars were to develop means of expression adequate for poetry. Since it was international in character, the development of medieval Latin lyric poetry is discussed in a separate chapter. Here it is sufficient to note that both the imitators of classical forms and those who practiced the new rhymed and rhythmical Latin verse contributed greatly to the development of the French lyric and were to some extent influenced by it. Nor should it be forgotten that the very numerous Latin hymns, more widely known than any other Latin poetry, passed on their imagery to the vernacular lyric.

It should be stated at once that all vernacular lyric poetry in the Middle Ages was sung. The author of the words was also the composer of the tune, or he fitted words to a melody already known. We do possess a few of these contemporary melodies, but the notation in which they were written down gives us very little evidence about the rhythm of the line. When we read vernacular lyric poetry, therefore, even if we understand it well, we are receiving only a part of the effect it conveyed to its medieval audience. There is, however, little alternative to reading the poems and supplying the rhythm mentally as best we can.

It is very hard to determine how much popular lyric poetry was in existence before the first extant works. There are numerous allusions to such songs, but they are too general to mean anything. Many nineteenth-century critics presumed the existence of a considerable body of folk songs and believed they had a great influence on the formal lyric. Much of this belief was based on the "ideal landscape" picture with which so many of the later lyrics opened and which, these critics believed, came from popular song; but the "ideal landscape" has now been recognized as a part of the Latin rhetorical tradition.

Modern critics, while not denying that there were popular songs, are inclined to the belief that the earliest French lyric, which comes from the *langue d'oc* region and already shows great sophistication, was influenced rather by classical and medieval Latin poetry and, curiously enough, by the poetry of the Arabs. It was, of course, by no means difficult for Arab poetry to become known. Provençal is very like the Catalonian dialect in Spain, and it has been shown that Arabic poetry frequently used the Romance vernaculars in its refrains. The reasons for believing that Arabic poetry affected Provençal do not, however, rest merely on geographical proximity. Several of the poetic forms used are very similar in both languages, and some types, particularly the dawn song, can be found in both.

Formal Love Poetry

A large part of the lyric poetry written in Provençal and later imitated in northern France was formal love poetry, the form for which was called the *canzon*. The lady is rarely named, but it is clear that she is always the wife of a great lord and that the poet treats her as a superior. This is true even if the poet was in fact superior in rank. The lady is described as the perfection of womanhood, and the poet regards himself as completely unworthy of her. Although his one desire is to love her fully, he knows that any such consummation is beyond his reach. He can therefore only live in hope of a smile or some slight sign of affection. Since, however, the most wonderful thing in his life is this love, he cannot give it up, for this would cause even more pain. He is in a constant state of tension, sometimes upbraiding his lady for her cruelty, sometimes saying that he will suffer anything if only he can stay in love with her. Love exalts him and gives him a special feeling (*joi*), which makes him capable of the most noble deeds. Nor can this love ever fade, for the lady's beauty has fixed itself in him and merged with the concept of eternal beauty in his soul. Here too is the theme of love service, as in the romance. But it is service without reward. The poet can do nothing but love the lady and tell of his love in song. The love expressed in the *canzon* has often been called spiritual, but except in a few cases, and later in Italian adaptations, this is not strictly true. It would be more accurate to call it unfulfilled love. Nor, in the *canzon*, is it adulterous (although it would like to be), since again it is never real. The stress on the difference in rank is very important, for in many poems one has the impression of formal praise and of subtle flattery. The poet was of lower rank than the lady addressed, and if he was not, he pretended to be.

It need hardly be said that the conventions just described were capable of widely differing treatment. In the best poets there is genuine analysis of the poet's own feelings, a desire to find the nature of true love and what it is that causes this agony-ecstasy. In others the *canzon* is merely a string of formal clichés. It may be noted here that there is little formal continuous argument in the *canzon*. Each strophe is complete in itself, giving a vivid picture of one aspect of the poet's feelings. Hence we often find different manuscripts giving the strophes in a different order. Scholarly reordering on any certain basis is difficult.

Certain concepts appear over and over again in this formal love poetry—the ecstasy of love, the wound of love, the glory of youth, the need for self-restraint, the danger from the lady's eyes (the light from them caused love!), the lady's cruelty, the need for mercy, the loss of self. These are present in all the poets.

The *canzon* began as a fairly simple verse form. It usually had six- or eight-line strophes of octosyllables or decasyllables, and the rhyme schemes were simple. This simplicity may be observed in the work of the earliest known troubadour, Count William IX of Aquitaine (1071–1127). During the twelfth century, however, strophic forms and rhyme schemes of great complexity were developed. Not only was the same rhyme scheme used for each strophe, but often the same rhyming sound in corresponding lines (*coblas unisonans*). Sometimes the rhyming sounds were in reverse order in the second strophe (*coblas retrogradas*), and other variations were attempted. The lines of an individual strophe were not always of the same length, but it became common practice to divide the poem into three parts, the first two of which had exactly the same rhyme scheme and metrical form, while the third was independent. These were known as the feet and the tail. The whole poem finished with a short *tornada* or personal appeal, sometimes to the lady, although not by name, sometimes to the *joglar* (jongleur, minstrel) who would actually sing the song.

Technical virtuosity was very important in the Provençal lyric, and it was not confined to meter and rhyme. The language itself varied. When the style was plain and used only common ornament, it was called *trobar plan* ("easy singing"). If large numbers of metaphors, unusual words, and especially rhymes were employed, it was called *trobar ric* ("rich singing"). Finally there was a cult of deliberate obscurity, where words were used in abnormal senses and outlandish metaphors were employed. This *trobar clus* ("closed singing") was often criticized by contemporaries, and some of it is quite incomprehensible to us. It has been stated that the poems were obscure because the authors were, in metaphor, putting in ideas from the Catharist (Albigensian) heresy, but this is unlikely.

There were, of course, other forms of love poetry beside the *canzon* (which enjoyed the highest reputation). Best known of these is the *alba* or dawn song, which tells of the sorrow of two illicit lovers parting at dawn. The scene is always the same—they have been awakened by the watchman or a bird, and the man must escape before he is observed by the spies of the jealous husband. Here the love is sensual and adulterous. But only the tearful parting is shown, and it has been pointed out that the situation is almost as fantastic as that in the *canzon*. The *alba* type has very close parallels in Arabic poetry. The other type of love poem, completely different, is the *pastourelle*. This type is more common in northern France, but there are a few examples, mostly of late date, in Provençal. Here the knight makes direct amorous advances to a girl he meets alone in the country. Since she is a peasant, there is no finesse. Bribes and even force can be used. The Provençal examples usually show the girl well able to hold her own and often outtalking her noble suitor. In northern France, however, the girls are usually simpletons, and the poems show the seamy side of love in the Middle Ages.

Several other types of poetry could be used for love poetry as well as for other purposes. They were the *tenson* or debate poem on a particular subject, between two or more persons, and the *partimen* or *joc parti*, where only one question is put and a second party criticizes the answer. The *sirventès*, of which more than two hundred exist, was a poem of personal opinion, often satirical or even insulting. Its satire could be personal, or generally political and social. The *planh* or lament was, of course, a poem of personal loss. The crusading poems in Provençal are usually actual calls to take part in a crusade and hence religious in nature. Elsewhere the crusade was often used as an excuse for expressing one's misery at parting from a lady.

After these general notes about the Provençal lyric we may mention the work of some of the more important poets. These were the troubadours (*trobador*). They were sometimes of noble birth, quite frequently lowborn professionals who depended on patronage. They wrote words and melody but, if they could possibly afford it, they had their works performed by a *joglar*. It is unlikely that the poems were *read* by contemporaries. Our manuscripts are collections made much later. We have a considerable number of biographies of the troubadours but, though often interesting and even sensational, they are unreliable and probably were made up largely from information drawn from the poems.

Provençal Poets

The first known troubadour was William IX of Aquitaine (1071–1127), whose adventurous life is reflected in his eleven poems. We know that he was constantly at war and in love and was several times excommunicated. Many of his poems are boasts; many are crassly sensual or obscene. But in some he presages the coming tradition of love as we find it in the *canzon*. Much more typical is Jaufré Rudel (c. 1150). His poems—only six survive—are all love poems of great tenderness. By far the most famous of these describes his wish for his distant love; the poem gave rise to the legend of his loving a lady in Syria whom he had never seen, traveling there, and dying in her arms. More likely his far-off love, for whom he yearns in hope and despair, is inaccessible but not distant.

Quite different from Jaufré was his contemporary Marcabru, a Gascon troubadour who was first at the court of Aquitaine and later at that of Alfonso of Castille. Marcabru was a skillful poet but often outspoken and deliberately crude. Few of his forty-four songs are *canzons*. He preferred the slashing *sirventès* where he could attack what he considered the growth of adulterous love at court and elsewhere. He is at his best in satire but he also wrote a charming *pastourelle* and a crusading song. He is the first writer of *trobar clus*—a strange thing for one usually so outspoken.

Although his contemporaries do not grant him the highest place among troubadours, most modern readers find Bernart de Ventadorn (flourished 1150–80) the most sympathetic. He was a servant at the castle of the Viscount de Ventadorn and had several other patrons. He also visited England (1154). All of his songs, about forty, are *canzons*, and he certainly gives the impression of being truly in love with the several great ladies whom he mentions under various *senhals* (cover names). His simplicity and sincerity are not his only claims to fame. He was a master of fine imagery (his comparison of his love to a lark greeting the sun is certainly the best-known image in

Provençal literature) and of controlled passion. A deep melancholy pervades his work but does not degenerate into sentimentality. That love is the center of his existence cannot be doubted. It is also pleasing that his poems are free of the excesses of virtuosity in form which—for our taste—mars the work of so many troubadours.

It is precisely this characteristic of overelaboration which we note in the two dozen songs of Peire d'Auvergne (fl. 1138–80). He is very fond of recondite rhymes and the tricks of *trobar ric*. Raimbaut d'Orange was proud of the obscurity of his *trobar clus*, represented by about forty pieces written between 1150 and 1173. His was an active life, much like that of William IX. To this group we may add Arnaut Daniel, who wrote between 1180 and 1210 and whom Dante regarded as the greatest of the troubadours. His eighteen poems certainly show great technical skill and even some innovations, but no originality of thought or deep feeling.

Closer to Bernart than these two but below him in poetic ability were Giraut de Bornelh and Arnaut de Mareuil, both of the late twelfth century. Arnaut's work is entirely conventional, and it is typical that he wrote a poem on manners, the *ensenhamen*. Giraut is better. He wrote seventy-seven poems, in which virtually all types are represented. Fifty of them are *canzons*, but his best work is in the *sirventès*, where he is serious and effective. He is most famous for a debate poem in which he and Alfonso of Castille discuss whether a king's love can be as noble as that of a knight.

Bertran de Born (1135–c. 1210) was a completely different man. As he says in a famous untitled poem, the pomp of war was his greatest delight. He certainly used his poetry to bring war about. His *sirventès* are designed to make trouble between Henry II of England and his sons. He eggs on Henry the younger and Richard to rebel against their father and switches sides unashamedly to gain his ends. Dante put him in Inferno for his promotion of discord, and the abrasive nature of his vigorous poetry makes this assignment quite understandable.

Peire Vidal (fl. 1180–1205) describes himself in his poetry as a complete eccentric. Although he sings his love for several women at the court of Barral de Baux, it was the lady he calls Loba, she-wolf, at Pennautier for whom, according to legend, he put on a wolf's skin and was torn by dogs. His poetry, which is always direct in style, reflects its author's idiosyncrasies in its boasts and parodies. He is the gayest of the troubadours but hardly characteristic.

As might be expected, the Albigensian crusade and the crushing of the civilization of southern France had a devastating effect on the production of lyric poetry. One poet, Folquet de Marseille, actually became a bishop and persecutor of heresy. Only one or two important names stand out. Peire Cardenal (c. 1190–c. 1290) is a serious poet, almost all of whose seventy poems are *sirventès*. His work shows the mark made by the events of his youth and takes to task the weaknesses of his contemporaries. The vocabulary and mannerisms of courtly love are gone. Guiraut Riquier (1230–c. 1300) moved between France and Spain. His work is not unlike that of Arnaut Mareuil but, in keeping with the spirit of the age, he writes *sirventès* of a religious nature.

The great period of Provençal lyric was over by 1215, but its inspiration produced important movements in Italy, as we shall see. As often happens with any genre, the theoretical, technical side of the lyric was organized long after the poetry had ceased to be a vital force. The *Breviari d'Amor* of Joan Estève and Matfoe Ermengau is an encyclopedia of terms in verse. In the fourteenth century societies were founded to further poetry, and one of these, at Toulouse, produced the *Leys d'amor* (second quarter of the thirteenth century), or laws of love. Earlier than this, Uc Faidit had written a *Provençal Donatus* (rules of poetry) for the Italians, and the *Razos de Trobar* ("Rules of Song"), originally written in prose by Raimon Vidal, was translated into Italian verse by Terramagnino about 1290.

Northern French Lyric Poetry

The forms of lyric poetry, including the discussed, were all imitated in northern France. In addition there grew up several forms which are hard to define because, although we have specimens of them, the form differs so much from one poem to another that it is hard to see what the essentials were. This is especially true of the lyric *lai*, which is a strophic poem with no fixed number of strophes or of lines within strophes. The *descort* is very similar. Its name implies lack of regularity. The motet was originally a musical composition for several voices. First Latin, then French words were added, and the type became very popular in the thirteenth and four-teenth centuries. Over five hundred are extant. Again there is an absence of fixed form; the stress was on the music.

During the later thirteenth century, some types of melody and verse form developed which were to dominate lyric poetry until the end of the Middle Ages. All, probably, were origi-nally dance forms. The most important were the rondeau, the virelay, and the ballade. The rondeau is distinguished by the use of the first line of the poem as a refrain, sometimes at the end of each strophe (usually three), sometimes also in other positions. The virelay was not, in the thirteenth century, distinguished from the ballade, except musically, but later it always uses "head" refrain, i.e. at the beginning of strophes, whereas the ballade has its refrain at the end. The *estampie*, another dance form, has no refrain. Although there are usually three strophes, these vary in length from four to thirty lines.

The French poets of the late twelfth and early thirteenth centuries follow their Provençal masters faithfully but with less ability. Conon de Bethune (died 1217) is best known for his crusading songs. He actually went on two crusades, and there is a personal note in his work. Blondel de Nesles, most famous for his legendary and quite unauthenticated search for Richard the Lion Heart, was a correct but uninspired poet, and the same may be said of Gontier de Soignies, Gautier de Dargies, the Castellan of Coucy, Gautier d'Épinal and others. Gace Brulé (died about 1212) is a much better poet, with at least the appearance of personal feeling in his love poetry. Jean Bodel of Arras (c. 1200) was a true poet, as is revealed in his five extant *pastourelles* and his *congé* or fare-well to the world (he died of leprosy).

There were numerous poets to carry on the tradition during the thirteenth century, not all of them nobles by any means. The *puys* or literary societies of northern France, particularly Arras, encouraged the production of poetry. The only names worth recording are those of Colin Muset, Thiebaut de Champagne, Rutebeuf, and Philipe de Rémi. Adam de la Halle is more properly discussed as a dramatist (see pp. 260f.).

Colin Muset (first half of the twelfth century) was appar-ently a professional minstrel with a wide range of skills and some originality. Thiebaut de Champagne (1201–53), later king of Navarre, wrote powerful love songs to an unknown mistress and also political and religious songs. He makes con-siderable use of allegory. Best known of all this group was

Rutebeuf (c. 1245–80), because his poetry takes on the personal flavor which was to be the mark of the fourteenth-century lyric. A great deal of his work is moralizing or satirical and belongs to the real, not the ideal world. He writes of his own poverty, of the problems of marriage and patronage, even of quarrels at the university of Paris. He also wrote formal didactic poetry, the *Battle of Virtues and Vices*, the *Dit d'Hypocrisie* ("Poem on Hypocrisy"), and *Miracles of Our Lady*. It is his wide range, irony, and personal note which most readers find attractive.

In the fourteenth century the Provençal conceptions of lyric poetry had largely disappeared. A poem was called lyric because it used a lyric form (usually rondeau, ballade, or virelay). Its content could be almost anything and very often it was a poem on the poet's own experience—or pretended experience—in love, war, politics, or some form of social life. Three poets stand out during this period, and we are fortunate in knowing a great deal about them, partly from documents but largely from their own work. They are Guillaume de Machaut, Eustache Deschamps, and Charles, duke of Orléans.

Guillaume de Machaut (c. 1300–c. 1377) was born probably near Rheims and was not a noble. Nevertheless he spent a great part of his life in the service of great men, including John, king of Bohemia, who died at Crécy in 1346; Jean of Normandy, later king of France; Jean, duke of Berry; and Pierre de Lusignan, king of Cyprus. All this gave him great opportunities for observing the contemporary world, both in and outside of France. His greatest love affair came when he was quite old—in 1361—when he wrote poems to a much younger lady described in his work *Voir Dit* ("True Poem"). He wrote a number of longer poems, including a description of the capture of Alexandria by his patron Pierre de Lusignan and several debate poems on the subject of love. Allegorical works are also common (*Poem on the Fountain of Love*, *Poem on the Lion*, *Poem on the Orchard*). His greatest contribution to literature by far, however, consisted of his motets and other lyric poetry. He wrote and composed twenty-three motets, seventeen *lais*, thirty-three *chansons*, and more than forty ballades. His topics, inevitably, are conventional—praise of ladies, the good life, and satire of society—but his treatment is skillful and varied.

Eustache Deschamps (c. 1346–c. 1406), sometimes called

Morel, was born in Champagne and was a pupil, perhaps a nephew, of Guillaume de Machaut. Eustache did not move in quite such high circles as his master, but he did occupy a number of what would now be called civil-service positions in the employ of the king and great nobles, particularly the duke of Orléans. These were not always without danger. In 1397 he was beaten and robbed while in Bohemia on a diplomatic mission. Throughout his life he was much concerned with getting and holding the means of livelihood, a fact which is reflected in his works. He looked back with yearning on his youth when he was president, in 1366, of a lighthearted literary society, and was desperately afraid of old age. His poetic output was enormous: more than a thousand ballades, one hundred and seventy-one rondeaux, and eighty-four virelays, as well as a few longer didactic poems (*Complaint of the Church, Mirror of Marriage*). These poems reflect every phase of his life, not only the events but his own changing attitudes and moods. He is fond of moralizing, like everyone else in his day, and much of his comment reflects commonplaces rather than experience. Nevertheless his work is a fascinating commentary on contemporary society.

Charles, duke of Orléans (1394–1465), might well have written less poetry if his life had not followed such a strange course. He was captured at the battle of Agincourt in 1415 and remained a prisoner in England until 1440, although several times near release. Only the kindness of many of his guardians, notably the duke of Suffolk, made life at all tolerable. His political actions on his return were unfortunate, and he finally settled at Blois with a literary circle. He had leisure for poetry (some of it in English) while in England and again at Blois. He wrote several cycles of ballades on various events. Like all his contemporaries, he addressed formal love poetry to ladies and commented on the events of his life. His work is very similar to that of Eustache Deschamps.

To these great names we can add two who are better known in other fields, Jean Froissart (1337–1410) and Christine de Pisan (1364–1430), both of whom wrote very well in the ballade form, he much in the manner of Machaut, she rather more personally of her home and friends.

The greatest lyrical poet of the French Middle Ages is the latest in time. François Villon (1431–after 1463) has become so much a legend that it is hard to sort out the facts. He was born in Paris, and his real name was François de Montcorbier or François des Loges. He took the name Villon from his tutor. After obtaining degrees at the Sorbonne, he gave up trying to progress in the church and joined the low life of Paris. He was banished in 1455 for killing a man in a fight and was in and out of prison for various offenses until 1463, when he was sentenced to be hanged for attempted murder, but the sentence was commuted to ten years' banishment. We hear no more of him after 1463. In spite of his constant association with criminals, he seems to have had protectors among the nobility, including perhaps Charles of Orléans.

His poetry reflects his life, for much of it deals with the strange events and characters of the low life of Paris. Some of it is written in their *argot*. But even more his poetry reflects the sharp contradictions of the fifteenth century—its religion and obsessive fear of death, its cruelty and tenderness, crudity and love of beauty—all gathered in one man. The *Lais* or *Little Testament* (1456) are a series of mock bequests to all manner of men and hence a brilliant comment on life. The *Grand Testament* (1461) contains some of his best work, including the debate between his body and soul. His two most famous works are the *Ballad of the Hanged*, in which he gives a haunting picture of his feelings on death, and the famous "Where are the snows of yesteryear," a lyric which conveys with great intensity the sense of loss of things past. It is easy to say what Villon treated and what were his violent changes of mood, less easy to say why he is a superb lyric poet. He had the very rare faculty, which characterizes only the greatest of poets, of lifting simple language from the banal to the sublime.

It is a curious fact that the history of medieval French lyric poetry begins with William IX and ends with Villon—two men of very similar character, turbulent, self-willed, and sensual. Both were in many respects uncharacteristic of what lay in between. For it is mainly formal skill rather than deep passion which characterizes the medieval French lyric. Its achievement was, in this respect, very great. Nor should it be forgotten that the love ideals it set up have remained to this day an important element in Western culture.

FABLIAUX

The fabliau or fable was a short (up to 1,500 lines) poem intended for amusement and laughter. It has none of the elements of courtliness and very rarely anything didactic. Its favorite subject was illicit love and, in particular, the tricks by which a jealous husband or a strict chaperon could be deceived. Its appeal was to the masses rather than to the court, although it was popular everywhere. The stories themselves were drawn from many sources, and parallels have been found in the mythologies of many peoples as well as in the numerous story collections of the Orient. There can be no doubt that these stories were well known long before the appearance of the extant versions, and that oral tradition played an important role in their establishment.

The fabliau reached the height of its popularity during the thirteenth century. After that the same material was used in prose stories. The first known fabliau, of about 1160, is *Richeut*, the story of a courtesan who foists her son off on a series of rich men and is delighted to observe that when he grows up he is as immoral and eager for love as she was herself. The story affords an admirable opportunity to poke fun at all classes from clerics to bourgeois and is typical of the fabliau. Of the 157 known fabliaux, some are by well-known authors, such as Phelipe de Beaumanoir and Rutebeuf. Many of the stories are better known from versions in later collections such as Boccaccio's *Decameron*.

ROMAN DE RENART

We have already seen how a single fable of Aesop developed, with the addition of much folklore and popular material, into the Latin poem *Ysengrimus* (1155). At the same time as this, a similar process was taking place in France and resulted in the great compilation called the *Roman de Renart*. This work is not a romance in any real sense of the word. It is a large number of different stories, by authors known and unknown, in almost but not quite all of which Renart (Renard) and his opponent the wolf, Isengrim, are the central characters. It is possible to arrange these stories to begin with the birth of the two main characters and end with Renart's death, but this would be highly artificial, since the stories did not appear in that order.

It is customary to divide the *Roman de Renart* into various *branches* according to author and date of appearance. The essential scenes of the sick lion at court and the flaying of the wolf (a scene which probably led to the "humanizing" of the beasts) and of Renart's pilgrimage were probably among the earliest of the *branches*. Of the total of twenty-six, it is fair to say that the oldest are those found in Latin and German versions and hence already formed, while the latest are those in which there is obvious imitation of known episodes or in which new characters are introduced. A large majority of the episodes, like those in *Ysengrimus*, are concerned with the tricking of the wolf by the fox so that he suffers at least disgrace or, more commonly, physical injury, such as the beating from the monks when he falls in their well in *branche* IV.

The early episodes are very largely funny stories about animals. The anticlerical satire which is so marked in the Latin *Ysengrimus* is largely though not entirely absent. In its place, particularly in the later episodes, is mockery of courtly adventure and the courtly world in general.

It is probable that *branche* II was written in about 1175 by Pierre de St-Cloud. It is the story of how Renart was tricked by some of the smaller animals (his only defeats) and of his adultery with Hersent, the wolf's wife. Richard de Lison is the author of *branche* XII and a priest of La Croix en Brie of *branche* IX. The popularity of the *Roman* was such that additional material was provided by the two works *Renart le nouvel* (1288/92) and *Renart le contrefait* (before 1342).

The world in which the animals live is not governed by any code of morality. Innocence is imposed upon, good faith is absent, selfishness is everywhere, from King Lion down. Everyone is corruptible, and those animals who are good are usually shown as too weak or stupid to be otherwise. Renart is the hero because he has no morals and is sharper than the others. It has been said that the *Roman de Renart* is a satire by "little people" of the great world. This is unlikely. Its primary intention was to amuse, and the satire, particularly in the early parts of the French version, is entirely incidental.

FABLES

Animal fables are closely connected with the beast epic. There are, however, few original collections in French. The fables of Aesop were known to the Middle Ages through prose versions of the fables of the Roman poet Phaedrus (fl. A.D. 15). The first collection was known as the "Romulus" group. It added a good deal of moral to each fable. A variation of the same called *Romulus Neveleti* has sixty fables in verse. There were numerous other reworkings in Latin. In French this collection appeared as the *Ysopet* of Lyons in the thirteenth century and, with additions from Avianus, as the *Ysopet I* of Paris in the fourteenth. The best-known collection, that of Marie de France, has already been noted. Two other Ysopets of the fourteenth century, *Ysopet II* of Paris and the *Ysopet* of Chartres, were based on the *Novus Esopus* in the Latin of Alexander Neckam.

DIDACTIC VERSE

A great deal of religious literature, particularly lives of saints and other devotional material, could be included under this heading; but these will be mentioned only if there is some special literary reason for doing so. Otherwise this section is restricted to works which had the specific intention of imparting information.

Such works begin to appear in French in the twelfth century. One of the earliest is the *Compoz* ("Calendar") of Philipp de Thaon, written about 1113, which gives a man's duties for every part of the year, often with allegorical interpretation. Problems of sin and the Christian life are treated in verse in Helinand's *Verses About Death* (c. 1195) and in *The Romance of Romances* of about the same period. Simon de Freine has a similar intention in his *Roman de Philosophie* (c. 1200), a verse reworking of Boethius' *Consolation of Philosophy*.

The thirteenth century saw the production of a number of works in praise of the Virgin. Poems on the Joys of Mary were written by Gautier de Coincy, Rutebeuf, and Guillaume le Clerc. Of the numerous collections of Miracles of Our Lady, the best is that of Gautier de Coincy in some 30,000 lines, written at the beginning of the thirteenth century. About 1240, Jean le Marchaut also produced a collection, but probably the best known of all is the charming story of the acceptance by the Virgin of the offering of the "Tumbler of Notre Dame," who had no other gift but the ability to perform for her.

During this century the poetic form known as the *dit*, a short verse narrative, became popular. Many of these were didactic in character, for example the *Poem of the Ring of Truth*, which gave the wearer power over men, and the *Poem of the Unicorn*. Guillaume le Clerc's *Coin of God* and *The Three Evils* written about 1226 and 1230, are obvious warnings against sin, cast in allegorical form. Attacks on contemporary evils are to be found in Robert le Clerc of Arras' *Verses on Death* (1260).

One of the most famous men of the fourteenth century, Jean Gerson (1363–1429), contributed to didactic literature by his own translations of his sermons. The Cistercian monk Guillaume de Deguilleville (fl. 1330–58) composed a huge moral-allegorical trilogy covering all moral and spiritual activities of man. The parts are called the *Pilgrimage of Human Life*, *Pilgrimage of the Soul*, and *Pilgrimage of Jesus*. Typical also is a poem by Phillipe de Vitry, *The Chaplet of the Fleur de Lis* (1355), allegorizing the lilies on the French coat of arms as knowledge, faith, and chivalry. Christine de Pisan (1364–1430), author of *Change of Fortune*, defended women against the numerous attacks on them in her *Letter to the God of Love* and *Poem on the Rose*. There was a great deal of literature about the position of woman. Martin le France defended them in his *Champion of Ladies* (1442), but advice was more common—as in *Parlement des Dames* of Olivier de la Marche (1425–1502)—and satire even more so. The best example of the latter is Antoine de la Sale's *Fifteen Joys of Marriage* (c. 1460), a witty attack on the institution. Alain Chartier (1392–1429) praises widows of heroes in his *Book of Four Ladies* and pleads for the poor lover in *La belle dame sans merci*. One of the most influential of the allegorical-didactic poems of the time was the *Roman de Fauvel* of Gervais de Bus (two books, 1310 and 1314). Fauvel is a horse, an image of wickedness, whose name is composed of the first letters of the French words for flattery, avarice, villany, fickleness, envy, and cowardice. Fauvel is a forerunner of Antichrist.

The great mass and apparent popularity of this didactic poetry, not only in France but throughout Europe, seems to be very largely a reflection of the influence of bourgeois culture and its desire for practical, sensible instruction and also of the increasingly uncertain moral and religious basis of life.

PROSE WORKS

In France as in all countries of western Europe, prose developed later than verse and even when it began to be used it was mainly for practical purposes. During the thirteenth and particularly the fourteenth and fifteenth centuries a large number of verse works, particularly the *chansons de geste* and the romances of adventure, were put into prose form. There is little point in mentioning the majority of these prose versions, since they were not independent works of art. History also began to appear in prose form, and some of the histories were works of considerable distinction, notably the *Conquest of Constantinople* by Geoffroi de Villehardouin (c. 1150–1212). Jehan de Joinville wrote a history of the reign of St. Louis under the title *The Holy Words and Good Deeds of St. Louis* (c. 1304–09). Best known of all is the brilliant pageant of the Hundred Years War, the *Chronicle* of Jean Froissart (1337–c. 1410), a work of poetic color based largely on personal experiences.

Two works should be mentioned here which are better known in their prose than their earlier verse versions. The *Story of the Seven Sages* goes back to a Latin and ultimately Oriental story in which an emperor ("Vespasian") sends his son to be educated by seven wise men. When he is recalled to court, the son and his advisers see that he will die unless he keeps silent for seven days. His wicked stepmother accuses him of attempting to seduce her, but his master attacks her trustworthiness with a story. She replies in kind, and by this procrastination the boy is saved. The verse form of this story goes back to about 1155; the prose versions are of the fourteenth century. The *Dolopathos*, originally in Latin but put into French prose by a certain Herbert about 1200, is very similar except that here the emperor is Augustus and the tutor Vergil. The stories are in part the same as those in the *Seven Sages*.

There are a few prose novels in the thirteenth century. In the *Daughter of the Count of Ponthieu* (late thirteenth century) the heroine goes through one adventure after another. She is cast adrift in a cask, sold to the Saracens, enters a harem, and finally releases her father and former husband from captivity and goes home with them.

A huge prose work, the *Perceforest*, was written about

1330. Its hero is pre-Arthurian but as always a model of knightly virtue. We find the influence of Boccaccio in Pierre de Beauveau's *Book of Troilus*. It is the fifteenth century, however, which sees the full development of the French *novella*. Antoine de la Sale's *Cent Nouvelles nouvelles* (c. 1460) is one of the finest collections of such stories, full of wit and charm. Finally we may note the work of Landri de la Tour, who about 1425 wrote, for his daughter's instruction, a book which combined moral stories and tales for pleasure.

German Literature

THE PRECLASSICAL PERIOD

General

IN CONSIDERING GERMAN LITERATURE, it should be remembered that it had already produced some important works before anything whatsoever had been written in the Romance vernaculars. This Old High German period has already been discussed (see pp. 36ff.). The impulse to write creatively died under the impact of invasion and political incompetence after the end of the ninth century. Furthermore the Cluniac reform, which tightened monastic discipline, tended to make writing for the laity less important than it had been under Charlemagne and his immediate successors. The result was a virtually complete absence of literature in the vernacular during the tenth and eleventh centuries. During this period there are a few works of a religious nature and the commentaries of Notker Labeo.

Religious Works

Of the religious works the following may be mentioned. *Ezzos Song* (c. 1060) is a hymn by a canon, Ezzo, dedicated to Bishop Gunther of Bamberg, which gives a brief account of the history of salvation, from Creation to Resurrection. Notker wrote a *Memento mori* poem about 1070/80, a call to repent. *Annos Song* (c. 1085) is a poem in praise of Bishop Anno of Cologne, preceded as was the custom in such works by a brief world history to "place" its subject. In 1127 a certain Lady Ava of Melk in Austria wrote a verse *Life of Jesus* and a *John* which have more poetic feeling than most similar works of the time. Songs about Judith, Solomon, and the young man in the fiery furnace also belong to this period, as does the *Memento mori* poem of Heinrich von Melk.

A few works in prose also survive from this period. Notker Labeo (950–1022) was a schoolmaster at the abbey of St. Gall and prepared for his pupils commentaries on Scripture and on Boethius' *Consolation of Philosophy* in German, an unusual and original feat. His works are based on Latin commentaries but show great skill in adapting German to this new purpose. Williram (1000–85) did the same for the Song of

Songs, and there is a further commentary on the same subject from the Abbey of St. Trudpert from the early twelfth century.

Waltharius

During this period several important Latin works were written in Germany, most of which are discussed elsewhere (see chapters on medieval Latin literature and on drama). One of them, however, is so closely tied to Germanic tradition that it must be mentioned here. The *Waltharius* is a long epic poem in the manner of Vergil and Statius. Its date and authorship have been the subject of much discussion. Some critics believe that it belongs to the late Carolingian period, mainly on the ground that it reflects the "spirit" of this period. The author calls himself Geraldus in the prologue, but no certain conclusion can be drawn from this. Ekkehard IV of St. Gallen (mid-eleventh century) tells of reshaping and polishing a school exercise of an earlier Ekkehard I about a certain *"Waltharius manu fortis."* In spite of everything adduced against the authorship of Ekkehard, this statement is still the most positive evidence we have of the date and authorship of the work.

The subject of the poem is a story of Walther and Hiltegunda which exists in later versions in German. Many familiar characters appear—Gunther, Hagen, Attila—and they have much the same characteristics as in the later *Nibelungenlied*, a fact which has given rise to the opinion that the two works grew up in the same cultural area. In this story Walther is, together with Hiltegunda, the girl betrothed to him as a child, a hostage of Atilla's court. He stands in high favor, leads the king's army in a successful battle, and, having a mind to escape, gets the court dead drunk at a great feast. He and Hiltegunda escape, taking with them a treasure. Their arrival in King Gunther's lands is reported by a ferryman, and the king takes Hagen and a number of picked warriors to capture the treasure. Waltharius has occupied a narrow cleft in the rocks and kills all attackers except Gunther and Hagen. He withdraws in the night, and after much persuasion Hagen is induced to join Gunther in attacking him. Everyone is wounded, Gunther by far the most seriously, and after a reconciliation with Hagen, Walther goes to his home in Aquitaine.

The story is vigorous and it is vigorously told. Most of it is devoted to carefully differentiated individual combats, very well described. The figures are all noble except Gunther, who has the same greedy and weak character we find in the *Nibelungenlied* and who ends in disgrace. Hagen and Walther are close friends as well as great warriors, a fact which explains Hagen's hesitation in attacking. The style is entirely that of Latin epic, with frequent verbal reminiscences of Vergil and Statius, but it would be hard to know what other style we could expect from a writer of the period. There is no reason for thinking that this work is a mere imitation with a freshly invented story. It is a free rendering in hexameters of an old Germanic story—and one of the most successful Latin epics of the Middle Ages.

There were very probably a considerable number of oral versions of stories circulating in the eleventh and twelfth centuries, from which there later developed the *Nibelungenlied*, *Gudrun*, and *Dietrich* epics. The extant material from the period before 1180 is, however, scanty and fragmentary. What survives is all written in a four-stress rhyming couplet which at first allowed considerable freedom in the number and position of unstressed syllables but later became regularized. Much of the poetry was copied, directly or indirectly, from earlier works.

Popular Narrative Poems

Two poems were taken from French originals which are known to us. A priest called Lamprecht of Trier translated about 1150 the Alexander poem of Alberic de Briançon from the French, of which only fragments remain. Lamprecht is a plodding translator, his only "original" contribution being theological commentary to show Alexander as the type of conqueror whose conquests fade like all things mortal. The content of his poem is that of the Alexander romances in general (see chapter on French literature). It exists in several versions of different dates. The second work is the *Song of Roland* of the priest Konrad, to be dated about 1170. The work is not a translation of the *Chanson de Roland* in the Oxford version but of one differing in a few respects. The author has changed the tone of the poem by emphasizing the role of Charlemagne and playing down Roland's pride. Emphasis throughout is on the Franks as warriors of Christ, not as seekers after fame. Thus one of the main points of interest, Roland's repentance, is lost. The conflict between Christian and pagan, although present in the original, is here emphasized to the exclusion of all else.

Other works, many of them fragmentary, are often called *Spielmannsepen*, epics of wandering minstrels, because they are clearly designed for entertainment only and rely on action, description of marvelous happenings, and crude comedy to obtain their effects. The only one which has survived complete in its original form is *King Rother* (c. 1150). It is a story of the wooing of a distant princess and, like many stories of its kind, falls into two main parts. Rother, king of Bari in Italy, woos the daughter of the emperor of Byzantium, first by messengers who are imprisoned, then in person, disguised. Harp playing gains him access to the lady, whom he carries off by a trick, only to lose her again. On returning he is almost killed but finally gains his prize. The stress is on adventure, the romantic East, clever tricks, and hairbreadth escapes. A giant, Asprian, who is kept on a chain like a dog and smashes lions against the wall, fights on Rother's side. There is no moral purpose to these stories.

Very similar in intent and style if not in content (so far as can be judged from fragments and later versions) were *Duke Ernst* (c. 1170), with its Arabian Nights atmosphere, *Count Rudolf* (before 1173), and *Solomon and Markolf* and *King Oswald of England*, both from the second half of the twelfth century.

The *Imperial Chronicle* (c. 1150) is an account in verse of the empire from Caesar to the author's own time. It shows the influence of the Augustinian view of history and is concerned with demonstrating the power of the church in the extension of this empire. It contains a great deal of material to illustrate each period and is thus a storehouse of legends, saints' lives, and folk tales.

THE CLASSICAL PERIOD

Most histories of German literature designate the few decades from 1170 to 1230 as the Middle High German classical period, and with good reason. In this short space of time were produced epic and lyric works worthy to rank with any in European literature. Both epic and lyric depend, with a few exceptions, on French models, and it is not necessary to repeat here what has been said above about the Arthurian romance and the Provençal lyric. Important differences, where they occur, will be noted in discussion of individual works. The literature of this period was courtly in two senses. It followed the conventions of courtly romance (see pp. 81ff.), and it was written to entertain a courtly audience. The great exceptions are the Germanic epics *Nibelungenlied* and *Gudrun*.

Narrative Poetry

EARLY WORKS

German literary historians usually use the term *höfisches Epos*—"courtly epic"—to describe those works whose subjects and manner of treatment are borrowed from French. With the exception of one work, Hartmann von Aue's *Poor Henry*, a French source is known for all the narrative works of the classical period. The borrowing extends to the subject matter, to the courtly background, and often to actual words. Yet none of the German works is a mere rendering of its French counterpart. All are considerably longer than their originals, and this increased length is due in part to a greater interest in the motivation of characters and in their moral background. Rarely is it caused by an addition of incidents. On the other hand there is less interest in social matters, and the German works lack the brilliant picture of court life painted by Chrétien de Troyes.

The author who connects the preclassical with the classical period is Heinrich von Veldeke (fl. 1180–1200), a Low German speaker from Limburg who changed to writing standard Middle High German in his epic *Eneit* (c. 1180). He also wrote lyrics and a life of St. Servatius. All contemporaries acknowledged Heinrich as the earliest master of courtly poetry. His *Eneit* is based on the *Roman d'Enée*, a Norman writer's version of the Aeneas story. Like his predecessor, Heinrich changes the nature of the story. He plays down the duty of Aeneas to found the Roman empire and stresses the features of romance-adventure and love. The evil love of Dido is contrasted with the pure love of Lavinia. Heinrich's greatest service to German letters was his introduction of smooth language and style. Although not distinguished by later standards, it is far superior to that of minstrel poetry.

HARTMANN VON AUE

We know nothing of Hartmann von Aue except what we can glean from his poetry. He lived in southwestern Germany and belonged to the service nobility (*ministeriales*). He wrote lyrics in his youth and a "Little Book," which is a debate on love. His epic works are of uncertain date, but we can be sure that *Erec* was the first. Then there came a crisis in his life—probably caused by the death of a dearly beloved overlord, about 1188—which produced the two religious poems *Gregorius* and *Poor Henry*. His last and, in form, best work is *Iwein*. *Erec* and *Iwein* are both modeled directly on the works of Chrétien de Troyes, and there is no need to repeat their stories here. Hartmann changes some details in the *Erec* but hardly any in *Iwein*. He is at pains, however, to underline and make perfectly clear the moral of Chrétien's work. Men must obey the imperatives of the courtly code if they wish to live in honor. There can be no sloth, no lower forms of love or adventure. The form of both poems is a game of tournaments or love making, but the purpose is to produce a perfect secular man.

This serious note in Hartmann's work is even more marked in his two legendary poems, *Gregorius* and *Poor Henry*. In the prologue to the former he explicitly renounces the follies of his youth and announces his intention to write a serious poem. He took his material from a French legend, *The Life of Pope Gregory*. The hero is not a historical pope. The story tells of a boy, born of the incestuous union of a brother and sister, who is put in a chest with gold and a tablet telling of his birth. He is brought up by a fisherman and an abbot. He becomes aware that he is of noble birth and decides to go into the secular world, in spite of the abbot's pleas to stay in the monastery. After a series of adventures, he rescues a queen from her enemies and marries her. She proves to be his mother. In bitter repentance he has himself chained to a rock and lives washed over by seas for years before delegates from Rome, told of his saintliness in visions, fetch him to be Pope.

Hartmann makes it clear that his purpose is to show that even the greatest sinner can be saved by God's grace, if he repents. What is fatal is to put off the repentance, since no one knows when death will strike. This is one of the favorite themes of medieval literature. Here, however, we have some unusual phenomena. What sin did Gregorius commit? Everything he did was in ignorance. At worst it can be said that he insisted on forcing his way into the secular world when acceptance of the abbot's advice would have saved him. When faced with the choice of the secular-transitory and the religious-eternal, he at first, like Parzival, chooses the former. Hartmann calls him a "good sinner," presumably because he was basically good. It is hard to avoid the conclusion that Gregorius thought of his birth as a stain, like original sin, and of his own incest as the result of a predisposition to sin. The stress is in any case on *timely* repentance and reward.

Poor Henry has no known source. Here the self-satisfied and perfectly decent man of the world is struck—undeservedly, he feels—by leprosy. He seeks vainly for a cure and is told that the only possibility is to find a pure virgin who will willingly sacrifice her heart's blood to cure him. Regarding such a thing as impossible, Heinrich returns home and stays with one of his free peasants. A daughter hears his story and determines to sacrifice herself. To her parents protestations she replies that this is a holy act and will have its reward. She goes with Henry to the doctor at Salerno, but at the last minute Henry cannot endure the thought of the sacrifice. He takes the girl back—much to her chagrin—and on the way recognizes that God knows the true course of action. At this recognition he is cured.

Clearly the outward affliction of leprosy is to be taken as an indication of the uncleanness of the soul. Henry was not bad, but his thoughts were fixed entirely upon the secular life. He refuses to recognize God's providence, and it requires an innocent child to show him the way to salvation. *Poor Henry*, too, is a warning against allowing the conscience to sleep.

Hartmann was renowned in his day as the clear stylist whose crystalline words made everything plain. He *is* a clear stylist, but also, often, a pedestrian one. Even his best work, *Iwein*, is heavy when compared with its French original. *Poor Henry* has charming features, but it is also full of rather obvious moralizing. We would perhaps be kinder to Hartmann if we did not have from the same period two works of genius, Wolfram von Eschenbach's *Parzival* and Gottfried von Strassburg's *Tristan*.

WOLFRAM VON ESCHENBACH

We know nothing of Wolfram von Eschenbach (c. 1170–1220) except that he was acquainted with several poets of his time and that he was from Franconia. He wrote three narra-

tive poems, of which only the *Parzival* is complete, and several
lyrics. He denies that he used Chrétien's *Perceval* as a model
and says that his work is based on that of a certain Kyot.
Careful comparison has made it clear that the basic story and
several books of *Parzival* are in fact based on *Perceval*, though
perhaps in a form slightly different from the one we have. Of
Kyot, if he existed, we know nothing. Still, Wolfram made
far-reaching changes. Chrétien has no prologue to his work,
and we learn only during the course of the narrative that
Perceval's father had been driven from his kingdom into the
forest and that two older brothers had been killed as soon as
they became knights. Wolfram on the other hand provides a
long account of how Gahmuret, a younger son of the house
of Anjou, the same as that of Richard the Lion Heart, went to
the East, rescued and married the Negro princess Belakane,
then left her before she bore a son, Feirefis. In a great tourney
in Spain he wins his Christian bride, Herzeloyde. Before
Parzival is born he leaves on adventure and is treacherously
killed in the East. Gahmuret is a purely secular knight whose
life lies in adventure. From him Parzival receives his strength
and beauty.

Herzeloyde determines that her son shall never know the
world of knighthood. She hides him in a wood, forbidding her
servants to speak to him of the courtly world. But he meets
some knights and persuades his mother to let him go. She
dresses him like a fool, in the hope that he will be mocked and
return. She also gives him some advice. When he leaves, she
falls dead. Chrétien's Perceval turns and sees her fall, but
Wolfram's Parzival does not.

The young man sees a beautiful lady, Jeschute, in a tent,
and, following his mother's advice, he kisses her and snatches
a brooch, thus committing his first unconscious sin, for the
lady's lover, Orilus, returns, accuses her of infidelity, and
drives her before him half naked to find the offender. Parzival
later finds Sigune (his cousin) holding in her arms the body
of her lover Schionatulander, killed because of her insistence
on love adventures. (This episode occurs later in Chrétien.)
Promising revenge, he departs and outside Arthur's court
meets the Red Knight, whom Wolfram calls Ither. This knight
sends in a challenge to the court, which Parzival takes up, but
not before he has unwittingly caused a maid, Cunneware, and
a squire, Antenor, to be punished by Kay, the seneschal.
Parzival, whom Ither considers beneath his notice as an oppo-

nent, is provoked into killing Ither with his hunting spear. He strips off Ither's armor and puts it on over his own clothes.

He arrives at the home of a good knight, Gurnemanz, who teaches him to look and behave like a knight. The boy is much attracted to Gurnemanz' daughter, Liasse, but leaves again and, in classic fashion, rescues Condwiramurs from the armies of her unwelcome suitors. Here again there is a marked departure from Chrétien, who has Blancheflur spend the night in love-making with Perceval, while Wolfram emphasizes the innocence of the pair even during the two nights after their formal marriage. Parzival is now much like Erec and Yvain. He has a beautiful wife and a fine castle. But he does not rest or set out on adventures. He goes to find his mother. In the course of his wanderings he is directed by a fisherman to a mysterious castle where he sees a strange procession—a lance from which blood drips and a precious stone called a grail which magically feeds all present. (There is considerable difference between the descriptions of the Castle of the Holy Grail, or Grail castle, by the two authors. Chrétien's Grail, for example, is a dish with a wafer in it.) Parzival also receives a splendid sword. He is surprised at the strange occurrences, but asks no questions since Gurnemanz has told him that curiosity is not becoming to a knight. The next day he finds the castle deserted and leaves. A squire mocks him from the wall.

He again meets Sigune, still lamenting her dead lover, and is cursed by her for not asking the question which would have cured the Fisher King at the Grail castle, who suffers from an incurable wound. He defeats Orilus, thus restoring Jeschute's honor. At Arthur's court, when he is about to be admitted to the Round Table, the hag Kundrie, an emissary from the Grail castle, appears and denounces him as heartless and a dishonor to the company. He departs in sorrow. Gawain, greatest of Arthur's knights, is challenged by Kingrimursel for allegedly killing his brother.

We are now given a long account of the deeds of Gawain. He becomes the champion of a little girl, Obilot, and makes love, elsewhere, to Antikonie, sister of King Vergulaht of Ascalun, an event which leads to a most unknightly scramble. He then meets Orgeluse, a scornful damsel, with whom he falls violently in love. She deliberately leads him into a series of dangerous situations, from all of which he escapes, and ultimately to the Castle of Wonders belonging to the magician Klingsor. Here he spends an uncomfortable and rather ludi-

crous night with a rolling bed and a lion. He is able to release
the ladies imprisoned there, including Arthur's sister and
Gawain's. After a challenge from the lover of his sister (at
which point Chrétien breaks off), Gawain returns to Arthur's
court, losing a battle with Parzival on the way, and finally
marries Orgeluse.

Parzival appears only once in this account. There is an
interval in the story of Gawain in which Parzival, in full
armor, is reproached by pilgrims, who tell him it is Good
Friday. He goes to a hermit's cave and confesses that he is
angry with God, who refuses to reward him however great
his services. He has sought in vain to find the Grail castle
again. The hermit, who is Trevrezent, brother of Anfortas,
the Grail king, endeavors to learn his story and soon determines that he is the person destined to be Grail king. He
also tells him that the angels who had remained neutral in the
struggle between God and Lucifer had once guarded the Grail,
but that it is now in the protection of a specially chosen
company. Anfortas is no longer truly king because he pursued earthly love (actually Orgeluse). He tells Parzival of the
death of his mother and his various sins but forgives him,
warning him that humility is the most important of qualities.

Chrétien, by contrast, makes this visit to the hermit short.
The hermit is not named and gives Parzival only formal advice. After the fight with Gawain, Parzival returns to Arthur's
court, amid great rejoicing, but this court is no longer the
object of his wishes. He departs sadly and meets (but naturally
does not recognize) his brother Feirefiz, seeking his father.
They fight, and only the generosity of his heathen foe saves
Parzival. Feirefiz is made a member of the Round Table and
then, with Parzival, now approved by Kundrie, goes to the
Grail castle. There are no difficulties. Parzival asks the question "What ails you, uncle?" and Anfortas is cured. Feirefiz
is baptized and marries Repanse de Schoye, the chief guardian
of the Grail, and to make all complete, Condwiramurs arrives
with her children Loherangrin and Karduz. Sigune is found
dead over the coffin of her lover.

This powerful and moving story clearly shows a search for
some ideal higher than Arthurian knighthood. We never know
what the Grail company is, except that it guards a stone upon
which a dove from Heaven lays a wafer each Good Friday
and which can give and preserve life. It is not the sacred vessel of Joseph of Arimathea but nevertheless something very

precious. The Grail company is clearly a body of knights whose morality is based on Christian principles. The Templars are mentioned as a parallel. To be Grail king is the highest earthly honor.

Parzival achieves this honor by a series of mistakes, most of them due to innocence or advice which, while well meant, was not understood. Parzival, like Gregorius, sins unknowingly. He has been told to kiss women, so he kisses the first he sees, Jeschute. He has been told to obtain armor by killing a knight in combat, so he kills one. His desire to be a member of the Round Table springs from ignorance. Once he has knowledge, he rejects this desire.

The hero's greatest mistake is to confuse the service of men with the service of God. A liege lord rewards services, and Parzival understands that God should do the same. When he does not receive his reward—the second visit to the Grail castle—he is angry with God. He has to learn humility, to place himself in God's hands. He finally reaches the Grail castle through no effort of his own. Wolfram speaks frequently of *zwivel*, a word whose exact meaning is doubtful. It can mean the sin of despair but more likely it means here the inability to choose the right path.

Love of one's fellow creatures is most important. Parzival had shown this love when he wept over the death of birds shot by his crossbow. The instruction he receives makes him unlearn it—formal love of women, suppression of spontaneous sympathy (learned from Gurnemanz), killing other men in jousts—all these were contrary to his natural feelings as expressed in his love for Condwiramurs. He has to learn charity again before he can be Grail king. Mere winning of battles will do no good.

It is easy to see *Parzival* as a novel of development, but this is too facile. In fact he does not develop. He suffers and learns what men have to endure, but he attains the Grail castle when he has, though more mature, returned to the state of natural charity he showed as a boy. Nor is the poem an allegory of the Christian life. Certainly it begins with a kind of Eden and Fall situation, but Parzival is not *any* Christian man. He is a chosen instrument of God.

Parzival shows many sharp contrasts with courtly romances. The Gawain scenes are, of course, put in to show the other level of achievement, the lower, worldly, more easily satisfied level of earthly joy. Parzival rises above this, just as he rises above the outside world. There is a similar contrast between Gawain's love, Orgeluse, and Condwiramurs. Orgeluse is the sensual temptress, leading men into adventure merely to test her seductive powers, while Condwiramurs shows the pure, faithful love of the true wife. Between the two is Sigune, bitterly repentant of her role in the death of her lover and showing a patience and fortitude which were models to Parzival.

There is little evidence of formal religion in Wolfram's poem, yet there is deep piety. The Grail is a precious stone, not a religious vessel, and of the Grail tradition of Robert de Boron there is no trace. *Parzival* is one of the most religious poems of the Middle Ages, yet it has many passages of earthly humor and personal involvement which are absent from almost all other courtly romances.

The *Titurel*, written after *Parzival*, takes up the story before the opening of the earlier work and concerns itself with Sigune and Schionatulander and hence, once again, with the nature of love. It remains a brilliant fragment.

Willehalm is a work on a completely different subject. Although incomplete, it is a long poem which combines stories from various poems of the cycle of William of Orange. It begins with the defeat of Willehalm and the death of Vivien, then continues with the shattered hero's return to his noble wife Gyburc, his visit and appeals for help to the weak king Louis, his return to his lands with help, and his defeat of the pagans, with the aid of Rennewart, a giant kitchen boy who proves to be Gyburc's brother.

Here, as in *Parzival*, we find toleration for the pagans. They are noble knights of chivalry and good manners, but the highest thing they have to fight for is love, whereas the Christians, fighting for God, are bound in the end to prevail. Once again there is noble married love, that of Gyburc and Willehalm. But the chief characters here are really martyrs—Vivien, and Willehalm himself, who, although he does not die, sacrifices the whole of his existence to the ever continuing conflict between good and evil.

GOTTFRIED VON STRASSBURG

The other great master of medieval German romance was Gottfried von Strassburg (fl. c. 1210). Nineteenth-century criticism, while conceding the superiority of Gottfried's style, regarded him as "frenchified," celebrating courtly love and

adultery, and hence less solid and moral than the more masculine—and German—Wolfram. More recently critical views
have shifted. While not denying the greater religious depth of
Wolfram's work, most observant readers believe that Gottfried
was not, after all, writing about courtly love; that his style,
while apparently clear, is invested with secondary and allegorical meanings; and that he presents some of the most advanced
thinking of his day. Curiously enough, Gottfried and Wolfram
were well aware of being rivals, and each refers to the other
with scorn, although not by name. They held strongly opposed
views of the purpose of epic poetry.

Gottfried's *Tristan*, written about 1210, is based directly on
that of Thomas of Britain, and there are very few important
differences in the story (see pp. 92ff.). Gottfried states cate-
gorically that he based his work on that of Thomas of Britain,
and careful studies have shown this to be true, though there
is some influence from the *Tristrant* of Eilhart von Oberge
(c. 1170). Yet the differences in treatment are very marked.
Gottfried says in his prologue that he is writing for a special
group of people, whom he calls *edele herzen*—"noble hearts"
—people different from the normal courtly audience, which,
he says, seeks only joy. For him love is a compound of joy and
sorrow, and the two parts cannot be disentangled. So basic is
this concept in Gottfried's work that he constantly illustrates
it stylistically by pairing such words as love and sorrow, death
and life.

In Thomas' work Tristan had been trained in the arts, but
Gottfried carries this idea much further. He devotes much
time to describing the training his hero received, particularly
in detailing his musical and literary education. It is his artistic
powers which recommend him to Mark's favor and which prevail upon Isolde's mother to cure his wound and to employ
him as tutor for her daughter. Since that daughter has already
received a good education, it is advanced work which she
receives from Tristan.

It was probably this attempt on Gottfried's part to describe
Tristan as an artist rather than as a knight that provoked
Wolfram into his declaration that *he* at least was a knight
and not a man of letters. Although Tristan *can* fight well, it
must be admitted that there is a good deal of cunning and
some downright trickery in his dealings with his opponents,
particularly Duke Morgan.

The nature of the love between Tristan and Isolde is, of

course, the greatest point of difference between Gottfried's
work and all others. What had been little more than sensual
passion in the early works with him becomes a permanent
bond between two people, the highest form of affection, en-
during through life and death. It is hard to tell whether there
was love between Tristan and Isolde before the drinking of
the love potion. Gottfried has his hero plead a wife as the
excuse for his leaving the Irish court at the end of his first
stay, a motif not found elsewhere. Certainly when Isolde finds
the notch in the blade and is prepared to strike Tristan dead
with his own sword, it is not the thought that he alone can
save her from marrying the seneschal which prevents her but
Tristan's reminder that she is a woman. Yet there is no clear
evidence that Gottfried intended them to be attracted.

The love potion they drink is described by Gottfried as
"death." It causes their death, of course, but death can be
simply the opposite of life and hence welcome to them. They
alone drink the potion. Brangaene throws the remainder into
the sea, and Mark drinks none of it, for his love for Isolde—
and he does love her—is quite different. Tristan and Isolde's
love is sensual and needs gratification. Yet it is at its noblest
and most refined when they are separated and when they are
in the "other world" of the love grotto. Both lovers struggle
when they feel the effects of the potion. Each thinks of loyalty
and tries to resist. Yet they cannot. They have to love on
earth, sensually—whatever the cost to themselves and to
others—as well as spiritually.

It is some time before they or others realize that their love
is something higher than a courtly intrigue. Brangaene thinks
it is courtly and acts accordingly, never with success. The
sensuality which overcame them with the love potion and
which was the earthly, transitory, darker side of their love
grows less as the poem progresses but never disappears. It is
when they are banished from court that their love reaches its
highest point. The life in the woods in earlier versions (though
not in Thomas') was a dreary episode which both were glad
to bring to an end. In Gottfried's work it is the closest thing
to perfect harmony they can attain. The grotto is situated, like
the earthly paradise, far from the haunts of men. It is a shrine
dedicated by pagans to the goddess of love, found by Tristan
by accident. Gottfried describes it in allegorical terms, as the
commentators described a church. Each of its parts repre-

sents one of the facets of love, as each part of a church represents an article of Christian faith. The center is a crystal bed. Only the lovers who attain "Tristan-love" can sleep here. The approach is through a door which no force can open, only a little key in the possession of the right people. At the end of his allegory, Gottfried shows that the cave is really the human heart—for he says that, although he has never been to Cornwall, he has known the cave well since his eleventh year, adding, however, that he has never slept in the crystal bed.

In the cave, as throughout the poem, Gottfried emphasizes that the harmony of the lovers rests on the arts as well as on sensual attraction. There too they play and sing together and their music rises in perfect unison. Tristan is, in fact, much more an artist than a conventional knight.

Gottfried's style presents none of the difficulties that we find in *Parzival*. Yet it is difficult to translate or reproduce, since the basic meaning of the words is only part of the effect. Juxtaposition of words to produce shades of meaning and antithesis are two of his favorite stylistic devices. He intends us to read not only the words but the pattern of the words. When these patterns seem interwoven, as they often are in speeches and soliloquies, it is because he wants us to understand that the character's own mind is torn between conflicting and unresolved ideas. For Gottfried, too, these characters are often more than persons. They represent a level of understanding. Brangaene represents the love of the court and the true confidante. Tristan's father is the perfect "joyful" courtly knight.

The poem breaks off at line 19,552, shortly after Tristan meets Isolde of the White Hands. It is hard to tell how Gottfried would have completed the work. Probably the story would have followed Thomas, with variations in treatment. As it stands, Gottfried's *Tristan* is one of the highest achievements in medieval literature and second only to Dante's *Divina Commedia* in its treatment of love.

Two poets, Heinrich von Freyberg (about 1290) and Ulrich von Türheim (about 1230), attempted continuations of Gottfried's poem, neither with any great success. It is clear that they did not use Thomas of Britain's work but turned back to the totally different poem of Eilhart von Oberge. In these continuations Gottfried's concept of love is, of course, totally absent.

OTHER ROMANCES

Numerous other romances were, of course, written by Germans during this period. Many of these writers are competent, if not brilliant, and suffer only because they are content with writing romances of adventure and do not seek to impose their own views upon the form. The *Lanzelet* of Ulrich von Zazikhoven (died 1214), a Swiss, was taken from a lost French original and is not based on Chrétien's poem. It begins with Lancelot's youth, then goes on to his struggle to join the Round Table, his acceptance, his tournaments, two rescues of Guinevere, and a mass of wild adventures. Lancelot has three brides at different stages, but the adulterous love affair with the queen is absent. The work is at once old-fashioned (it dates from about 1204, the same time as *Iwein*) and anticipatory, for many romances were to show a turn for wild adventure.

Although Wirnt von Grafenberg (c. 1200) intended to contrast the rewards of God and the world in his romance *Wigalois*, he also piles one adventure on another. His hero was Gui Galois, son of Gawain. Like Ulrich, he is fond of magic and fairyland. Two other works carry to extreme lengths the type of unorganized adventure story: *The Crown of Adventures* of Heinrich von dem Türlin (c. 1215) and *Daniel of the Flowering Vale* by "Der Stricker" (c. 1215).

The court of King Arthur was not the only subject of romance. Otte of Hesse wrote about 1205 the *Eraclius*, based on the work of Gautier d'Arras. Benoît de Ste-Maure's Troy romance was translated (and shortened) about 1210 by Herbort von Fritzlar in his *Trojaroman*, while Albrecht von Halberstadt translated Ovid's *Metamorphoses* directly from Latin, with none of the usual medieval moralizing or modification. A much more interesting work is that of Moriz von Craûn. Nothing is known of the author or of his source. He seems to have written about 1210, for his hero, a French baron, did not die until 1196. The work is partly parody, partly fabliau, but is apparently intended to be a warning against infringement of the courtly code. *Floire and Blanche-flur* (c. 1220) by Konrad Fleck is a tale of childhood love, taken from a French original.

The next group of narrative poets show very clearly in their work that they are merely following in a great tradition. Rudolf von Ems (died c. 1250) produced a mass of work on various subjects. His *Good Gerhard* is a moral legend, *Barlaam and Josaphat* is a long Christianized version of the widespread Buddha story, *Wilhelm von Orlens* is based on the William of Orange cycle, *Alexander* is, of course, based on the French romances, and finally the *World Chronicle* is a versification of the Old Testament. All are markedly didactic. Ulrich von Türheim wrote a continuation of Wolfram's *Willehalm* as well as Gottfried's *Tristan*, while Reinbot von Durne imitated Wolfram in his legendary *Saint George* (c. 1235–40). Another *Willehalm* was written by Ulrich von dem Türlin about 1260, and romances of adventure and love by Berthold von Holle (c. 1260), Augustin (*Duke Frederick of Brunswick*), and Der Pleier. Ulrich von Eschenbach wrote new versions of several themes: *Alexander* (c. 1250), *Herzog Ernst* (c. 1286), and *Wilhelm von Wenden*.

Konrad von Würzburg (died 1287) was the best narrative writer of this period. The very intensity of his efforts, however, show how far the ideal knighthood of the Hohenstaufen courtly period lay behind him. He sincerely wished to accommodate these ideals to the morality of the rising bourgeoisie, but he did not understand them well enough. He is, however, a fluent and able writer. His short verse narratives, such as the *Heart Story*, *The World's Reward*, and *Otto with the Beard* are attractively written. He followed these with verse legends and a long, courtly poem, *Engelhart*, which is a tale of friendship like *Amis and Amiloun*. He also wrote an allegory, *The Complaint of Art*, on the sad state of poetry. His last work was an enormous, unfinished *Trojan War*. Its 10,000 lines show that it was not a mere copy of the earlier romances, but an attempt to be more historically accurate. His *Partonopier* and *Tournament of Nantes*, on the other hand, are clearly of French inspiration.

Except for those of special interest, there is little point in listing the mass of adventure romances of the late thirteenth and fourteenth centuries. A certain Albrecht, perhaps Albrecht von Scharpfenberg, wrote in 1275 a *Titurel* modeled after Wolfram's work. It is in a highly rhetorical style and inclines heavily to allegory. The tendency to pile on adventure is well illustrated in Heinrich von Neustadt's *Apollonius of Tyre* (c. 1291). In 20,000 lines he tells the same story as the Latin romance but fills in any gaps in time with a mass of uncoordinated and irrelevant adventure. Between 1473 and 1478

Ulrich Fueterer combined most of the well-known adventures into his *Book of Adventure*.

In Germany as in France, the romance had, so far as written remains show, a rapid rise and a long, slow decline. Its greatness sprang very largely from the ideals fostered by the more cultivated courts of the Hohenstaufen period. The material was borrowed from France, but the German masters, especially Wolfram and Gottfried, showed themselves superior in many respects to their French predecessors, particularly in moral seriousness and depth of psychological perception. The romance did not, however, survive the decline of courtly society. Germany suffered much more than France from internal discord in the thirteenth and fourteenth centuries, and the rich bourgeoisie who emerged as the new audience for literature had little feeling for the finer points of the romance. It was coarsened both in material and in morality. The material was swollen and distorted so that all sense of structure was lost, and the morality was made more obvious so that the ends of both formal religion and social behavior would be served.

POPULAR NARRATIVE POEMS

The term *Volksepos* ("popular epic") is used by German literary historians to denote narrative poetry which draws its material from Germanic rather than French or classical sources. Although it thus classifies works by subject matter, there is also a basic difference in style and treatment between the courtly and popular epic. The latter tried hard to take on the fashionable courtly veneer, but the social code under which its earlier forms were written was unresponsive to change, and the works look back to earlier generations even more markedly than the French *chansons de geste*.

We have already seen (pp. 124f.) that the Latin *Waltharius* was modeled on a German story and that Icelandic literature contains stories which clearly date back to the Germanic migrations of the fourth, fifth, and sixth centuries. There can be no doubt that such stories were handed down in Germany by oral tradition just as they were in Scandinavia, and such a supposition is confirmed by the accidental survival of the *Hildebrandslied*. In view of the large amount of heroic literature which has survived in Icelandic, there is surprisingly little in German, a fact which is no doubt due to earlier conversion to Christianity and also to the invasion of French culture, which attracted the best writers.

Of all the popular epics, the *Nibelungenlied* is by far the most important. Its author is unknown but was certainly an Austrian, and the *Nibelungenlied* was written down in the first decade of the thirteenth century, perhaps around 1203. There are thirty-four manuscripts of the poem, ranging in date from the thirteenth to the sixteenth century, a fact which has not made the task of scholars any lighter. For it is clear that these manuscripts are not copies of the same work but of at least three versions. The oldest, C (Hohenems-Lassberg), clearly represents a version which has tried to impart a courtly polish to the work. The other two main manuscripts, A (Hohenems-Munich) and B (St. Gallen), are much closer, and most critics now agree that A, on which Lachmann based his famous edition, is a carelessly written, shorter version of B. Modern editions are based on the B manuscript. There is also a *Klage* ("Lament"), appearing in all but one manuscript, which tells of the burial of the dead and of their exploits. It is regarded as a separate poem.

Any reader of the *Nibelungenlied* will observe immediately that it bears striking resemblances to the *Edda* poems, the *Prose Edda,* and the *Völsunga saga.* Yet the differences are equally striking, for many of the stories relating to Brünhilde and Siegfried are absent and Kriemhilde (the name given to the Scandinavian Guthrún) does not revenge her brothers on her second husband, Attila, but her husband Siegfried on her brothers. Obviously the German version was either drawing on different source material or had deliberately changed the course of the story. Many theories have been advanced to explain the composition of the *Nibelungenlied* as we have it, but that of Andreas Heusler has received most support. He believed that the Siegfried-Brünhilde and Kriemhilde revenge stories developed separately. There were brief lays on each subject in the fifth and sixth centuries, which developed into longer poems in the twelfth. Heusler does not try to determine the intermediate stages, except to say that at some point the rescue of Brünhilde from the ring of flame was replaced by the battle tests we find in the *Nibelungenlied*, and that there was an eighth-century song of the Burgundians in which the revenge of Kriemhilde on her brothers was introduced. There may well have been an earlier "Nibelungennot" about 1160, telling of the downfall of the Burgundians.

This theory, which admits that there may have been influences from other, especially Scandinavian poems, gives to the author of the extant work the credit for joining the two parts together. It is certain that they appear very unequal in technique. The first part, to the death of Siegfried, is interesting but full of loose ends and unexplained references. The second part is far better motivated, and its structure is careful and well planned. (It is perfectly possible to follow the Burgundians on their journey to Attila's court on a map.) There are, furthermore, startling discrepancies of characterization and sympathy between the two parts, as will appear from the following summary of the story.

We are told that Kriemhilde was a beautiful girl, sister of Gunther, king of Burgundy. She tells her mother, Gudrun, of the dream she had, in which eagles tore to pieces a falcon she had tamed. Her mother says that she will marry a noble husband but soon lose him. We then hear of Siegfried. He is made a knight with full ceremony. The account is quite different from that in the Scandinavian versions, for his mother and father are still alive. The hero sets out to win Kriemhilde, knowing of her only by reputation. When his company arrives, Hagen, a retainer of Gunther and the most experienced of his knights, tells all he knows about Siegfried. He obtained the Nibelungen treasure (in a way altogether different from that in the *Eddas*) and the cloak of invisibility from Alberich and killed a dragon whose blood made him invulnerable except in one spot.

Siegfried is brash at his first meeting with Gunther but later helps him in a war against the Saxons. He sees Kriemhilde, but before he can win her, he has to help Gunther win for himself Brünhilde, a queen in Iceland. When the party arrives there, Brünhilde clearly expects Siegfried to be the wooer, but he pretends to be a mere retainer, a fact which is to have important consequences. By using the cloak of invisibility, Siegfried helps Gunther beat the queen at three tasks, hurling the spear, throwing a stone, and jumping. The parties return to Burgundy, Siegfried marries Kriemhilde, and Gunther marries Brünhilde. Gunther is ignominiously hung on the wall by his mighty wife, and Siegfried is again called in to tame her. He does so but takes away her ring and belt, which he gives to Kriemhilde.

After some years, Brünhilde says that a mere retainer such as Siegfried should not be allowed to be away for so long from his master's court. She fails to convince her husband, but Siegfried and his wife are invited to court. The two queens quarrel over precedence on entering church, and Brünhilde finally learns that Siegfried had only pretended to be a mere retainer. She calls for revenge. Gunther is supine, but Hagen is eager to avenge his queen's honor. He gets Gunther to agree to a hunt. He also persuades Kriemhilde to put a cross on her husband's shirt over the spot where he is vulnerable. After getting Siegfried hot in a race, he leads him to a spring and strikes him down as he stoops over the water. Kriemhilde first hears of her husband's death when the body is thrown before her door. Of Brünhilde we hear little more. There is no mention of her suicide, as there is in the Norse versions.

In spite of her knowledge of the murder, Kriemhilde elects to stay at Worms. She uses the Nibelungen treasure to win support, until Hagen has it taken from her and dropped into the Rhine. Rüedeger comes as emissary to ask for Kriemhilde as second wife to Etzel (Attila). In spite of Hagen's protest, this is agreed upon. Her journey to the Huns' court is carefully described. She bears Etzel a son, Ortlieb. She prevails on Etzel to invite her brothers, and, again over Hagen's protest, they go. Two mermaids, whose clothes have been taken by Hagen, at first prophesy a successful return to Worms but later, when they have recovered their clothes, they say that only the chaplain traveling with them will return. To defy fate, Hagen throws the chaplain into the river, but he swims ashore. The journey, again described in detail, is interrupted for ceremonies at Rüedeger's castle at Bechelare, where Giselher, Gunther's youngest brother, is betrothed to Rüedeger's daughter.

When the Burgundians arrive, there is little pretense at friendliness. Hagen and the minstrel Volker anger Kriemhilde by displaying Siegfried's sword. Etzel and his noble retainer Dietrich keep the peace until one of the Huns, egged on by Kriemhilde's promises of reward, attacks. Ortlieb, Etzel's son, is killed by Hagen, and a great battle takes place which the Burgundians win. Subsequent attempts to crush them, including the burning of the hall, weaken but do not defeat Gunther's men. Rüedeger is now in a dilemma. Shall he help his liege lord Etzel or his newly acquired relations, the Burgundians? As usual, loyalty to the lord triumphs, and he is killed.

Dietrich von Bern, who cannot believe the news, sends his

man Hildebrand to confirm it. In a general melee which follows, only Hildebrand, Gunther, and Hagen are left alive. After a demand for surrender is refused, Dietrich captures the two Burgundians and hands them over to Kriemhilde, asking her to spare them. When Hagen refuses to reveal the whereabouts of the treasure while Gunther is still alive, she has her brother executed. Then Hagen defies her, and she personally cuts off his head with Siegfried's sword. Hildebrand, disgusted that a noble knight should die at the hands of a woman, cuts her down in turn.

At first sight, revenge is the dominant motif of this work. Revenge by Brünhilde for Siegfried's slight, revenge by Kriemhilde for Siegfried's death. Yet there is much more to the poem. The dominant motif is honor, of which revenge is a part, and not the least important part of honor is the honor of a king. Hagen cannot have a high opinion of Gunther, for he is shown as a weak king from the outset. Hagen tries to save him from the consequences of his actions, even at the price of being accused of cowardice. In all this, his concern is with the honor of kingship, not with Gunther personally, and he crowns his acts by having the king killed to save the honor of the kingdom. In thus keeping the king's honor, Hagen dominates the second part of the poem as Siegfried had dominated the first. Hagen's character does not change. He is always hard and practical, but his role, and hence the importance of his attitude, expands through the book.

Siegfried is by no means the same character as Sigurd in the *Eddas*. He has no apparent link to Brünhilde, though there are one or two hints, and his love for Kriemhilde is natural and unforced. In spite of his great power, he is a pleasant and youthful hero, with no dark background to overcome. The affair with Kriemhilde, though cast in the mold of courtly love, is a spontaneous love story, while his death by treachery at the hands of a man he regarded as a friend is pathetic and deeply moving. His weakness was his inability to resist telling Kriemhilde how he broke Brünhilde's resistance. He thus fell victim to the women's rivalry and Brünhilde's injured pride.

Kriemhilde's character undergoes the most change. In the first part of the poem she is naive and innocent, an impression intensified by the fact that the author goes to much trouble to give his work a courtly veneer and especially to make

Siegfried win his bride in courtly fashion. In the second part she is a monster, desiring nothing but the blood of her brothers.

Two or three characters appear to rise above this general gloom. Giselher, the pleasant young brother of Gunther, Rüedeger, noble and generous yet loyal to his lord, and Dietrich, more powerful than anyone yet concerned only with preserving peace. Significantly, both kings are weak. Etzel follows the "southeastern" tradition in this poem and is gentle but ineffective. Gunther, like his counterpart in the *Waltharius*, desires gain and a handsome bride but has neither the power nor the courage to get them by himself.

Over all the poem hangs the doom of the treasure. No one needs it, for Siegfried, Gunther, and Etzel are already wealthy and powerful. Yet it brings about their deaths. Hagen dies for refusing to reveal that it is inaccessible at the bottom of the Rhine. Here again we have the Germanic concept of fate. A man may struggle, but he cannot avoid it. The author of the *Nibelungenlied* was too sophisticated to use as a theme the defiance of death which earlier heroes showed, despite the fact that his hero Hagen does, deliberately, defy both fate and the Christian god by throwing the chaplain in the river. The characters in the poem are professedly Christians. They go to church and perform the necessary rites. Yet the morality of the poem is virtually unaffected by Christianity, less perhaps than *Beowulf*. The Germanic material moves inevitably to a tragic conclusion, and the "courtly" apparatus which the author imports sits uneasily in such company.

As has been mentioned, the structure of the *Nibelungenlied* is far from perfect. There is evidence of imperfect assimilation of material, of conflicting motifs, of changes in intention. When, for example, did Siegfried perform all the exploits described by Hagen? We first see him at Xanten, his parents' home, about to become a knight, and from there he goes directly to Worms! This material is almost all Germanic, but it is not by any means all paralleled in the Scandinavian versions. Some critics have found influence from the French *chansons de geste* and from Slavic sources. Even if these were proved, the story would still remain essentially a Germanic poem, born in the period of migrations and developed into a long epic with increasing sophistication but little change in morality.

The poem is written in a peculiar strophe consisting of four long lines which are probably intended to have eight stresses each. In fact, only the fourth has the full number, the last stress in the first three lines being represented by a pause. The use of a strophic form in narrative works is virtually certain to produce a series of pictures rather than a continuous narrative, and this is precisely the effect of the *Nibelungenlied*. Furthermore, the last line of each strophe is frequently a general comment by the author, which gives a gnomic, almost didactic effect. The language is much simpler and more old fashioned than that of the courtly epics. There is an almost total lack of abstraction. Much of the action is sustained by dialogue.

In spite of its obvious shortcomings, the *Nibelungenlied* is the greatest of the Germanic epics. It has power and sweep, its characters are well drawn and interact violently, and it is, in the end, a fine story.

OTHER POPULAR EPICS

The *Nibelungenlied* stands alone as a representative of Germanic epic. The other works we possess are late, fragmentary, or much changed from their Germanic originals. The nearest in date is the *Gudrun*, written about 1230. It is a strange mixture of near-history and fantasy. Hagen, son of the king of Ireland, is stolen by a griffin! He kills its brood and after spending some years with three kings' daughters, also stolen, he returns home and marries one of them. His daughter Hilde is sought by Hetel of Hegeling in marriage. Hagen refuses, and two of Hetel's men spirit her away. There is a fight and reconciliation.

Then Hilde's daughter, Gudrun, is sought in marriage by Hartmut of Normandy and Herwig of Zeeland. She favors the latter, but while he is away helping her father in battle, she is kidnaped by Hartmut. The Hegelings pursue, Hetel is killed, and the Normans escape. There is a long wait until enough new men are grown for a successful attack. Meanwhile Gudrun refuses to marry Hartmut and is crassly mistreated by his mother, Gerlind. At last the rescuers arrive and are recognized. Gudrun pretends to yield to Hartmut in order to be well bathed and clothed when her rescuers arrive. In the battle the forces of Herwig are successful. Gerlind is killed, but Hartmut is pardoned and there is universal rejoicing.

Gudrun is a strange mixture. The early parts are clearly Eastern in origin. The double wooing story, though with different brides, is characteristic of *Spielmannsepos*. Yet the chief virtues set forth in the work are patience and forgiveness. Although the material is partly Germanic, and the fight between the Normans and the Zeelanders (at Wülpensand) is historical, the work is Christian in tone and largely didactic in purpose.

Ortnit and Wolfdietrich, a much better work, dates from the same period but unfortunately is extant only in fragmentary form. It too is a double story. Ortnit wins a bride from an unwilling father and is killed by a dragon sent against him in revenge. Wolfdietrich is the son of Hugdietrich and is exposed in a wood because a treacherous woman, Sabene, says that he is the devil's son. His name comes from the fact that during his stay in the forest the wolves play with him. Sabene's treachery is exposed, but on his father's death he, his mother, and those faithful to them are again exiled by two older brothers—at Sabene's instigation. After many adventures Wolfdietrich goes to Ortnit's castle, marries his widow after killing the dragon, and brings back an army to defeat his brothers. This is a good adventure story, unpretentious but well told.

A number of incidents from the story of Dietrich are used in other works. *Alphart's Death* (c. 1250) is the story of one of Dietrich's young warriors, treacherously killed by a man whom he had defeated and spared. The *Eckenlied* (mid-thirteenth century) is a confused story of Dietrich's victories over giants, dwarfs, and others. *Biterolf* (c. 1260) begins like an Arthurian story with Biterolf, king of Toledo, at Etzel's court. He has left a son, Dietlieb, at home, who goes to seek his father. On the way he is attacked by Gunther and Hagen and fights with his own father. There is a great battle between Huns and Burgundians, who are, however, reconciled in the end. It is apparent that the author wanted to get every known story into his work. In the *Rose Garden of Worms*, the author shows Dietrich's forces clearly defeating the semicourtly Franks and driving Siegfried to take refuge in the arms of Kriemhilde. Several different versions exist but they are all much later than the original thirteenth-century work.

The Dietrich material was collected about 1280 by Heinrich der Vogler in *Book of Verona*. It is merely adventure entertainment, as is the *Ravenna Battle* of the same period. After this the heroic epics become part of popular literature and appear again as chapbooks.

The later Middle Ages produced a considerable amount of comic verse not unlike the French fabliaux. *Pfaffe Amis* (c. 1220) by an author known as Der Stricker is a collection of strange tales much like the later *Till Eulenspiegel*. The peasant wedding was a favorite subject. There are several anonymous poems on these crude festivities, which always end in fights, but it was not until the fifteenth century that a really great poem on this theme was produced. Heinrich Wittenweiler, a Swiss, wrote his comic epic *The Ring* around 1410. The poem is divided into three parts—the courtship, wedding feast, and riot—and is full of the crudest comedy and realism, with much parody of "courtliness." But there is nevertheless a serious purpose in pointing out the follies not only of the peasants but of all classes of society. Hence the title *Ring*, which shows that all the world is the object of the satire.

As has been noted, there were two main streams of narrative poetry in medieval Germany. In spite of some superficial resemblances—adventure, honor, love—they are completely different. This difference lies much more in the approach than in the source material. The writers of the Arthurian romances had a moral purpose. The world they portrayed was idealized, but the conduct they depicted was intended to lead men to higher goals in real life. Just as the Christian Heaven was not of this world but was nevertheless to be sought by men, so the courtly world provided a secular ideal to strive for. The great romances reflect some of the highest moral and religious thought of the period, yet they are also entertainment of the highest order.

It is hard to find a similar moral purpose in the popular epic. Its foundations were indeed in real life, but it was the real life of a past age. The exemplary force which the epic may have had for an earlier age was largely lost on an audience educated, at least formally, in Christian morality. The popular epics in all countries reflect the whole life of the ruling class of the period they describe—war and peace and the fate of nations. Thus they are close to history in the impression they make, and their value for later generations lay largely in their glorification of history. The romances on the other hand are concerned with the leisure occupations of the aristocrat—love, the tourney, and the court—and through their description of the knight's activities in these leisure occupations they are able to study the development of individual character and what would now be called the psychology of their heroes and heroines in a way which the popular epics neither attempted nor achieved.

Lyric Poetry

EARLY *MINNESÄNGER*

There is very little evidence of lyric poetry in German before the twelfth century. To say that popular songs "must" have existed is easy but tells us nothing of their nature. The occasional references to *cantilenae vulgares* or *winileodi* may be interpreted according to the critic's fancy. The earliest works still extant do not antedate the twelfth century. A few of them are anonymous and simple in theme, the most famous being a short love poem: "You are mine, I am yours, that you must know. You are locked in my heart. The key is lost. There you must always be." This charming and spontaneous poem certainly seems to be a native product.

The same may probably be said of the works of two authors whose names we know—Der von Kürenberg and Dietmar von Eist. Apart from their names, we know nothing of them, except that they lived around 1150 in Austria. Der von Kürenberg wrote his poems in the same strophe as that of the *Nibelungenlied*. The works are love poems, but the conventions of the troubadours are absent. Whether the man or woman is speaking, there is a frank directness of approach and a real desire for love fulfilled. Both poets use figures, such as the falcon as lover, which are found elsewhere in native German poetry. For them, love is natural, not a matter for theoretical speculation, and the man is perfectly prepared to leave a lady who is making too many demands on him. "Love service" is certainly not present. Yet there are some similarities to the Provençal lyric. Dietmar's best-known poem is a *Tagelied*, or dawn song, which, although simple, has the same features as the Provençal *alba*.

Direct influence from French models can first be observed in the so-called Rhineland school of poets, who flourished in the last decades of the twelfth century. Among them were some of the greatest writers of the *Minnesang*. This term means "love song" and strictly it should be used only for the German equivalent of the *canzon*. It is, however, often extended to mean all lyric poetry of the twelfth and thirteenth centuries and thus includes political and moral poetry as well as love lyric.

There can be no reasonable doubt that the *Minnesänger* were dependent on themes and melodies from France. Little contemporary music has survived for the poems of the early *Minnesang*, but even so it is possible to show that tunes were taken over and set to German words. Furthermore the verse form of the *canzon*, with its characteristic tripartite division, is also used consistently in these love poems. Troubadour love imagery also appears in the German poets. We find the same yearning, the same hopelessness, the same worship. It might be thought that German *Minnesang* is merely a pale reflection of Provençal lyric, but this is far from true. The German poets never acknowledge their French models or make any reference to them, and a close reader soon observes that the spirit underlying the poetry is completely different.

In German love poetry the lady is unimportant. This may seem like a paradox, but it is true. The praise of her beauty and qualities is formal and short. The poet is not concerned with her but with his own feelings or those of a lover. These feelings he analyzes with great care and detail. Thus the question, what is love? occurs over and over, with varying answers. Self-questioning and self-examination are the principal material of the *Minnesang*. Why am I in love? What is it my lady wants of me? Why do I despair and still love? Why is love always mixed with sorrow? And always there is the tension between the desire for love's fulfillment and the knowledge that such fulfillment would shatter the ideal of womanhood which the poet has set up for himself. The service which the German poet proposes to his lady is to sing her praise. Yet only a small part of any poem is devoted to this. It may be that the highest praise that could be bestowed was that the poet loved her. It is pointless to talk of adulterous love in connection with German poets, for they never say who their ladies were, and it is highly doubtful, in most cases, whether the ladies existed at all. The courtly love convention, which no doubt began with the panegyric love song to a married lady, becomes in German poetry a largely theoretical study of the love problem.

It is worth noting that the early poets of the *Minnesang* are, at least technically, noblemen. The earliest of them was the emperor Henry VI himself, but the first important poet was Friedrich von Hausen, who died on a crusade in 1190. His work derives directly from troubadour poetry. His most famous poem is a crusading song in which he subtly examines the separation of heart and soul brought about by the fact that his soul must go on a crusade but that his heart will stay behind with his lady. It is hard to determine where the poet would rather be. With Friedrich is associated a group of less important poets, all of whom were in Italy with him and who obviously came into contact there with French poetry. This group includes Bligger von Steinach, Bernger von Hoheim, Ulrich von Gutenburg, and Rudolf von Fenis. A few poems of each are extant. All of them are feeling their way toward a highly sophisticated type of lyric called *Minnesang*. The sadness caused by distance and separation is present and is, indeed, emphasized in the work of Albrecht von Johannsdorf (fl. 1180–1200), who uses the theme of the crusades to contrast his unrewarded service to the lady and his service to God. He is often critical of the cruelty of ladies and shows at times an unusual determination to have his own way.

The lyric poetry of Hartmann von Aue (c. 1160–c. 1210) is far below that of his epic, while the lyric of Heinrich von Veldeke (c. 1145–c. 1210) rather surpasses his epic. Contemporary with Hartmann were two truly great poets, Heinrich von Morungen (c. 1155–1222) and Reinmar von Hagenau (der Alte; c. 1160–1205). Both sing of the hopelessness of love and of their resignation, but their methods are different. Heinrich, a knight from Thuringia, was a fairly important man of affairs and not a professional poet. There is considerable personal feeling in his work, and all critics have commented on his brilliant use of visual metaphors and figures to describe the beauty and glory of his lady. In his dawn song he describes the white sheen of her body in the moonlight, elsewhere he compares her with the sun. This penetrating light from her person is what fixes her beauty on him forever. Yet his song, he recognizes, is futile because it is never acknowledged. The lady may like it, may command him to sing, but the singing never achieves its purpose.

The same may be said of Reinmar, an Alsatian, who wrote at the Austrian court in Vienna. His work lacks the plasticity and brilliant imagery of Heinrich von Morungen. It is more philosophical, more carefully argued and more subtle—so much so that it is not until one has looked behind the apparent monotony of expression that one notices the brilliant argument and careful discrimination. Hopelessness and resignation form the great part of Reinmar's work, but he occasionally lashes out at ladies for their cruelty (and straightway repents)—and at poets whose praise of their lady cannot match his.

WALTHER VON DER VOGELWEIDE

Heinrich von Morungen and Reinmar were the two greatest exponents of *Minnesang* in its purest form, and, indeed, exhausted the limited possibilities of the theme. Their younger contemporary, Walther von der Vogelweide (c. 1178–1228), trained by Reinmar at the Austrian court, showed how the love theme could be celebrated more naturally and yet use the full store of imagery which the earlier *Minnesänger* had perfected. We have one document about Walther which shows that he was in the employ of Bishop Wolfger of Passau in 1203. Otherwise our knowledge of him comes from his work. Fortunately, he makes numerous references to himself. While in Vienna, he wrote conventional *Minnesang* but was not particularly successful. It was when he was forced to leave Vienna in 1198 because of lack of patronage that he began to develop his true talents. These find expression in three main types of poetry: those referring to actual political events, those of social and theological comment, and those on love.

We can deal with the last group first. Walther quarreled—in several poems—with Reinmar over love poetry and later developed something completely new. Instead of hopeless love for an unattainable lady, he shows us a fresh young girl on a spring morning. Love is once again natural, yet there is in most of the poems just as much respect for the unmarried girl as for the highborn lady. She is described in terms of nature, in a way which owes much to Latin poetry but is more personal. Hope has replaced the hopelessness of *Minnesang*, although that hope is still mixed with shyness and idealism. The language of these poems abandons the formal dialectic and outworn imagery of the *Minnesang*. Natural description abounds, and Walther is the first German poet to make frequent and successful use of the *Natureingang* or "spring opening," the ideal spring landscape.

Walther's political poetry was something quite new in Germany. Similar to the Provençal *sirventès* in that it comments on current events, it uses the same general metrical form as the *Minnesang*. Groups of poems on the same general theme have the same strophic form and hence melody, even when written several years apart. In these political songs Walther deliberately attempts to serve princes with his pen as others did with their swords. No doubt there was a degree of personal interest in his actions, but clearly an even larger degree of genuine concern for the empire. The political situation after 1198 was confused. Frederick of Hohenstaufen, son of the emperor Henry VI, was too young to rule. Two candidates arose: Philip of Swabia, Henry's brother, and Otto of Brunswick. Walther regarded the former as the true candidate and used every poetical device at his command to win the German princes over to his side, particularly when the powerful Pope Innocent III threw his support to Otto. In a series of brilliant strophes, Walther made it clear that the empire should be independent of any outside interference and that firm government was needed.

Just when he seemed about to triumph, Philip II was assassinated (not at Otto's instigation) and Otto succeeded without opposition. After an interval Walther found his support was needed and gave it. Although he never liked the rather stingy Otto, he supported him once again when strife arose between empire and papacy. His attacks on Innocent III were so strong and personal that several authors reproached him. This was not the generalized satire on the papal curia so common among the Latin writers, but a slashing attack on the Pope's efforts to collect money—not for a crusade as alleged but to keep his Italian priests in luxury.

Walther's enthusiasm for Otto could not last. He turned to the rising sun of the third candidate, the brilliant scholar, patron of literature, and wonder of the world, Frederick II, and was finally rewarded by him in 1220 with a small property near Würzburg. This event he celebrates in a pure outburst of joy. It was not only in directly political songs that Walther gave utterance to his thoughts on the world. Many of his longer poems are contemplative and almost philosophical. They analyze the relationships of the various parts of the empire and the way in which it must be organized so as to serve the ends of God.

Even more important than his poems on the empire are

Walther's poems on man himself. What are the forces which drive and control him? The poet refers to the trinity of powers—material and worldly goods, honor and moral behavior, and, superior to the other two, the worship of God. How can these be reconciled? As he grew older, Walther became more and more pessimistic about the prospects of reconciliation. He saw a decline in standards, a young generation bent only on pleasure, even singing itself debased and coarsened. In his last great poem he sings a lament for the great days he has seen and speaks of present woes. Yet, he says, there is hope. Christian men should band together for the great crusade against the heathen and joy will once again come to the world.

Walther was a man of many parts. In his frequent travels he saw much of men and not all of what he saw was favorable. Some of the patrons for whom he sang—Hermann von Thüringen, for example—were political weathercocks who constantly sought their own advantage. Walther tried to support them but the task was often distasteful. He was not himself a man of easy temper, and some of his poems are very human explosions of wrath against personal enemies.

The scope and depth of Walther's poetry is tremendous. Like all truly great lyric poets, his language is simple, his versification uncluttered by excessive virtuosity of technique. He is thoughtful, deeply moral, and religious, yet can be playful and ironic when his subject demands it. His contemporaries Wolfram and Gottfried both mention him; Gottfried in particular praises him as the greatest living lyric poet. He is certainly the greatest lyric poet of medieval Germany and probably of the whole Middle Ages.

LYRIC POETRY AFTER WALTHER

As might be expected, Walther's influence on later poets was immense, but this influence was not all to the good. On the one hand, he had broken the tyranny of the restricted *Minnesang* form and thus opened the door to greater and sometimes pernicious liberties with theme and language. On the other, he had provided models to imitate. Every love poem after his day begins with a conventional spring opening.

Of the large number of lyric poets of the thirteenth and fourteenth centuries, only a few deserve more than passing mention. Walther's younger contemporary, Neidhart von

Reuental (fl. c. 1217–37) was the first of a completely new group of poets. His poems are dance songs, with dance tunes, very different from the staid *Minnesang*. Instead of knights, we see peasants and their girls, dancing outside in the *Summer Songs,* inside in the *Winter Songs.* Eroticism is always present. The mothers warn their daughters at the spring festivals but sometimes take part themselves in the dances. In winter there is rivalry, quarreling, and fighting among the peasants. Neidhart frequently presents himself as a suitor and is virtually always worsted by some crude boor.

The poems are all satirical. The witty picture of peasant life is obviously ironical. But more important is the fact that into the mouths of these louts Neidhart puts the choicest language of the *Minnesang,* so that there is deliberate parody. The peasants are shown aping the manners of the nobles and thus making fools of themselves. Yet at the same time the nobles, including Neidhart, are laughed at, for these same peasants defeat them in the game of love. One can understand why Walther von der Vogelweide complained about the coarsening of taste. The young men at court doubtless roared with laugher at seeing the *Minnesang* so mercilessly pilloried. Yet, with all his coarseness, one cannot deny Neidhart vigor and wit and a great deal of originality. With his pictures of peasants aping the courtly lover he sealed the doom of the *Minnesang* and acquired for himself a reputation as peasant-baiter which lasted for centuries.

The older tradition of *Minnesang* was pursued by, among others, Ulrich von Lichtenstein (c. 1200–75). He gives his opinions on the service of love in a kind of biography, *The Service of Women,* in which he describes his life as a servant of courtly love, the tourneys he has fought (two separate series) and the ladies he has served. He preserves the old forms, but the effect is hollow and often grotesque, for the service of love was for him a literary motif, not a part of life.

Tannhäuser (early thirteenth century) is much more like Neidhart. He uses dance forms, and much of his work is parody. At about the same time Gottfried von Neifen, Burkart von Hohenfels, and Ulrich von Winterstetten were engaged in making a more natural kind of folk poetry from both elements, the *Minnesang* and Neidhart poetry. Steinmar von Klingenau (1251–93) produced crudely realistic poetry on the peasant level, while still using *Minnesang* forms.

Johannes Hadlaub (c. 1293–1340) may be said to mark a turning point. A bourgeois of Zürich with no feeling for aristocratic poetry, he combines in his work all the types of his predecessors, from pure *Minnesang* to imitation of Neidhart. He tells of his own love life with rather heavy realism. Although there were many other imitators, the *Minnesang* was now merely form. It had been succeeded by realistic poetry.

In the thirteenth and fourteenth centuries there were a large number of wandering professional singers, whose stock in trade consisted largely of formal panegyrics and poems of comment on events or morals. Most of these were unimportant, but one stands out: Heinrich von Meissen (born about 1260). He was a singer of great virtuosity in form and melody. Most of his work was of a didactic and even religious nature, but his love songs were good enough to earn him the name Frauenlob ("Praiser of Women"). It is not surprising that he is credited, although probably incorrectly, with setting up the first school for professional singers.

Heinrich von Mügeln (fl. 1346–69) of Meissen composed works, some in lyric form, some longer, on moral subjects and the events of his day. He wrote a 2,600-line poem called *Garland of Maidens* which is an allegorical description of the liberal arts, and he covered much of medieval learning in his shorter poems. Oswald von Wolkenstein (1377–1465), a more vigorous poet, lived a full life of wandering and adventure, all of which finds its way into his numerous poems. The one fairly constant thing in his life was his love for Sabine Jäger, the daughter of a political rival, and this brought him only trouble, for she lured him into a trap which cost him time in prison. Oswald was a master of every poetical form and treats a wide variety of subjects from longing for far-off love to coarsest obscenity, from pastoral duets to political adventures. His near-contemporary Hugo of Montfort (1357–1423) wrote similarly but with more self-restraint and less power.

The change from a courtly to a bourgeois audience produced considerable changes in form as well as in content. The carefully constructed strophes of the earlier lyric poetry gave place in German literature, as in French, to more direct forms of expression. The *Minnesang* gave way to the *Minnerede*, a poem on love which was similar to the French *dit*. Where earlier forms of the lyric persisted, they became very stereotyped. Although the earliest definite record of a *Singschule* or school for songwriters dates from 1450, it is certain that there had been brotherhoods of singers before this, attached to churches. Their subjects were largely religious and allegorical, and at first they used only the twelve melodies of the great masters. Later, to qualify as a *Meistersinger*, they had to compose a new melody. Their poetry counted syllables rigidly and often distorted natural word accent to obtain a line. Their work is full of formal learning and rhetoric but is rarely spontaneous. A large number of the works of early singers are preserved in the Colmar manuscript, together with a description of how a potential mastersinger was tested.

Many of the poets of the late fourteenth century and fifteenth century write in the fashion of *Meistergesang*, even though they were not necessarily trained in its schools. Muskatplüt (c. 1390–1441), with his moral poems and topical commentary, and Hans Volz (1433–1513) fall into this category. The number of *Singschulen* increased rapidly, and they attained their greatest influence in the sixteenth century, particularly in southern Germany.

Didactic Poetry and Satire

During the great period (1170–1230) of courtly writing there is little didactic poetry—a few moral poems by Spervogel or Herger (late twelfth century), of whom we know nothing. But with the decline of the Hohenstaufen period there begins a stream of works which reaches a flood in the later Middle Ages. This didactic poetry takes various forms. We have already noted its appearance in the lyric. There were also longer, professedly didactic works and narrative poems with a didactic purpose. Later, allegory is used, as it was in French literature, to teach the essentials of a particular subject.

A complete guide to living was given in the form of a father-to-son poem by a knight of Winsbeke (c. 1220–30). He describes in order the duties of a knight, of a gentleman, and of a Christian. Much longer is the work of an Italian, Thomasin von Zerklaere, at the court of Wolfger of Passau, the patron of Walther von der Vogelweide. In ten months in 1215/16 he wrote a 15,000-line poem, *The Stranger from the South*, which covers the whole of human manners and morals, from how to behave at table to God's empire on earth. He knows the work of contemporary poets, including Walther, but his approach is that of a trained theologian. A more elementary (and more widely read) work of the same type was the *Bescheidenheit* (c. 1230) of Freidank. The title means "distinction" and the purpose is to show how a Christian can recognize good and evil. It is a straightforward moral work.

One of the most important didactic works is *Meier Helmbrecht* (c. 1280) by Wernher der Gartenaere. It is the story of the son of a solid farmer, spoiled by his mother and sisters, who against his father's advice decides to join robber knights. He plunders successfully and returns home loaded with booty. His father ejects him, and he is caught, punished for his crimes, and finally hanged by outraged peasants. The moral is well driven home—everyone should stay in the place to which God appointed him. Yet there is social criticism too— of barons who rob, of mothers who are not content with a hard-working son, of fathers who will not perform a harsh duty. This is a very fine narrative, not without effective comic overtones.

Satire of contemporary manners is also to be found in the *Book of Complaint* (1276/7) and in Heinrich von Berlingen's *Chessbook* (c. 1290), which uses chess figures as models of the classes of society. The works which go under the name of Seifried Helbling (the actual author is unknown), written between 1283 and 1299, are of the same order but with more personnal feeling. Hugo von Trimberg's *Renner* ("Runner") (c. 1300) is a work not unlike that of the knight of Winsbeke already mentioned. It is very long (24,000 lines) and less certain of its social intention than its predecessor. Bourgeois morality was already making itself felt. The popularity of *Renner* is shown by the existence of more than sixty manuscripts.

Another chess allegory, Konrad von Ammenhausen's *Chessboard Book*, was written in 1337. Like its predecessors, it makes symbolic use of chessmen to make a sharp attack on contemporary morals. In spite of its moralizing and enormous length it was very popular. Moral teaching was also the purpose of a rendering of Aesop's fables by Ulrich Boner, a Swiss, about 1345 under the title *Precious Stone*.

Heinrich der Teichner produced around 750 *Reimsprüche*, short moral poems on the relation between man and God, man's free will, his means of salvation, and the sin which besets him. In the course of these he severely criticizes his contemporaries. Peter Suchenwirt's formal elegies on dead

nobles and on Heinrich der Teichner (a rare piece of contemporary criticism) and Gerhard von Minden's versions of
Aesop's fables also belong to the fourteenth century.

Several allegorical works were also written in this period.
One of the best is Hadamar von Laber's *Hunt* (c. 1335).
Here the formal terms and ceremony of hunting deer are used
to describe pursuit of the lady. The desires and feelings of the
lover are allegorically represented by his hounds. Obviously,
the hunter can never catch the lady, but it gives the author
an opportunity to display great virtuosity in allegory. Another love allegory is the *Smock* (c. 1380) of "Meister
Altswert," who pursues his love with less finesse. The rules
of love are stated more explicitly in Eberhard von Cersne's
Rule of Love (1404). He uses the work of Andreas Capellanus (see chapter on Latin literature) as a basis but moves
the scene outside the French court and makes the rules of
love applicable to society in general.

We have already mentioned Muskatplüt. Besides his shorter
poems, he wrote the long *Complaint of the Empire*, a pessimistic poem of the triumph of materialism. Equally gloomy
is a late-fourteenth-century work called the *Devil's Net*, in
which the devil explains how he has lured all classes of
society into his clutches. Similarly Hans Vintler in his *Flowers
of Virtue* (1411) is more concerned with attacking vice than
praising virtue.

At first sight it may seem strange to classify the German
versions of the *Roman de Renart* as didactic poetry, but such
in fact they are. There is a strong satirical element in the Latin
version, as we have seen, and this becomes very pronounced
in the Low German works of the late Middle Ages. The
earliest work in German was Heinrich der Glichezaere's poem
(c. 1180), of which only 685 lines survive. An anonymous
reworking of about 1240 is extant. The incidents are those
familiar from the *Ysengrimus*, including that of the sick lion.

The most significant works in the Renard cycle are those
in Middle Dutch. There are several variants which seem to
stem from a version written about 1270 by a certain Willem
of Hulsterlo. All versions center around a trial of Renard at
court and not around the sick-lion scene, which does not
appear. All the animals complain of Renard's behavior, and
messengers sent to fetch him are badly treated. He escapes
hanging by a tale of treasure which excites King Lion's cu-

pidity. His deceit is uncovered, and to escape the consequences he proposes to go on a pilgrimage, but turns aside to his castle. He is put under the ban, that is, made an outlaw.

Although this Middle Dutch work is not a didactic poem, it does attack the whole medieval system of justice. The lion, under his wife's thumb, is a corrupt judge and the whole court corrupt with him. These elements become even more marked in the lengthened prose versions printed at Gouda in 1479 and at Delft in 1485. The Caxton translation into English was made from the Gouda version. In 1487 in Antwerp a modernized verse version was printed, of which only fragments remain. Its author was Hinrik van Alkmar, and from this a Low German version printed in Lübeck in 1498 was made. This poem, *Reinke Vos*, was by far the most popular of the German versions and has remained so. A prologue to the Dutch original makes it very clear that the poem is intended as a satire on the follies of men. There is no direct moralization, but the attacks on the behavior of the various classes of society are plain enough. Such a method of satirizing society is certainly more amusing than the heavy didacticism of many contemporary works.

Prose Works

In Germany, as elsewhere, early prose is entirely technical in character. The earliest which can be called literary is the preaching of the great Franciscan Berthold von Regensburg (c. 1215–72). During the thirteenth century he was followed by a series of great mystics whose work, while not strictly literature, deserves mention because of the magnificent style in which it was written. Mechtild von Magdeburg (died 1282) wrote between 1250 and 1265 the visions called *Flowing Light of God*, in which she felt deeply drawn to love of the Heavenly presence. A far deeper thinker, indeed one of the greatest mystics of the Middle Ages, was Meister Eckhart (c. 1260–1327), most of whose works were written in Latin but whose sermons (collected by his followers) and *Book of Divine Consolation* (1308) mark him as a master of German prose. Two other remarkable men followed him, Johannes Tauler (c. 1300–61), active in Strasbourg and Cologne, and Heinrich Seuse (c. 1293–1366). The *Book of Truth* (1327) and *Book of Eternal Wisdom* (1324–34) are Seuse's greatest works. All of these authors had virtually to create a new style. They borrow images from poetry, translate from Latin, allegorize, and use metaphor. The result is a highly luminous and flowing prose style.

There was also prose of a completely different kind. Elisabeth of Nassau-Saarbrücken (1397–1456) put into German prose adventure stories already popular in France. Two of them, *Loher and Maller* and *Herpin*, tell of princes exiled and brought up in the wilderness and their return after many adventures. *Hug Scheppel*, another tale of even wilder adventure, purports to be the story of how Hugh Capet gained the throne of France. Except for a rather confused *Prose Lancelot* of the thirteenth century, these were the first prose adventure stories in German. Johannes Hartlieb wrote a prose *Alexander* in 1444, taken from the Latin. A number of other German works were put into prose form in the second half of the fifteenth century—*Wigalois*, *Tristan*, and *Duke Ernst*—as well as more popular tales like *Melusine* and *Fortunatus*.

This section is properly concluded with some account of the most famous prose work of the German Middle Ages, the *Ackermann aus Böhmen* ("Plowman from Bohemia"), written about 1403 by Johann von Tepl (c. 1351–1415). This is a formal dialogue between the plowman (he plows paper with his pen!) and Death. The plowman accuses Death, in legal form, or robbing him of his wife. Death replies that this is his duty. The dialogue develops into a discussion between the two on the function of death and the usefulness of life. Death at first claims that he clears away excess so that life can go on but, as the plowman forgets his personal loss, he attempts to show life is useless anyway. This the plowman refutes, for life is God's creation, and he must therefore love it. Although God awards Death the legal victory, to the plowman goes honor for upholding so nobly the goodness of human existence. The work is finely written, with great learning and sense of form, and also with a feeling for the purpose and importance of life which seems to bridge the gulf between the Middle Ages and the Renaissance.

The observant reader will note many similarities between the literary history of France and that of Germany. There is in both a great period of courtly romance and lyric at the turn of the twelfth century, paralleled by the existence of a national epic. Then follows a period of imitation and decline, relieved by a few poets with a gift for describing their own times realistically. Yet it would be a mistake to regard German literature as merely following French. Each was responsive to the intellectual and social currents of the time—the court as intellectual center, scholasticism, the Gothic, decentralization and social upheaval, the rise of the bourgeoisie. But, given these same conditions, each produced its own peculiar works. Even when the subject matter was substantially the same, the treatment was varied. *Perceval* is not *Parzival*, and the *Minnesänger* were not *troubadours*. Each brought his own contribution.

Italian Literature

GENERAL

WE HAVE NOTED that English literature started late in the Middle Ages and suffered from the fact that for several important centuries English was not the language of the cultured. Italian literature experienced a similar fate but for almost the opposite reason. The language remained for centuries very close to Latin. It was not difficult for Italians to learn to understand and speak Latin of a kind. The idiom and style of Cicero and Vergil were, of course, beyond them, but for everyday purposes Latin was readily comprehensible. Thus Italian developed no vernacular tradition like that of the languages of northwestern Europe. Its numerous dialects were not considered worthy of literature, and for centuries there developed no language which could even remotely be called standard.

There was also a rather important social reason for this retard. Italy in the twelfth century did not develop feudal courts with a small cultivated élite like those found in many parts of France and Germany. On the contrary, there was a great deal of political upheaval in many Italian cities, and patronage was hard to come by. This factor undoubtedly had an effect both on the development of vernacular literature and on the themes it used. It can be stated at once that the courtly romance found no great welcome in Italy. There are no national epics such as are found elsewhere, and drama, in the sense in which it developed across the Alps, is also lacking.

Until the Renaissance, Italian literature is much more religious than that of other countries. It missed the "secular" twelfth century and was deeply affected by the religious movements of the thirteenth—the begging orders and the rational theology of Thomas Aquinas. Thus the following survey contains considerably more references to religious poetry and prose than earlier chapters.

EARLY LYRIC POETRY

The earliest appearance of literature in the vernacular in Italy was in the form of lyric. It is possible to trace fairly accurately the influences which led to its development. We know of several troubadours who paid visits to Italy—Pierre Vidal, at the end of the twelfth century, among others. They brought with them the forms and conventions of the Provençal *canzon*, and it is perfectly possible that not only Italians but Germans first learned of troubadour poetry in Italy. The first lyric love poetry by Italians was written in Provençal—by Folquet de Marseile (c. 1180–1231), a Genoese, and by Sordello (c. 1200–69).

The ideas of the troubadours and the language in which they expressed them found a warm welcome in the highly cultured and cosmopolitan court of the emperor Frederick II at Palermo in Sicily. Here, for the first time, a school of Italian poetry flourished. Its chief service was to mold the language as a poetical instrument and to start the development of the sonnet form. The *Lament of a Crusader's Lady* by Ciullo d'Alcamo, although put into the mouth of a woman, has many of the characteristics of the troubadour crusading song. Similar works were written by Ruggerone da Palermo and Odo delle Colonne, all in the first half of the thirteenth century.

The two most famous members of the Sicilian school were Guido delle Colonne (fl. c. 1280), who produced the Latin prose version of the Troy story, and Jacopo da Lentino, "the Notary" (c. 1240), credited with inventing the sonnet. The former shows that considerable mastery of language and form had already been attained. Another and more interesting feature of Guido's work, however, is his introduction of the scientific imagery which was to be so characteristic of Italian lyric and which distinguishes it from that of other countries. Even at this early date, fire, water, air, light, and earth are presented in a series of images to illustrate the course of love. The use of such imagery naturally increased the tendency already evident in Provençal and German poetry to treat love impersonally, without reference to any particular lady.

Jacopo's work follows the same general pattern, but with even more emphasis on learning. The sonnet form grew naturally out of what was virtually the standard form for the *canzon*: two groups of lines corresponding exactly in length of line and rhyme scheme, followed by another group of a different pattern. All that was needed was to fix the number of lines in each group and make them of a regular length, and this Jacopo did. The Sicilian school served a useful purpose in acclimatizing the ideas of France to the Italian language. If it did not itself produce any great poetry, it prepared the way for others.

The poets of Tuscany were among the first to imitate, without any great subtlety, the Provençal forms of the debate poem and the *canzon*, using in these the familiar conventional style. Pleasant though the early poems of Ciacco dall'Anguillara and Alesso Donati are, they do not present anything specifically Italian.

Guido Guinizelli (c. 1230–c. 1276) was a poet of a completely different cast. Well trained in science, he was yet a master of poetic language. His subject is the nature of love and its relation to the human heart, his imagery that of natural science. He is completely impersonal. No real lady seems to be the object of his affection. Hence there is no flattery, no worship, except that implicit in his belief that love itself is the highest of spiritual experiences and is worth describing in terms used of the most refined features of the universe. Guido's style, like that of many poets of the Tuscan school, is a series of intricately interwoven comparisons in which it is not always clear which is the more important element. A good deal of skill—and knowledge of such things as Aristotelian science and the allegorical properties of precious stones—is needed to understand the images properly. Thus his style has defects. Striking as his comparisons are, subtly as he compares love with flame, light, the sun, the heavens, the reader is left with a sense of coldness. His words are melodious, his ideas beautifully expressed, but his poetry is to be interpreted, not absorbed.

There is no doubt that Guido Guinizelli surpasses the troubadours in his analysis of love. Guittone d'Arezzo (d. 1294), writing with similar ideas and intentions, was less successful because of his inferior ability with language. Moreover, Jacopono da Todi (c. 1230–1306) can hardly be reckoned as one of the Tuscan school, even though he lived in the area. His verse is enthusiastically religious. He attempts none of the fine discriminations of the Tuscan school but seeks to express in clear and unequivocal language his devotion to Christ and the Virgin. His poetry is intensely personal, even mystical. It is full of concretely detailed visions. Naturally it owes much to the tradition of the Latin hymn, but there is little of the elaborate allegory so often found there. Rather it derives its images from popular speech and from the best of the poetry of secular love.

There are two other great Tuscan poets, both contemporaries of Dante and, like him, pupils of Brunetto Latini (c. 1220–94), the author of the encyclopedic *Treasure*. They are Cino da Pistoia (1270–1337) and Guido Cavalcanti (c. 1250–1300). Cino was a lawyer and weaver of logical arguments. His poetry shows it. His sonnets and *canzoni* are well constructed, rational, and uninspired. He uses with great skill the image of the power of the lady's eyes to create love, inspire the soul, and destroy the man. In this image too is science—for light is the source of life, of love, and of destruction.

Guido Cavalcanti seems to be the person celebrated by Dante as the creator of the "sweet new style" (*Purgatory*, Canto XI). It is still far from clear what is meant by this famous expression. Certainly Cavalcanti is unsurpassed in the polish of his language and brilliance of his rhetoric, but it is impossible for any judicious reader to see a break so sharp (with, say, the poetry of Guido Guinizelli) as to constitute a new style. Cavalcanti was extremely learned, a philosopher and dialectician, and his poetry reflects it. Yet he could, on occasion, be brilliantly personal and brilliantly poetic, for, when dealing with a subject not susceptible of philosophical treatment, his mastery of language produced a vivid and impressive style.

One common characteristic is evident from this brief study of the Tuscan poets. The love which for the troubadours was directed at an unattainable but actual lady is now analyzed as love for an abstraction—Woman. From this it is not a long step to the visualization of the eternal Feminine of Dante. The use of scientific and, especially, light imagery to describe the state of love, and the removal from this description of any trace of sensuality, meant that such love must, inevitably, become religious. It is often hard to determine whether secular or religious love is being discussed in Italian lyrics. With Cavalcanti the way was prepared for Dante, whose lyric poetry is discussed below with his other works.

Lyric that can be called medieval had a short if brilliant life in Italy. After Dante the next great name is Petrarch, and he must be classed as a poet of the Renaissance, despite the numerous medieval elements in his work.

DANTE

Life

Dante (1265–1321) dominates medieval Italian literature even more than Chaucer dominates Middle English. He is one of the very few unquestionably great geniuses of world literature who is so universal, so concerned with moral behavior, and such a fine artist. It is tempting to see in Dante the epitome of everything medieval and the greatest artist in all fields. Such a judgment would be unfair. Gaiety and comedy were alien to his temperament, and he falls far short of Chaucer and many other writers in this respect. He was not such a gifted observer of the social and political scene as Walther von der Vogelweide, nor does he study the problem of *human* love so thoroughly as Gottfried von Strassburg. Yet even with these reservations he towers above other artists both in the majesty of his language and in the sweep of his imagination.

Dante Alighieri was born in Florence in 1265. His family was important, although not particularly wealthy. He was betrothed as a boy to Gemma Donati, daughter of an aristocratic family, and he later married her. Nothing is said of his marriage, but it is significant that she did not accompany him into exile. His education was excellent, for he studied under the learned Brunetto Latini. Even if we did not know this, his works would be proof enough that he had absorbed all the theological, scientific, and literary learning of his time. His experiences in politics began early. After a short spell of military service, he was a member of the council of six for two months in 1300, then ambassador on several missions for the city.

His subsequent life of wandering was caused by factionalism in Florence. The Ghibellines, theoretically supporters of the emperor, had been driven out of Florence, but the Guelfs, supporters of the Pope, had split into Blacks and Whites who quarreled among themselves. Generally the Blacks were the old aristocratic families, the Whites the newer bourgeoisie. The Pope, Boniface VIII, caused further trouble by making demands on Florence which were rejected by the Whites. Dante was one of the Priors, the ruling body of Florence, at this time (1301) and voted with them to exile the leaders

of both parties, among them Guido Cavalcanti, a close friend.
Dante himself was sent to the Pope to try for a reconciliation,
but while he was away the Florentines accepted Charles of
Valois as "mediator." Once in control he handed the city over
to the Blacks. Dante was condemned to exile and loss of
property for misconduct in office and never returned to
Florence.

His hatred for those who had exiled him and, perhaps
unreasonably, for Florence itself grew with the years. He described himself as a Florentine by birth but not by nature.
The rest of his life was spent as a penniless exile, which for a
man of his proud temperament was almost unbearable. He
found patrons—Can Grande della Scala at Verona was
one of the most consistent—but he was also at Bologna,
Lunigiana, Padua, and Lucca. He spent the last years of his
life at Ravenna with Guido Novello da Polenta and was there
joined by three of his four children. He died in Ravenna on
September 14, 1321.

Early Works

Dante's earliest work was lyric poetry, and the most famous
work containing lyric poetry was the *Vita nuova*. This is a
prose book giving an account of the famous love for Beatrice,
with interspersed lyrics. As is well known, the lady whom
Dante calls Beatrice was probably Beatrice Portinari (1266–
90), whom he first met when he was nine. There was no love
affair in the usual sense of the term, and Dante's lyrics, even
those which celebrate Beatrice when she was alive, use celestial and religious imagery. After her death her spirit becomes
merged in the poet's mind with Truth itself. His yearning
for her is also a yearning for virtue and for heavenly beauty.
In these lyrics Dante uses the forms and concepts evolved by
the other writers of the *dolce stil novo* ("sweet new style")
and applies them to a personal love which is yet not the
personal love of a man for a woman but of a man for a
personified ideal. Beatrice, typically, is not described, but the
impressions she makes on other people—and particularly, of
course, her effect on the poet—are detailed many times.

His next work was the *Convivio* or *Banquet* (c. 1290),
which purported to be a learned commentary on lyric poetry.
It is a rather unformed work, full of learning, but it is quite
apparent that Dante had not mastered the art of clear exposition in prose. The same may be said of his Latin work *De*

vulgari eloquentia ("On the Use of the Vernacular"). Here he tries to discuss the differences in the various non-Latin languages and the various levels of style. He then shows how the highest form of literature which could be written in the vernacular was the *canzone*, the formal love lyric, and he goes into great detail about the construction and style of such lyrics. *De vulgari eloquentia* is an incomplete study. Its chief interest for us lies in its exposition of Dante's own views on lyric poetry. Clearly, for him form in the lyric was of the greatest importance, a judgment borne out by his selection of the greatest troubadours—those whose form was most elaborate. The work is not easy to follow, for Dante's Latin style is tortuous.

His famous political work in Latin, *De Monarchia* (before 1313), was written for a special occasion. Henry of Luxemburg, elected emperor as Henry VII, had high hopes of unifying the empire. Enthusiastic about the possibility of firm secular control and a limitation of the power of the Pope, Dante wrote a tract in which he reasoned that the secular part of the empire was coexistent with and equal to the spiritual part—that is, the papacy—and not subject to it as the papal authorities claimed. He refutes the parallels the latter used to support their claim—that the sun is the spiritual power and the moon of secular power shines by its light.

He also hopes for a restoration of the true Roman empire, which seemed to him to embody all that was good in secular rule and to have obtained its dominion by the special favor of God. In *De Monarchia* Dante is seeking that "Roman peace" which was always his ideal and an end to the strife which had wrecked his life. His hopes were doomed to disappointment, for Henry failed and died in 1313.

Divina Commedia

The *Divina Commedia*, or simply *Commedia* as Dante himself called it, was written in the years of exile. It sets forth Dante's thoughts and emotions, his objective and subjective feelings about man on earth and man's ultimate destiny as part of the universal plan. It is an allegory of man's life, but the poet himself participates and thus injects into the allegory personal considerations which make a great impact on the reader. The *Commedia* is a complex work, and before discussing it further, it will be best to give a brief summary.

Dante, at the age of thirty-five and thus in the Jubilee year of 1300, finds himself wandering in a dark wood (of error). He looks toward a beautiful mountain just beginning to be illuminated by the sun's rays but finds his way blocked by the beautiful leopard (fleshly delight), the lion (ambition), and the she-wolf (avarice). He can make no progress until Vergil (human reason) appears and offers to be his guide through Inferno and Purgatory. After that a blessed woman will guide him through Heaven. Dante, afraid at first, is assured that the divine will has chosen him, and he sets out.

The vision of Hell embraces a large number of sections, but when examined closely they are seen to conform, as do the parts of Purgatory and Paradise, to a number system. There are three main sections, in which the sins of incontinence, violence, and fraud are punished. Incontinence is subdivided into four divisions, violence into three—against neighbor, against self, and against God. Fraud is broken into two main categories, the simple and the treacherous. The simple contains ten subdivisions, the treacherous four. Various combinations of these can be made to produce the numbers 3, 7, 9, and 10.

There are nine circles in Hell itself, but before Dante is transported over the river he sees the souls of those who took no active part in good or evil. They are now stung into perpetual activity but are not actually in Hell. Most souls are ferried over the river directly to Hell by the mythological Charon, but Dante, after fainting, finds himself transported to Limbo, the first circle of Inferno, where dwell the unbaptized and the noble pagans. Their only punishment is being deprived of the sight of God.

The sins of incontinence—lust, gluttony, avarice, and anger—are punished with winds, foul liquids and filth, rolling of weights, and self-injury respectively. Then Vergil and Dante move to the city of Dis, where the violent are punished. Demons who will not let them in are scattered by an angel, and the first thing they see are burning sepulchers in which heretics are confined. The seventh circle is guarded by the Minotaur, symbol of violence from classical mythology. In a river of blood, guarded by Centaurs, stand those who have committed violence against others, including famous tyrants, while the suicides have taken root in the form of trees and are gnawed by Harpies. The blasphemers and those who have done violence against nature and art are being slowly tortured by fire, among them Dante's master, Brunetto Latini. Usurers are also punished here.

The monster Geryon takes Dante and his guide to the eighth circle. Here the worst crimes are punished—fraud and malice. Panders and seducers are lashed by demons, flatterers live in filth, and those guilty of simony, including high ecclesiastics, are held upside down while their feet are burned. False prophets are made to walk looking backward, while those who have perverted public office for gold are set in boiling pitch and rent by demons. Hypocrites in leaden cloaks are also in this circle, as are the thieves. Evil counselors, including Ulysses, are even farther down. Sowers of discord, both in politics and religion, and falsifiers, such as forgers, are the last group in this circle, which is called Malebolge.

The four divisions of treacherous fraud are punished in the last and most terrifying place, the very bottom of Hell and the center of the earth. There is no light and movement here, all is frozen horror. In it are punished Cain and those who have done violence to their kindred, betrayed their country, or infringed the laws of hospitality. Last of all are those who betrayed their master and benefactor—Satan, frozen in all the sins that seep down to him, Judas Iscariot, and Brutus and Cassius, the murderers of Caesar.

Satan is in the very center of the earth. Vergil and Dante climb his sides and turn so that they may make their way out again to the antipodes and the hill of Purgatory.

The above account deals only with the general structure of Hell and the punishment of sins. But the actual journey is a personal experience. Dante describes himself in these horrible surroundings. He is terrified of Charon, of the demons who block the road to Dis, of the dreadful crowd at the bottom of Malebolge. The passage is a nightmare for him, and only the presence of Vergil saves him from complete collapse.

Many of the persons who are punished in Hell are figures from mythology, the Bible, classical literature, and earlier medieval history. But much more important are the numerous persons from contemporary Italian history, some of them not even dead by 1300, the time Dante's journey was supposed to have occurred. With very many of these Dante was personally involved. The famous story of Francesca da Rimini is the story in which we can observe most clearly the human pity which Dante feels even for those whom he knows to be sinful, and on account of which he is rebuked by Vergil for implicitly questioning the divine justice. Francesca's love affair with Paolo da Verucchio, her husband's brother, ended tragically when both were murdered by the outraged husband about 1285. It is the tragic perversion of true love as much as the fate of the lovers themselves which moves Dante. There are several other instances of Dante's regret for perverted love, of which perhaps the best known is his grief for the fate of his old teacher, Brunetto Latini, who is confined in the seventh circle for his sin against nature, presumably homosexuality. There are other passages, however, where Dante takes a fierce delight in the punishments, particularly those inflicted on political opponents—some of them still alive when he wrote!

It is these conversations which are the life of the *Inferno*, as they are of the other sections, for they remove the account from the realm of abstract description to that of personal experience. The same may be said of the descriptions of the tortures and of the landscape of Hell. These are not things appreciated by the mind but by the emotions, and their impact on any sensitive reader is tremendous. Dante has used elements from the Christian and the pagan descriptions of the underworld—Dis, Phlegython, Charon, and Geryon are classical. The devils, the frozen center, the stream of blood are Christian. All contribute to the idea of increasing distance for life, from light, and from God.

The mount of Purgatory rises in the southern hemisphere, immediately opposite Jerusalem. Its guardian is Cato of Utica, a strict moralist. When Vergil and Dante arrive he is suspicious, but on hearing of the heavenly command he allows them to proceed. They see a group of happy souls arrive, some of whom Dante knows. They are directed by a group of those who, though repentant, died outside the church. Among them is Manfred, king of Naples, excommunicated by Clement IV. Then follow the souls of those violently killed who repented at the last moment. As they seek a place of rest under the guidance of the poet Sordello, they meet kings repenting lives spent in ease instead of duty. During the night no souls can ascend the mount, and the three stars of the theological virtues (faith, hope, and charity) shine, while during the day Dante sees the four stars of the moral virtues (justice, bravery, temperance, prudence), which are the guides of the pilgrims' purification.

The next day Vergil and Dante are admitted through a gate to Purgatory proper and ascend a path which winds around the mountain. On its side are carved biblical scenes. The first penitents they meet are the proud, bending under weights in their search for humility. Dante is reminded of the transitory nature of earthly goods. As he leaves this circle an angel's wing wipes out one of the seven P's (for *peccata*, "sins") put on Dante's forehead by the angel at the gate.

In the next circle penitents expiate the sin of envy by being unable to look upon the things they enjoyed in life. On the third terrace the wrathful are punished. While engulfed in the black smoke which covers this area, Dante is given an explanation of earthly wickedness, which springs from human faults and the lack of true government. The fourth circle is that in which sloth is punished, and while they are waiting to enter it, Vergil explains to Dante the system of Purgatory, how the lower three circles are for the punishment of those who have misdirected their love so as to rejoice in the sufferings of their neighbors. The slothful have lost their desire for God's love, and those in the three upper circles have directed their love to earthly gratification. Vergil also explains the difference between good and evil love and the necessity of moral merit. During a sleep the slothful, now eager for activity, disturb Dante.

Avarice is the first of the false-love sins and is punished by holding souls close to what they once had desired. Among the avaricious is Hugh Capet, founder of the royal house of France, whose avarice cast a shadow over the whole of Europe. Statius, the Latin poet, is also being punished in this circle, but for prodigality. Opposite sins, thus, are punished together. At this juncture the poet tells how Vergil's own poetry had converted him to Christianity.

Those who were gluttonous on earth are punished—though they accept punishment gladly. On the way to the next circle Statius carefully expounds the doctrine that the human being obtains its soul from God, and when the body dies the soul retains the insubstantial powers of memory, intelligence, and will. In the last circle the sin of lust is being purged by flames, and it is here that Dante meets the famous poet Guido Guinizelli. Only the mention of Beatrice induces Dante to cross the flames. After another night they ascend the stairs to the top of Purgatory. All the P's are gone from Dante's forehead; he is free from the effects of the Fall. No longer does he need the guidance of Vergil, who now leaves him. He enters the Earthly Paradise and is instructed in its nature by Matilda, its guardian, the personification of the active life. Here he sees various phenomena symbolic of the spiritual life and Holy Scripture. A car arrives and in it a presence whom Dante, terrified, recognizes as Beatrice. He turns for support to Vergil, but he is gone. Beatrice reproaches him for his wasted life and lost promise. She tells him that the loss of her bodily presence should have made him seek the spiritual even more. He swoons and awakens in the stream of Lethe. He is encouraged by four star nymphs to be strong in order that he may look into Beatrice's eyes. Following the car in which Beatrice rides, although almost blinded by her glory, he goes to the tree of knowledge and is given a vision of the discord between church and state which keeps the world in misery. Beatrice tells Dante in symbols of God's judgments, but he begs for more clarity. The waters of Lethe have washed away things tainted with sin, and soon, after drinking the waters of Eunoe or true knowledge, he is ready for Beatrice's explanations of Paradise.

The *Purgatorio* is much more abstract than the *Inferno*. Although there are punishments, they are simple, and no effort is made to dwell on them, since they are accepted gladly by the penitent souls. Meetings with important contemporaries occur, but since these are souls of men saved, they are usually Dante's friends or at least people for whom he had sympathy. There is much stress on abstract explanation of moral law and science and of theology. Rather than the vivid sensory pictures of Hell, we are given the workings of the mind. The emphasis here is on the ethical. Cato is the guardian, Vergil the explainer. The purpose of Purgatory is to rid the penitent of those sins which resulted from the Fall, and it is therefore divided into three main sections, perverted, defective, and excessive love. The first and last of these, as already pointed out, are divided into three parts, each one of the deadly sins. Between them is defective love or sloth. To these seven are added two sections of pre-Purgatory, the excommunicated and the late-repentant, making nine. Above all comes the Earthly Paradise, and thus the 3, 7, 9, 10 grouping is effected.

Dante's journey through the various regions of Paradise under the guidance of Beatrice should be understood in the light of the Ptolemaic system. To Dante the earth was the center of the universe, and the planets were ranged in the order familiar to modern astronomy, except that the sun was where we would place the earth. These planets moved each in its own cycle around the earth and also in an epicycle around a point on that cycle. Thus progress would be from the earth to the moon, then to Mercury, Venus, the sun, Mars, Jupiter, and Saturn. Above these is the region of the fixed stars, then the *primum mobile*, and finally the empyrean or ultimate Heaven. Again Dante's laws of numbers are followed. There are three main planetary heavens, infrasolar, solar, and suprasolar, subdivided into the seven planetary heavens already mentioned. To these are added the stellar Heaven and *primum mobile*, to make nine, and the empyrean completes the ten.

After an invocation Dante describes his upward movement, accompanied by Beatrice. He is now freed of the encumbrances of the flesh but not entirely of its mental obstacles. When they reach the moon Beatrice explains how God's glory is reflected in all heavenly bodies, although in some more than others. Dante now sees souls as they really are. He is told that each, in whatever sphere, partakes of the joy of Heaven but at different intensity. In the moon sphere are those who have somehow not fulfilled their vows. Yet Beatrice hastens to explain that their *permanent* abode is in Heaven. They are meeting Dante in places suitable to their condition. He is further enlightened about the difference between the act of vowing and the substance of vows.

In the sphere of Mercury he meets the great lawgiver Justinian (this is the place for those who were proud and are now self-effacing). He expounds views (which are Dante's) on the wickedness of attacking the empire as an institution. There follows a careful explanation of the act of Redemption. Angels and Adam and Eve were made directly by God, and after redemption all men are restored to the privileges of unfallen man. The Redemption has to be achieved by God—man cannot do it himself, however humble he is—and therefore the incarnate part of God suffered the just penalty of men's sins on the Cross while his spiritual nature was outraged. In this act justice and mercy were combined.

On the planet Venus a meeting with Dante's noble friend Carlo Martello gives an opportunity to show that human character is part of God's order and is determined by celestial influences, not heredity. Italian politics again appear, but then

Folco says that in Heaven sin is remembered only as the occasion for God's grace.

The arrival in the sphere of the sun is the occasion for a discourse on the divine wisdom which ordains that it shine as it does. Twelve spirits encircle the travelers, to heavenly music, and one of them, Thomas Aquinas, tells Dante of the ever increasing power of love. He also praises the great worth of St. Francis, but not most of his successors. Bonaventura, the Franciscan, does the same for St. Dominic. Thomas also points out the various kinds of earthly wisdom and warns against drawing unjustified conclusions. Solomon tells Dante of the effect of the resurrection of the body—the making of perfect man, body and soul yet freed of the grossness of earth.

In the red sphere of Mars are the warrior spirits praising Christ crucified, among them Dante's great-great-grandfather, killed on a crusade, who describes the glories of the Florence of his day. He also interprets the hints which Dante has received in Hell and Purgatory about his own fate and tells him in detail what will happen.

As they rise toward Jupiter, Beatrice's beauty becomes greater. Here is the sphere of justice. The just kings, forming an eagle (of Rome), try to explain to Dante the mystery of the exclusion of the just pagans from Heaven. No one can hope to fathom God's justice, but at the Judgment Day the pagans will receive their reward. Ripheus, a Trojan, and the emperor Trajan, who in different ways believed in Christ, are already in Heaven.

At the sphere of Saturn, where Jacob's Ladder leads to the *primum mobile* of the angels, Dante is met by the bright spirit of Peter Damian, the Italian mystic, who again warns of the dangers of attempts to penetrate into the mind of God. Here also he meets St. Benedict and other spirits of the contemplative life but notes that none mounts Jacob's Ladder because of the degeneracy of the monastic orders. He is warned of the brilliance of the new spheres he is approaching.

Still in the sphere of Saturn, the poet is granted an overwhelming vision of Christ and of those who on earth worked for him. Here too he sees the Mystic Rose, the Queen of Heaven. At the request of Beatrice, he is given to drink from the divine table, sees the saints, and is questioned about his faith by Peter. His replies reveal his dependence on Thomas

Aquinas. James questions him on hope, which Dante refers to as the hope of salvation based on Scripture. John's glory is so great that Dante cannot see. He is reassured and answers the questions put to him on love. His sight is restored, and he sees the spirit of Adam, who tells him of Paradise. Peter denounces Pope Boniface VIII, Dante's particular enemy, and others on earth. As he rises with Beatrice to the *primum mobile*, she tells him that here is where space and time begin. She also laments the state of earth.

In the *primum mobile* Dante becomes aware of the nine concentric circles of brightness, representing orders of intelligence or angels, revolving about the bright light of love, and Beatrice explains to him how the inmost circle is the swiftest and brightest and knows most of love, whereas, since all heavens have an amount of excellence proportionate to their size, the outmost is the greatest. Angels who are pure form or act were created in eternity and at the same time as time and the heavens. The angels always have the joy of direct contemplation of God's love, which created them.

The angelic rings fade, and Dante and Beatrice move into the empyrean. Here Beatrice achieves her full dazzling beauty. Here there is no time and space, and the glory of God, reflected from the *primum mobile*, shines upon the elect, who thus may gaze on God. There is a space among the saints for that Emperor Henry for whom the *De Monarchia* was written, but a grim doom is forecast for Clement.

Dante now enjoys the final vision of heavenly light, the glory which is perfect peace and complete love, free from fear of loss. Beatrice leaves Dante to take her place, and he prays that she will continue to guide him, realizing now that perfect love means perfect love of her in God. St. Bernard of Clairvaux, the figure of contemplation, now stands at his side. He shows the poet Mary Queen of Heaven and the other saints, divided into those who looked forward to Christ and those who looked back to him. Bernard prays to Mary to grant Dante power to gaze on the final mystery and to keep himself true to the vision ever after. Mary looks to God, and the poet has an ineffable vision of all the universe joined in a bond of love. This vision he cannot describe but feels the wonder of it still.

Thus end the hundred cantos of the *Commedia*, three times the thirty-three years of Christ's life on earth plus one—the bottom pit of Hell which stands outside. It should not be thought from the above summary of the *Paradiso* that it is a series of theological expositions. Although the third part is much more concerned with philosophy and theology than the other two, the language is poetic throughout, and the arguments are advanced more by poetic figures than by the methods of logic. Moreover, the exact meaning of many passages is disputed. Boccaccio was already writing commentaries to clarify Dante's work in 1373.

The poem is, of course, a vision, although it does not follow the conventions of that genre by having the poet fall asleep. It is also an allegory, but not in the sense that the only actors are abstract personifications. Rather the poem must be allegorized by the reader in the way that Dante himself recommended in his famous letter to Can Grande. We can consider the places and persons Dante meets literally, or in their historical context, or as allegorical figures. Many of them, in fact most, are by their very nature types of sin or virtue, but the personal element which binds the Italians of his own day to the poet makes them more vivid than any allegorical figure could be. The figures outside Dante's personal experience are usually chosen as symbols of a particular characteristic, as St. Bernard of the contemplative life. Probably the most important of these is Vergil.

For Dante, as for most men of the Middle Ages, Vergil occupied a special place. His poem called the "Messianic eclogue" was universally, though wrongly, held to be a prophecy of the coming of Christ. Furthermore, he had written of the underworld with power and imagination in the sixth book of the *Aeneid*. He was credited with being a magician, so that a more perfect guide could hardly have been found. Yet in the allegorical sense he is something much more: human reason, that reason which is itself capable of distinguishing right from wrong and of establishing moral virtue. Hence Vergil can be Dante's guide until the Garden of Eden is reached but not after; for here man is back to primal innocence, and human reason can do nothing. Beatrice, who, as we have seen, had long been regarded by Dante as Heavenly, takes over his guidance, personifying revelation, the higher knowledge, while at the last Bernard, the contemplator, is to be interpreted as intuition.

The journey which Dante takes shows us all the possible

destinations of the soul. Yet no one soul, now that the patriarchs have been rescued from Hell, could, in fact, ever make that journey. Dante has been specially privileged. Allegorically, however, every soul must take the journey if it wishes to be saved. Hell represents man in a state of sin, victim of fleshly desires. Hence the highly pictorial descriptions. He moves out of sin, guided by reason, to the other side of the world, and, by a long and painful process of discipline and repentance, he regains his state of innocence. He is now pure in heart and can indulge in the contemplative life, that is, the contemplation of virtue, guided by revelation, until he achieves his heart's desire. Thus Dante, in his own pilgrimage, represents all that part of humanity which wishes to break away from sin and arrive at the truth.

Science, philosophy, and theology play a great part in Dante's work, and it is a tribute to his genius that he was almost always able to present his ideas in poetical form. His science and moral philosophy is basically that of Aristotle, seen through the eyes of medieval scholastics. Much of the plan of Hell and Purgatory is derived from Aristotelian categories. His theology, though eclectic, is largely in agreement with that of Thomas Aquinas. The universe is a place of law and order—much of it, though by no means all, accessible to human reason. Yet Dante is the last person who could be accused of mere conformism. His ideas, finally, are based on his own learning, and his attitude to the church and its administration is unorthodox in the extreme. His personal opinion of their qualities is what determines the destination of the souls of those men whom he knew, and there are many high ecclesiastics in Hell.

For all its theological and allegorical features, the *Commedia* is an intensely personal poem. It is the experience of a poet, a seer. Dante suffers and rejoices and loves and hates. There is always personal contact with other people at every stage. The world to which he will return is always in his thoughts, and one's final and strongest impression is that Dante's deepest urge is to bring peace back to this earth by restoring the harmony of church and state.

It is in the *Inferno* that Dante's poetic qualities are easiest to see, for here he had unlimited freedom to draw upon his imagination and create characters who, while terrifying, are not without comic elements. But it is in the *Paradiso* that his vision is most sublime. The poem, it should be remembered, is a *Commedia* in the medieval sense (see discussion p. 245). It begins in the wood of error and ends before the majesty of God. It is thus the most sublime and the most optimistic of poems.

MINOR LITERARY WORKS AND PROSE

Except for certain types of plays, which will be treated in the chapter on drama, there is little Italian literature, apart from that already discussed, which is not in prose. Italy imported the Arthurian romances from France in the *Tavola ritonda* ("Round Table"), a prose version of the late thirteenth century of the French prose Arthurian material and Prose-Tristan, and the *chansons de geste* in the *Reali di Francia* ("Kings of France"), but these are not much better than translations. The rhymed romance *Giulio Cesare* ("Julius Caesar") by Jacques de Forest is based ultimately on Lucan's account of the civil war but has the usual chivalric form. There are collections of courtly stories in Italian, as in other languages, but they show the lifelessness of late imitative literature—the *Novelino* and *Stories of Ancient Knights* (both late thirteenth century) are typical.

Religious and didactic prose makes up a great deal of the bulk. Brunetto Latini put together a work called *Flowers of the Philosophers and of Many Learned Men* (thirteenth century), an anthology of excerpts, mainly classical. Bono Giamboni's *Garden of Consolation* (c. 1270–80) is a similar work, except that it is concentrated on pieces about the virtues and vices. Most famous of such works was Brunetto Latini's *Trésor* (Treasure), a huge encyclopedia in French, of which an adaptation, the *Tesoretto*, was later put into Italian. More original, though dependent on Boethius' *Consolation of Philosophy*, is Bono Giamboni's *Introduction to Virtue* (1270–80), which shows a young man lamenting changes in fortune and considering the consolation which philosophy and religion can bring.

Religious prose, though largely following old forms, takes on new life in the fourteenth century. The most famous of all such Italian works was the *Little Flowers of St. Francis*, an artless account of the deeds of the saint which is lively and fresh to this day. Different in kind is Iacopo Passavanti's

Mirror of True Penitence (c. 1300–57), which is a carefully selected group of moral sermons meant to bring home the terrors of Hell.

The century of mystics is represented in Italy by Catherine of Siena (1347–80). In spite of her illiteracy, she dictated letters to the most powerful statesmen and clerics of her day, in attempts to produce by exhortation an end to the conflicts which tore the world. Like Hildegard von Bingen, Mechtild von Magdeburg, and Margery Kemp, she was an ecstatic visionary, describing in lyrical prose her mystical attachment to the vision of Christ. Like most such persons, she uses a highly figurative and allegorical language abounding in the metaphors of spiritual love.

It is hardly necessary to add that there were chronicles of some importance written at this time. Ricordano Malespini's *History of Florence* (down to 1282) is a strange mixture of fact (when he spoke from experience) and the wildest imaginings (when he used books). Albertino Mussato (1261–1329) of Padua, a man of great literary eminence in his day, wrote Latin works on the emperor Henry VII and on the events in Italy after Henry's death. Almost as historical is *Eccerinis*, his Latin play on the tyrant Ezzelino, which brings home the horrors of the tyrant's reign.

One of the most important of the chronicles, because it deals with the Florence of Dante's day, is that of Dino Compagni (1260–1324), who covered, from personal experience, the affairs of the city from 1270 to 1313. He was himself a notable participant in these events and speaks of them with inside knowledge. There is little art to his work but it has for that reason the more immediacy. In his chronicle of Florence Giovanni Villani (d. 1348) covers events to 1348, and his son and grandson continued his work. He is a careful but uninspired author.

Middle English Literature

GENERAL

ENGLISH HAS A HISTORY very different from that of the other vernaculars of western Europe. While they evolved steadily from the period of the Carolingian empire and gradually developed a literature of their own, English, after a period of literary production which occurred much earlier than that of any other vernacular, found itself forced into a subservient position for more than two hundred years. In France and Germany, as we have seen, the twelfth and thirteenth centuries were the greatest centuries of literary production and were followed by a long period of decline, with only an occasional major work. In England these centuries were a period of almost total literary barrenness. Norman French was the language of the court and consequently of vernacular literature. Any courtly literature written in England during this time was in French. Thus England took no part in the period of courtly literature, except through the works of such writers as Marie de France and Thomas of Britain. The courtly works written in English were, with some notable exceptions, late and inferior. No national epic developed in England as it did in France, Spain, and Germany. Secular lyric poetry shows very little influence of the forms and traditions which originated in Provence.

Yet this late start was not without its advantages. The language of the Anglo-Saxons was enriched from the Norman conquest to the fourteenth century—when it emerges as a vehicle for serious literary work—by a vast number of French and Latin words, so that it became a remarkably subtle and flexible literary instrument. Such groups as loose, release, relax, and kingly, royal, regal—the first in each group being from Old English, the second from French, and the third directly from Latin—show how the same basic idea can appear with subtle variations according to the root from which it came.

In literature, too, English had a vast European reservoir on which to draw. The French romances and allegories were the common property of Europe by the end of the thirteenth century. Dante and later Boccaccio were available to Chaucer and his successors, so that the great period of Middle English literature was written when what is usually called Renaissance literature was beginning in England. It has already been noted that in the later Middle Ages patronage of literature passed from the princes to the bourgeoisie, and this is as true in England as on the Continent. Thus, this literature reflects the tastes and attitudes of the middle class rather than those of the aristocracy.

It is less easy to categorize medieval English literature than the literatures of the other vernaculars. We shall retain the divisions of romance (by now a general term for prose and verse narrative) and lyric poetry but make a special section for allegorical and didactic poetry and, of course, for Chaucer.

NARRATIVE

Some of the works important for Authurian literature which appeared in England—Geoffrey of Monmouth's *History of the Kings of Britain* and Wace's *Brut*—have already been mentioned. The latter work was put into an English form by Layamon, an English priest (fl. 1189–1207). He tells the story of the kings of England but, like his predecessors, lays most stress on King Arthur and the Round Table, the building of which he describes in detail. His poem is over 30,000 lines long, more than twice the length of Wace's poem. It is written in alliterating verse but with some conventional rhyme.

Almost all the great characters of Continental Arthurian romance appear in English form in the late thirteenth century and fourteenth century. It will be sufficient to note one or two of them which are typical of all. *Sir Perceval of Galles* (c. 1340) is a reworking of the story which Chrétien de Troyes made into a great romance (see pp. 88ff.), but it clearly draws on other sources besides the French writer. Amazingly, the work says nothing of the Grail. Perceval sets out in much the same fashion as in Chrétien's work, except that he is even cruder. After killing the Red Knight and burning him to get his armor off, he has to kill the knight's mother too (she is a witch). The wild adventures go on like this. There is no Gawain parallel story and no hint of any duty higher than the Arthurian. Similarly in *Sir Tristrem* (c. 1300) the emphasis is on the rivalry between Tristan's father, Rouland, and Duke Morgan. So much time is devoted to this that the Tristan and Isolde love episode is relegated to the background.

This treatment is characteristic. The Arthurian romances become pure adventure stories, most of them of little or no literary merit, in which the Arthurian court is no longer the mecca of all knights and the touchstone of knightly virtues. Such romances are of interest principally because they open new source material for the Arthurian scholar. We may mention such works as *Arthour and Merlin* (1250–1300), *Yvain and Gawain* (c. 1350), *Alliterative Morte d'Arthur* (c. 1360), *Libeans Desconus* (c. 1340), and *Prose Merlin* (c. 1450).

Sir Gawain and the Green Knight

There are, however, two Arthurian works which bear comparison with any written on the Continent—the anonymous *Gawain and the Green Knight* and Malory's *Morte d'Arthur*. The former was written in the last half of the fourteenth century by a gifted poet who was almost certainly the author of another work, *The Pearl*, found in the same manuscript (see pp. 195ff.). He uses an archaic alliterative verse form which enjoyed a revival in the fourteenth century but combined it into a strophe with rhyme. The first half of each strophe has a varying number of four-beat alliterating lines like those used in Anglo-Saxon literature. The second half has five lines rhyming *ababa*, the first with only one stress, the remainder with three each. The dialect is West Midland, which, to a modern reader at least, sounds harsher and more primitive than the more polished East Midland of Chaucer.

The story of *Gawain and the Green Knight* is simple and consists primarily of two motifs—the beheading test and the temptation to adultery. The time at Arthur's court is New Year—not the usual Pentecost, the beginning of the adventure season. A fantastically dressed Green Knight bursts in and offers to let anyone strike a blow at him, provided that he may return the blow one year later. Gawain is the only man brave enough to accept the challenge for the honor of the court—although Arthur offers to do so. The ax cuts off the knight's head, but he picks it up and walks away. Almost a year later Gawain sets out through winter weather to meet the knight.

On the way he is entertained at a castle. The lord, Bercilak, proposes an exchange. He will go hunting and at the end of each of three days will exchange with Gawain whatever he has gained for Gawain's winnings during the day spent with

Bercilak's wife. At the end of the first day Gawain receives a deer—a noble quarry, wise and sagacious—and gives the lord the one kiss he has received from the lady. At the end of the second day he receives a wild boar, symbol of his courage in resisting the lady's wishes, and gives two kisses. On the third day, however, the quarry is a fox, symbol of cunning and duplicity. For although on the third day Gawain has, indeed, continued to resist the blandishments of his beautiful hostess, he has accepted from her a green scarf which will protect him from all wounds. This gift he does not declare.

When the time comes for him to face the Green Knight, two blows are deliberate misses, and the third merely nicks him to show the tiny mark on his honor. The Green Knight is, of course, Bercilak, and the whole stay in the castle was designed as a test of honor by the magician Morgan le Fay. Gawain returns to Arthur's court and confesses his weakness. In his honor the knights all agree to wear green sashes around their waists.

The poem is an interesting moral dilemma of a type different from that posed in Continental Arthurian romance. Although Gawain is here, as elsewhere, the noblest of knights, and although the apparatus of leaving Arthur's court for an adventure in a strange world is here also, the problem is nevertheless a personal one. Gawain is able to maintain his honor before the court, and he maintains it against the lady's wiles by cunning and humor on the first day and by moral strength on the second. But he is not quite strong enough to withstand the temptation to be *sure* he will not be killed by the Green Knight. Here, and not in his relations with her, he shows his weakness. Nor will he admit it to Bercilak, even though he does not know at the time that he and the Green Knight are the same person.

Another moral could be drawn—that the creatures of nature, of the outer world, are in the end superior to the knights of Arthur's court. For the strange-looking, apparently half-human knight is merciful to Gawain in a situation where an Arthurian might not have been so. He pardons his weakness and admires his courage. Yet there is no question but that the author wants us to admire Gawain. The pentangle (five-pointed star) on his shield shows his devotion to the "five fives"—fingers, virtues, wits, wounds of Christ, joys of Mary. He is a truly Christian knight.

All critics have commented on the brilliant description—of winter, of the hunt—and characterization in this poem. It is a mature and well-constructed work which is undoubtedly the finest single piece of Arthurian romance in English.

Malory

Sir Thomas Malory's work is of a very different kind. Caxton printed it as a continuous narrative, starting with the parentage and birth of Arthur and ending with his death, and it is in this form that all modern versions of the stories of King Arthur and the Round Table are arranged. Malory, however, appears to have written the work in a series of different adventures, drawing them from a number of sources, mostly French prose but including the alliterative *Morte d'Arthur*. He found these stories intertwined in highly complex fashion but himself preferred to tell the stories of the knights individually. He finished his work in prison about 1469, and Caxton printed his version in 1485.

Malory is concerned with storytelling. In his work Arthur is not the weak king we often find in French and German romances, but vigorous and the true head of his kingdom. Although courtly love is important, it is a convention rather than the driving force it was in the twelfth-century writers. Adventure is more important, as can be seen in the stories of Lancelot and Tristan, whose knightly exploits are much expanded. The Grail quest follows the vulgate version (see above, pp. 90f.). It is Galahad alone who sees the Grail and, also as in the vulgate version, is the final destruction of Arthur's kingdom.

Malory is not so concerned with moral problems as the author of *Gawain and the Green Knight*. Yet it is impossible to escape the conclusion that he regarded adulterous love as the cause of the collapse of a great civilization which was founded on knightly companionship. Arthur himself is the child of an adulterous union, Modred is his son by another. The rift caused by the love of Lancelot and Guinevere is the ultimate cause of destruction, a fact which they acknowledge by withdrawing from the world.

Malory's fluent prose and Caxton's organization have made the (misnamed) *Morte d'Arthur* by far the most available and the most readable of Arthurian romances. Even if none of its parts approaches the great French and German masterpieces, the whole is a fine keystone to the great arch of Arthurian romance.

Minor Romances

The romances of antiquity are poorly represented in England. *King Alisaunder* (c. 1300), in octosyllabic couplets, represents the French romances. The English Troy stories were not taken from Benoît de Ste-Maure's French romance but from Guido delle Colonne's moralizing Latin version. The *Seege of Troye* (early fourteenth century) and John Lydgate's *Troy Book* (1412–20) are the English representatives. Much more important was Chaucer's treatment of one incident which he received indirectly from Benoît, the story of Troilus and Cressida.

The material from the French *chansons de geste* fares little better. Perhaps because of national rivalry, there is only one extant reworking of a story from the *matière de France: Sir Ferumbras* (before 1380). This is the French *Fierabras*, the story of the Saracen giant defeated by Oliver and converted to Christianity who becomes a staunch supporter of Charlemagne. There are also Middle English versions of other romances already mentioned, *Floris and Blancheflur* (c. 1250) and *Amis and Amiloun*.

We noted that several English stories found their way into French literature during the twelfth and thirteenth centuries. These stories usually have a setting in or near the British Isles and are marked by stress on adventure and romantic rather than courtly love. *Havelock* (mid-thirteenth century) is based upon an Anglo-Norman version of about a century earlier, but the material is English. Havelock, while still a child in Denmark, is deposed by the wicked Earl Godard. As usual he is spared by the man deputed to kill him and raised as a fisherman. A strange light about the boy's head shows him to be of royal birth. He is taken to England and becomes a cook's helper. An English heiress, Goldborough, is forced by another wicked regent to marry him. She also sees the light around his head. Ultimately Havelock's prowess is such that he conquers England and Denmark.

Some of the motifs here are familiar—the exiled prince, the poor upbringing, the powerful cook's helper. But *Havelock* has vigor and honesty. It is less stylized and therefore more convincing than the courtly romances. On the other hand, it is less sophisticated. Much the same may be said of *King Horn*, written about the same time and also based on an earlier Anglo-Norman work. Again we have the exiled prince on a foreign shore. This time his love for the local princess Rimenhild leads to further banishment. After numerous adventures, he returns to rescue her from another suitor. Then back to save his own land of Suddene from the Saracens and again a rescue of Rimenhild, whom he finally marries. The "double jeopardy" so evident in many romances is here carried to almost absurd lengths.

Guy of Warwick and *Bevis of Hampton* (both c. 1300) describe the struggle of warriors against the infidel. Two noteworthy works deal with British historical figures. *Richard Coeur de Lion* (c. 1300) is a loud patriotic romance of wild adventure. John Barbour's *Bruce* is a more worthy effort. It tells the praises of the heroic Scottish king in his struggle against the English invaders.

Several narrative poems are classified, for not very obvious reasons, under the rubric "Breton lay." We have already noted that several of Marie de France's short poems are called Breton lays because they seem to be based on Celtic fairy stories. The term was used in the Middle Ages both for stories taken from those of Marie de France and for others where the Celtic connection is far from obvious.

Sir Orpheo (c. 1320) takes its title from the Greek legend of Orpheus and Eurydice, and there are some similarities in the plot. On a beautiful spring morning Sir Orpheo's wife Heroudis is kidnaped by the king of the fairies. Orpheo, with only his harp, sets out to find her and does—dancing in a company of knights and ladies. Orpheo's music persuades the king of the fairies to grant Heroudis to Orpheo—reluctantly, for Orpheo looks like a poor minstrel. They return to their native land, and the steward, who has faithfully looked after the kingdom, is horrified when told a false tale of his master's death but overjoyed when he reveals himself.

The author appears to have changed all standard motifs—instead of Hades, fairyland, instead of Eurydice's return to Hades, a joyful return home, instead of a scheming steward, a faithful one. It is hard to see why this story should be Celtic, for the Orpheus legend is clearly recognizable. It has simply been made to conform with medieval ideas. Certainly the result is a pleasant poem.

There are other lays, of which the best is *Sir Launfal* (c. 1350), a free adaptation of Marie de France's poem of the same title. It is concerned with the common fairy story of the lover who has a fairy mistress who will desert him if he reveals his love. In rejecting the advances of Queen Guinevere, Launfal does reveal it; he loses his mistress and regains her only when threatened with death by Arthur for an alleged attempt on the queen's honor.

LYRIC POETRY

Although the origins of Continental lyric poetry in the vernacular are obscure and much disputed, there is little difficulty in recording and classifying those lyric works which are extant. The poets are for the most part known, at least by name, and their works can be dated with reasonable accuracy and shown to be part of a definite tradition. The secular poetry is distinct from the religious, even when, as in Italy, there is use of religious thought and imagery. Moreover, certain themes dominate this secular poetry, and of these by far the most important is that of *fin amors*, the love of the troubadours and their successors.

No such clear-cut treatment of Middle English lyric poetry is possible. Its origins are disputed, and critics agree very little either on this or any other aspect of the lyrics. Most lyric poetry in Middle English is anonymous. It is hard to distinguish between the secular and the religious poetry, since many works seem to partake of the peculiar characteristics of both. The question of origins is complicated by lack of evidence about the native lyric in the twelfth and thirteenth centuries, that is, the period of dominance of French. There had been lyric poetry during the Anglo-Saxon period (see pp. 34f.), although hardly in the sense of what we would call lyric in later Continental literature. The works of the great French *trouvères* were certainly known to many people in England, as those of Guillaume de Machaut were known, for instance, to Chaucer. Yet it cannot be said that the formal French love lyric was imitated to any extent in Middle English. The type had lost its vitality by the time Middle English became a literary language. There is evidence of influence, but nothing more.

Lyric poetry in England, as elsewhere, meant poetry with

music. Most critics are still of the opinion that Middle English lyric originated with the importation of the *carole*, a round-dance tune, from France. We do, indeed, have evidence that the *carole* existed in France, and it is true that the earliest English lyrics are called carols. Yet it is a little hard to see why this particular import should have taken root when others, of far greater reputation, were ignored or were of slight influence. The alternative suggestion, based on evidence in some manuscripts, has more plausibility. This theory contends that the earliest *caroles* were in fact ecclesiastical, that they were inserted in the Gradual of the Mass, and that they followed church usage in the three-part pattern: burden (refrain), stanza, burden. This would make the origins of the lyric rather native than foreign, rather religious than secular, and these findings would accord well with its subsequent development. Whatever conclusions are reached about the problems of origins, there can be no doubt that English lyric poetry shows far more influence of popular poetry than do the lyrics of the Continent. The language and verse forms never attain—or even seek—the virtuosity of Provençal. It is sometimes difficult to determine whether a poem is directed to an earthly or heavenly person (although this need not mean that the language is obscure).

The Continental "spring landscape" opening was much used in Middle English lyric and gives its name to a type called the *reverdie*, the new green of nature. Even so, the rigid formality of the Continental ideal landscape is rarely present. The details mentioned are those which could in fact be found in England in the spring and not those of a prescribed Mediterranean scene. The well-known lyric from the late thirteenth century "Sumer is icumen in" breaks all the formal rules. A cuckoo is mentioned (not a nightingale or lark), the meadows blow (they never do in French poetry), and seeds grow (never mentioned on the Continent)! Most English lyrics follow this "native pattern." Many, of course, use the clichés of courtly love. They breathe sighs, tell of love's agonies, chide their merciless lady. But there is never the attempt at subtle analysis of love which is the staple of *Minnesang* and, as we have seen, of the Italian lyric. The lover may sigh in the famous lyric *Alysoun*, but he is in no danger of becoming metaphysical.

In England as on the Continent, the fourteenth century

saw a great deal of lyric poetry written on the events of everyday life. As in the love lyric we have at least the illusion of personal experience of love, gambling, drinking, and disappointment rather than the formal moralizing of much contemporary French and German poetry.

The surviving religious lyrics far outnumber the secular, and even allowing for the accidents of transmission and the fact that religious poetry was more likely to be copied, it seems likely that the major effort in lyric poetry was made by clerics. A study of the religious lyrics, particularly the devotional ones, shows the great influence of the situations and imagery developed over the centuries in Latin hymns. These latter poems had evolved a system of allegorical meanings for words and expressions which enabled every hymn to be read on several levels. For example, the Cross was scarlet because it was at once bloody and imperial, *patibulum* ("wood"; "Cross") is at once the place of death and of life, of cruelty and mercy, of sacrifice and expiation. Such figures as these and the mystical language developed in the praise of the Virgin appear in a large number of the religious poems written in England.

The favorite, though by no means exclusive, themes of the hymns were the sufferings of Christ on the Cross, the yearning to share His suffering, and praise of the Virgin. In this last type we find, as in Continental poetry, the language of courtly love used in her praise. Mystical love, the desire to be at one with the sacred persons, is the emotion which permeates the best of this lyric poetry. Probably the best known example is the lyric with a Latin refrain *Quia amore langueo* ("Because I languish with love").

The other type of religious poetry is of less interest. It leans on the tradition of the Latin *De contemptu mundi* ("scorn of the world") and is devoted to pointing out the vanity of human wishes and the transience of earthly joys. The subject is treated on much the same lines in all instances—and with much the same examples drawn from the contemporary scene or, more often, from the great men and women of the past.

Lyric poetry never achieved the eminence in medieval England that it did on the Continent. It may be described as "charming" or "moving," but a close comparison of English lyric reveals that much of its charm lies in a predisposition of modern readers to consider good that which is merely simple or naive. Most medieval secular lyrics fail to rise above the commonplace. The religious poems have more depth of feeling and a more sophisticated use of language, but they are usually at their best when they keep closely to Latin hymn tradition.

ALLEGORICAL AND DIDACTIC POETRY

We have had occasion to note earlier that allegorical poems are frequently didactic. This observation certainly holds for English literature, for some of the most important attempts at teaching and social commentary are cast in an allegorical framework.

The *Proverbs of Alfred* (probably twelfth century) and the versified sermon *Moral Ode* (c. 1170) are undistinguished works. The first is merely a collection of proverbial sayings to which King Alfred's name has been attached, the second a work on Hell and Heaven, with appropriate descriptions of horrors and joys. *Ormulum* (c. 1200) is a work of 20,000 lines of scriptural material with moral comment. There exists also a Middle English *Bestiary* (c. 1240), with the usual allegorized descriptions of animals.

Debate Poems

Much more important than any of these—in fact one of the best poems in Middle English—is *The Owl and the Nightingale* (c. 1200). This work falls into two classifications. It is a debate poem, but also it may very well be an allegory. The poet wanders into a valley where he hears the owl and the nightingale debate their claims to superiority. The basis of the debate is that the nightingale's song is essentially sensual and leads men into the wrong paths. The owl on the other hand, although melancholy, is wise. The nightingale's reply is that she sings for the delight of married lovers and that the owl has no voice and a quite unfounded reputation for sagacity. The fierce debate is mediated by the wren, who declares that the dispute shall be settled by Master Nicholas of Guilford.

The only clear facts about this amusing and vigorous debate are that the nightingale represents the sensuous world, possibly that of courtly love, and the owl, more mature, perhaps represents Christian wisdom. Certainly the allegory could be a parable of pleasure and duty, active life and contemplative life, art and thought, secular poetry and religious poetry. Since the debate is unresolved, we are not likely to find out. The poem's merit lies in its naturalness (rare in a debate poem) and skill in using dialogue. That it is a debate between two aspects of life is clear. More we cannot say.

The *Debate of the Body and Soul* (late thirteenth century) offers no such problems. It shows the soul of a dead knight rebuking his body for the sins it had committed. The body reminds him that the soul is responsible for sin, a verdict which is confirmed when his soul is plunged into Hell. This is a powerful piece of moralizing in a traditional form. Equally to the point is Robert Mannyng's *Handlyng Synne* (before 1303), but the method is different. Like many medieval writers, he decided that the most effective—and entertaining—way of warning people against sin was to describe the sins which should be avoided. This he does in 12,600 lines of octosyllabic couplets. The material is drawn from the vast collection of *exempla* or moral tales drawn up during the thirteenth century by the preaching friars. Many of his "illustrative stories" are highly unedifying, but since they are specifically stated to be things one should never do, the moral is preserved. By far the best known of his tales is that of the dancers of Kolbek. For dancing in the churchyard during Mass, a group of people are condemned to dance continually for a whole year. Since the dancers themselves are unaware of what is going on, it seems that the spectators are being warned rather than the dancers being punished.

The most prolific of the didactic authors was John Gower (c. 1330–1408), a man of great learning. His French *Mirror of Man* is a description of the cardinal virtues and the deadly sins and is intended to make a man lead a Christian life. A Latin work, *Vox Clamantis* ("The Voice of One Crying Out"), written after the Peasant's Revolt of 1381, is an attack on that revolt, but it covers many more problems. The work is a general criticism of the moral state of England and of its rulers, particularly Richard II.

Gower's work in English has a Latin title, *Confessio amantis* ("Confession of a Lover"). The work has the typical framework which Jean de Meun had made fashionable in the *Roman de la Rose*. The poet is wandering in the springtime thinking of his ill success in love. Venus, whom he meets, will not help him until she is sure he is her true servant. Genius, called to hear his confession, helps him by recounting the things of which he may be guilty, with illustrative examples. This affords a pretext for relating a mass of tales about unfortunate lovers and the reasons for their misfortune. Gower is chiefly interested in the moral conclusions to be drawn from these tales, but his book was an interesting and useful collection of stories, much appreciated by later writers.

The Pearl

It has already been noted that the author of *Gawain and the Green Knight* almost certainly wrote the other great poem in the manuscript, *The Pearl*. This is a vision poem and also an allegory—a favorite combination. The poem opens with the return of the poet to a garden where he had lost a precious pearl. He falls asleep, and the pearl appears to him in the form of a girl in white. He laments her loss but is chided for doing so, for she is now one of Heaven's queens. She is separated from him and cannot rejoin him in an earthly state. To his question about the possibility of one so young attaining Heaven, she replies that she was innocent, a state even better than that of repentance. He is, however, granted a vision, imperfect since he sees it as a mortal, of the new Jerusalem. So overwhelmed is he that he attempts to cross the stream which divides him from it and from his pearl, but he is prevented. He wakes and resolves to wait in patience for his reunion.

A great deal of the symbolism in this poem is drawn from Revelation. There the pearl is the emblem of purity and crowns the temple. Clearly, then, it can here stand for the pure perfection of religion and for the eucharist. Yet this would hardly seem to be enough. The reference to the girl, to the fact that the pearl was only two years old when it was lost, seem to indicate rather the loss of an innocent daughter, and there is a great deal in the work which supports the view that it is an elegy for a lost daughter. This view does not, however, prevent our interpreting the pearl allegorically. Dante's long-dead Beatrice showed him a vision of Paradise. There is no reason why the *Pearl* poet's innocent daughter should not show him the new Jerusalem and, in doing so, make use of the symbolism of the pearl—which may have been her name.

The Pearl is certainly very far from being an impersonal

allegory. Its depth of emotion, both in regard to the pearl and to the heavenly vision, transcend the allegorical frame. The possibility of mystical union with the Lamb is coupled with the desire for pure reunion with the pearl. In fulfilling this goal the poet will, like all good Christians, regain the innocence lost at the Fall and share in the redeeming sacrifice of Christ. The brilliant descriptive language which is a feature of *Gawain* is used even more effectively in *The Pearl*, for the author has moved from the courts of earth to the courts of Heaven.

Similar virtuosity is to be found in the versification. There are nineteen groups of five strophes and one of six. Each strophe has twelve lines, rhyming *ababababbcbc*. The last word in each strophe within each group is always the same, and this same word appears in the first half line of each strophe. Thus in each group one word appears ten times. This system is obviously used to form harmonious closely linked groups. Number symbolism was a common principle of arrangement in medieval poetry.

The *Pearl* poet may have written two other pieces: *Purity*, a verse sermon on the need to come to God clean in body—as those in various biblical incidents did not—and *Patience*, the story of the impatient Jonah, another *exemplum* in reverse.

Piers the Plowman

The Vision of William Concerning Piers the Plowman is even more difficult to discuss than the *Pearl*. It exists in three versions, called the A, B, and C texts. The A text is the shortest and earliest (c. 1362, 2,567 lines), the B text is next (c. 1377, 7,242 lines), and the C text is latest and longest (c. 1387 or later, 7,357 lines). The two longer versions are not mere expansions but reworkings. Most scholars regard the B text as the greatest. There has been much discussion of the authorship, and some authorities have seen three different writers at work. The majority, however, would now agree that William Langland, a West Midlander, was the author.

The work is, as its title implies, a vision poem. It is also an allegory and a work of social and religious comment. The first vision of "Will" is of a "field full of folk," which is a device for describing the contemporary social scene. The main action in this vision is the marriage of Lady Meed (Bribery) with False. She is brought to trial in London, but only Conscience and Reason persist in their opposition to her. In the next vision we see Conscience preach such a sermon that all turn to repentance, even the Seven Deadly Sins. A pilgrimage is started to the shrine of Truth, but no one knows where she lives. Piers the Plowman does know, but he must first finish his plowing. Truth gives Piers a brief statement (a pardon), which says simply that those who do good will be saved, those who do evil will be damned. This ends the vision, and then comes the search for Do-well, Do-better, and Do-best.

These three types of life are hard to define, and it is not easy to see exactly how they are being sought. There are constant digressions from the idea of progress. Many allegorical figures are used to question the poet and provide ideas for the definition of the various ways of life. Wit, for example, says that Do-well is to fear God, Do-better is to suffer, Do-best partakes of the nature of both. Again and again, however, we are reminded of the snares of the world that prevent the attainment of the good life. This leads to a great deal of satire and condemnation of contemporary life, particularly the pride of the great and the worldliness of the clergy. This is probably the best-known element in Langland's work, and it was certainly the one most imitated by his successors. Yet it is only incidental to his main purpose, the search for the good life and its characteristics, such as Charity. As the poem progresses, more and more attention is given to the church itself, to the incidents in the life of Christ, to parables (the Good Samaritan to illustrate charity), to the Harrowing of Hell, to the founding of the church and its struggles with worldly men who will not accept it, and finally to Antichrist and the sins which accompany him.

It would be idle to pretend that *Piers the Plowman* is an easy poem to understand. Probably even contemporaries with more understanding for and sympathy with the form and ideas would have found it hard. Langland is a poet, not a theologian, so that his visions are truly visions of aspects of Christian truth, not rational arguments. Yet at the same time a good knowledge of theology is necessary in order to understand the numerous references in the work. The use of abstract figures, while normal in allegory, is also distracting. Piers himself is not a constant figure. He appears to start as a simple, religious plowman, changes to a priest in the likeness of Christ, and then to a leader of the church.

Nor is the main theme of Do-well, Do-better, and Do-best at all clear. It would be easy if we could say that these are the equivalents of the active, the contemplative, and the truly religious life. So, to some extent, they are, but there is no simple equation.

The work is of very uneven poetical quality, and there is no disguising the fact that even by the standards of its time, it is formless. Langland was as unsystematic an artist as he was a theologian. At its best, however, it offers some of the finest religious visionary poetry in English.

CHAUCER

It would be possible to select one or two outstanding authors from any of the national literatures, but nowhere except with Dante in Italy can it be said that one figure towers so high above all other authors as Geoffrey Chaucer does above the other Middle English writers. He wrote a great deal—though many of his works are incomplete—and covered a wide range of subjects, but his greatness can be attributed directly to his extraordinarily sharp observation of human nature and his ability to set down what he saw with freshness and humor.

Life

The main facts of Chaucer's life are fairly clear. He was born around 1340, the son of John Chaucer, a London wine merchant in comfortable circumstances. He became a page to the earl of Ulster, and was taken prisoner in France around 1360 and ransomed. He married Philippa Roet, a lady with influential connections, secured a royal annuity, and was many times in Europe on diplomatic business. In the course of his travels he visited Italy and France. From 1374 to 1386 he was Comptroller of the Customs for London, a lucrative position. In 1386 he was a justice of the peace and Knight of the Shire in Parliament from Kent. After three years of inactivity he became Clerk of the King's Works in 1389 and deputy forester in Somerset in 1391. When Henry IV ascended the throne, Chaucer petitioned him in a poem for financial aid and was granted a substantial annuity.

Thus, it is clear that Chaucer was far from being a professional poet. His career is not dissimilar to that of Eustache Deschamps, but he was more fortunate in his patrons and his positions. The relative freedom from financial worry which he enjoyed for most of his life enabled him to avoid the pitiful complaining and wheedling which mar the work of some contemporaries. It also gave him an opportunity to become acquainted with men of all classes and countries.

Early Works

The *Canterbury Tales* are, of course, Chaucer's greatest work. Although the sources of many of the tales are to be found in Continental literature, the work as a whole is markedly English. The earlier works show far more evidence than the later of French and Italian influence. Moreover, it should not be overlooked that in Chaucer's day the earlier romances of the twelfth century were hardly known. The Arthurian cycle, although still productive, was rather unfashionable. Courtly love was viewed as something belonging to a past age, still indeed noble and worthy of imitation but not closely connected with real life. The works which most influenced Chaucer were the *Roman de la Rose*, (significantly, the latter part of Jean de Meun rather than the truly courtly beginning by Guillaume de Loris), the works of Boccaccio and of Guillaume de Machaut, and, besides the Latin classics, such works as the *Dream of Scipio* and Macrobius' comments on it, Guido delle Colonne's Troy story, and Dante's *Divina Commedia*. It will be noticed that many of these are allegorical works and, further, dream visions. This was to prove to be Chaucer's favorite literary type.

Probably Chaucer's first essay at literature was to translate the *Roman de la Rose*. Only a very small part, if any, of the extant version is his, but it is significant that he chose a dream vision as his first work. His next work was the *Book of the Duchesse*, an elegy in octosyllabic couplets on the death of Blanche, the wife of John Gaunt, duke of Lancaster, Chaucer's patron. He uses the dream-vision framework. The poet is thinking about love when he sleeps and dreams of a hunt on a bright May morning. He sees a knight in black who recites a lay about his bereavement, which he follows with an account of his love for Blanche. The dreamer can hardly believe she is dead. Waking, he looks at the story of sad love he had been reading in Ovid when he fell asleep, the story of Ceryx and Alcyone, who were turned into birds. He decides to write an account of his dream.

Chaucer, here and in other poems, has suffered from the efforts of critics to find something "different" in his poetry. The work is, in fact, fairly conventional. The three stages of sad love are contrasted—Chaucer's unfulfilled love, the Ovid story of metamorphosis, and the duke's fulfillment and deprivation. That Blanche is a model woman and that her love for the duke was perfect goes without saying in a poem of this type. In this respect the poem is a kind of courtly *exemplum*.

Because of its connection with a historical event, the date of the *Book of the Duchesse* is fairly easy to establish at 1369–70. The date of *The House of Fame* is not quite so easy to fix, but it is probably around 1379. Again we have a dream vision. In the first part there is a description of the Temple of Venus, with appropriate decoration on the motif of Dido and Aeneas. Then the poet is swept upward by an eagle, who proves to be most learned, for he tells Chaucer a great deal about love, science, and other matters. The third part shows us the petitioners' voices floating up to the House of Fame, where they are accepted or rejected according to whim. Nearby is the House of Rumor, whirling around with stories of gossip. The manuscript breaks off as a "man of great authority" is about to tell Chaucer about love.

It is hard to see how Chaucer was going to conclude this incomplete poem. It is full of reminiscences of French and Latin poetry. An eagle bore Ganymede up to Zeus, and the complaint of the eagle about Chaucer, the heavy burden, may well be a contrast between him and the slim youth. But the eagle was also a symbol of the soaring intellect—and of St. John. There are numerous classical references to the effects of rumor and to the prayers which reach Zeus. The fragment has a good laugh at learning, particularly while Chaucer is on his heavenly journey, and we should perhaps enjoy the parody and leave it at that. The poem is written in octosyllabic couplets.

The Parlement of Foules (c. 1380) is again a dream vision and, one suspects, has the same elements of parody. Again Chaucer describes himself as meditating on unsuccessful love —a favorite pose and in itself a jest at the numerous *serious* poems which begin this way. This time he turns to the *Dream of Scipio*, hardly a work calculated to help him with love problems. In a dream which follows (does the book put him to sleep?), he is taken by its chief character, Scipio Africanus, to a garden. This is not the garden of the *Roman de la Rose* but bears inscriptions on gates like those of Dante's *Inferno*. Love, say the notices, can lead to gay adventure or to misery. Inside the garden it is mating day for the birds—St. Valentine's Day. The eagles, being the noblest of birds, have to be mated first. Three males vie for the hand of a female in a long-winded courtly style which irritates the other birds. They want her to make up her mind so that their turn can come. Nature finally gives the female a year to make up her mind and assigns suitable mates to the other birds. The satire of courtly love is obvious. After long debate, there is no union— it is put off for a year. The highest nobility are thus sterile, confined to talk. The lesser birds, following the dictates of Nature, have no time for such nonsense. It is hard to avoid the conclusion that Chaucer has a good deal of sympathy with Jean de Meun's attitude, and the introduction of personified nature shows his kinship with Jean and with Alain de Lille. Comedy and irony, it will be noted, are already among the chief characteristics of Chaucer's works. The poem is written in rhyme royal, a strophic form. Each strophe is made up of seven five-beat lines rhyming *ababbcc*.

Troilus and Criseyde

Also written in rhyme royal was the work which, next to the *Canterbury Tales*, is regarded as Chaucer's best: *Troilus and Criseyde* (c. 1385). Chaucer did not take this story directly from its source, Benoît de Ste-Maure's *Roman de Troie*, but from Boccaccio's *Il Filostrato*. He may also have used a French version of Boccaccio's poem. Criseyde was a beautiful Trojan widow whose father, Calchas, a priest, had gone over to the Greeks. Troilus, a notorious antifeminist, falls deeply in love with her in the best courtly style. His agonies are finally ended by Criseyde's uncle, Pandarus, who brings the lovers together. They delight in each other's company for several years, until Criseyde is returned to her father. They part with mutual protestations of love and undying affection. But Criseyde is soon approached by the handsome Greek hero Diomedes, and it is not long before she yields to him. When Troilus hears of this he plunges into battle and dies. His spirit ascends to the eighth sphere and he is able to comment on the folly of earthly love.

By medieval definition this work is a tragedy, for the

happiness of the lovers is upset by Fortune, and Troilus dies. Yet the thing he dies for is shown in his own words to be futile. In this poem, as elsewhere in Chaucer's work, it is hard to tell exactly what Chaucer the poet, as distinct from Chaucer the narrator, really thinks. Certainly Troilus' condemnation of his own actions is severe. He sees that he directed his love to a frail and unworthy object, when he should have concentrated on the permanent joys of Heaven. In other words the last note sounded is that of Christian renunciation of earthly joys (though Troilus was a pagan!). Even the worldly Pandarus had warned him how transient were the joys he sought.

It would therefore seem logical for us to view Criseyde as the typically hollow, unfaithful woman seeking only her own immediate pleasure who is a stock figure in medieval anti-feminist literature. There is a good deal of basis for such an interpretation. She rejoices in her free status as a widow; she plays coy with Troilus, but once her interest is aroused, she has no moral scruples. Once in the Greek camp, she is im-pressed by Diomedes, a figure whose charms are entirely sensual.

Yet, Chaucer obviously has great sympathy for both Troilus and Criseyde. Because he is aware of human weakness, he refuses to pass moral judgments on their actions. Even if they sought the wrong kind of love, he could be sorry for them. Criseyde was weak, but he will not say that she was vicious. After all, circumstances beyond the control of either (For-tune) led to the tragedy. Neither could help the war or Criseyde's departure.

In this poem more than any other Chaucer is concerned with details of character and environment. He takes his time in letting us see the development of Troilus' love, which rises like a storm, and the much more calculated, wavering, uncer-tain interest of Criseyde. He here shows himself a master of the technique of revealing the "divided mind." Pandarus, in Chaucer a middle-aged man, is not merely a go-between. He likes life himself and will make it as pleasant as he can for others, but he has no illusions. Pleasure soon fades—and there is in the end no such thing as idealistic love. Thus, Pandarus' point of view, however perversely, approaches that of Troilus in his eighth sphere.

Chaucer's own moral code, the one he would like the world to live by, is clear. Yet he is sympathetic to those who cannot measure up to this standard. Further, he takes great care to leave final judgment to the reader. In brilliant detail he unfolds the story—let the reader make of it what he can.

Between *Troilus* and the main body of the *Canterbury Tales*, Chaucer wrote, at the instigation of Queen Anne, a prologue and nine stories called *The Legend of Good Women* (c. 1386). It tells of ladies, largely classical, who were deceived by men. The prologue is amusing, for Chaucer is required by "Queen Alceste," who perhaps represents the English Queen Anne, to do penance for maligning women in his poems. He quotes (not in his own person) authorities who speak for women, and very strange ones they are—notorious antifeminists. Chaucer clearly soon tired of the subject, for he broke off the series.

Canterbury Tales

Chaucer's *Canterbury Tales* are among the very greatest works of English literature. Quite probably he had already written some of them before he evolved the brilliant connecting idea of the pilgrimage to the shrine of St. Thomas à Becket in Canterbury. It should be noted at once that such a pilgrimage was a perfectly natural event and that Chaucer makes of it much more than a mere framework. The pilgrimage moves, it is lively, events take place outside the stories themselves (such as the arrival of the canon and his yeoman and the equally sudden departure of the former). The gathering of the pilgrims at the Tabard Inn at Southwark, near London, is the occasion of perhaps the best collection of character portraits ever penned in English. After a brilliant description of the April season (like the Arthurian adventure-season opening), Chaucer describes his pilgrims. His technique is magnificent. He pretends to utter objectivity. Yet by a careful selection of characteristics for each, he enables the reader to form a moral judgment on the characters. There is, of course, an element of the conventional about the portraits. Each profession in the Middle Ages, as at other times, had its type. If Chaucer had described an honest, handsome, generous miller, he would have been a laughingstock. The same is true for the friar, the pardoner, and others. Everyone knew how they were supposed to be represented, and Chaucer so represents them. Our principal delight is in the details.

The highest-ranked—and first-named—pilgrim is a knight.

He is given the conventional knightly attributes, but sincerely. He is a fine man. His squire, deep in the throes of courtly love, is treated with more irony. Their attendant we see through his attributes as a working man. Only a few other characters are so sympathetically handled. Greatest praise goes to the simple country parson, who taught Christ's love, but first followed it himself. The clerk of Oxford, although Chaucer feels that he carries learning a little far, is also treated sympathetically. The plowman and franklin, good country people, also come off well. The medical and legal professions have their weaknesses exposed, and the dubious conduct of the shipman and reeve in their professional activities are noted.

It is when we come to the portraits of those connected with the church (other than parish priests) that Chaucer's irony becomes harsh and his sarcasm more biting. Some characters —the pardoner and the summoner are the best examples—are attacked viciously. Their physical characteristics are made to reflect their evil souls. The friar is handled a little less roughly, but his perversion of his order's rules for his own profit, his utter disregard of the most solemn obligations of religion in order to gain the goods of this world, make him a reprehensible character. The monk and the prioress are treated differently. They are not bad people—just a bad monk and a bad prioress. Chaucer's most sympathetic characters are not only good people but good at their chosen work. The author is at his ironical best in describing the monk. He doesn't like the cloister—so why should he stay in it? He does like hunting, falconry, good food—so why shouldn't he indulge in these? The only trouble is that at some point in the past he took vows of obedience, poverty, and chastity. Nor is the prioress bad. On the contrary, she is a well-mannered, well-dressed, handsome lady who pays great attention to the effect she makes on the company—which is just what a prioress ought not to do. She would make, in fact, a very good lady in a courtly romance.

Low life is well represented by the miller and the cook, and it is typical that here Chaucer uses a great deal of physical description. Warts, hair, growths on legs appear. Probably the most famous of all the portraits in the General Prologue, certainly one of the most extensive, is that of the wife of Bath. Once again Chaucer is discussing the subject of love. The wife talks about nothing else and thinks about nothing else. She has had five official husbands and is looking for a sixth. She is flamboyant, sensual, often crude, but nevertheless rather touching. She cannot live without men and yet, apparently, she cannot live with them very well either. She is forever seeking the perfect mate who will be gentle and courteous (courtly?) and at the same time dominant and masculine so as to win mastery over her. Chaucer was obviously fascinated by his creation. He gives her a long prologue of her own when her turn comes to tell a tale.

It is the professed intention of the host, as stated in the prologue, to have every pilgrim tell two tales on the way to Canterbury and two on the way back. In fact there are only twenty-four tales extant, and some of these—including Chaucer's own!—are incomplete. The order of the tales has usually been determined by that in the Ellesmere, the most famous of the ninety-odd manuscripts in which all or part of the tales appear. There have been many suggestions for re-shuffling, particularly in order to make groups of similar tales, but these are matters for specialists. The poems are written in various poetic forms—some common, like rhyme royal strophe and rhyming couplets, others unusual, like that in the monk's tale.

It is impossible to give here even a brief summary of the individual tales. We shall merely attempt to characterize the more important ones. The knight's tale, which comes first, is a long and stiff tale of the rivalry of two knights for a lady. They are very close friends, their love shatters the friendship, and one dies. The romance, if such it can be called, is cool and has the obvious moral that fate settles all things and we must bow to it. The miller's tale, which follows, seems almost a satire, for it tells of love in highly indelicate and immoral terms. Everyone is either stupid or vicious. Yet the story is very funny and very much alive. It is the earthy answer to courtly love.

The reeve follows with a tale against millers, again on illicit and very unspiritual love affairs, there perpetrated in the miller's house by two students. Chaucer makes ample use here of traditional rivalries and enmities. The man-of-law tells the tale of Constance, patient under a most extraordinary series of trials but finally, because of her faith, triumphant. The wife of Bath's prologue is a great deal longer than her tale, and in it she justifies her sensuality by brilliant parodies of scholastic argument. The antifeminists are routed in her long and jolly description of her own marriages. Yet in her tale she does give a formula for a "perfect marriage." The hero is a knight of Arthur's court condemned to death for rape. To escape he must find out what women most desire. After many failures, a hideous hag promises him the answer if he will marry her. He is forced to agree and hears that it is mastery over men. On the wedding night he complains that his wife is ugly and is offered a choice—ugly and faithful or beautiful and doubtful. He leaves the choice to her, and now that she has won she decides to be both beautiful and good. The wife of Bath has won her point.

The friar and summoner, who have quarreled during the wife of Bath's tale, now tell in turn tales in which the other comes to a bad end, the summoner to the devil and the friar puzzling over a disgusting gift which he is supposed to divide. The clerk tells the tale of patient Griselde, another paragon of virtue; the merchant the much less edifying but more amusing story of January and May, the old husband, the young wife, and the inevitable lover. After a tale by the squire, which reaches no conclusion, the franklin tells a very pleasant tale of married love, which is in sharp contrast to that of January and May. A pretty wife, hard pressed by a model courtly lover, says in jest that she will yield if he moves some rocks from the coast. A magician is hired and the deed apparently done. The wife, in a quandary, appeals to her husband, who tells her she must keep her promise. Moved by this, the lover repents. The story shows how love's problems can be handled if all have true "gentilesse"—good breeding.

Many of the tales which follow are of a moralizing nature, several on familiar themes. The pardoner tells the old tale of the three men who find a treasure and kill each other to obtain a bigger share. He preaches a hellfire sermon in conjunction with it. The prioress tells of a boy killed by Jews miraculously kept alive until his murderers are hanged; the monk a series of "tragedies" about various great people. The second nun tells a life of St. Cecilia, while the parson, in prose, preaches a sermon on the seven deadly sins. This is the last tale of the day, suitably moral. In between the serious stories there are the shipman's tale, a fabliau of a wife who pays for her clothes with money a monk gives her in exchange for her favors—money he borrows from her husband. The nun's priest's tale is a fine rendering of one of the stories from the *Roman de Renart*—Renard's attempt and failure to carry off Chanticleer the rooster. It is a pretty sermon on flattery. The canon's yeoman tells of his master's wicked experiments in alchemy and, just before the parson's tale, the manciple, after a quarrel with the cook, tells a tale from Ovid about the punishment of a tattletale bird—the white crow who became black.

Immediately after the prioress, Chaucer himself attempts two tales. His first is an extravagant parody of the contemporary romance called the *Tale of Sir Thopas,* which the host, Harry Bailey, soon stops. Then, in prose, Chaucer tells the *Tale of Melibee.* This he manages to finish. It is a debate on private revenge and true justice, well supported with quotations. Very typically, Chaucer assigns to himself an almost ludicrous role as storyteller.

Numerous attempts have been made to see an overall intent in the *Canterbury Tales* as we have them. Firstly, we can hardly judge from what was completed whether Chaucer really meant to carry out his plan. Secondly, if there is such an overall purpose, it is far from obvious. That love and marriage are of great concern is clear; they are important in all of Chaucer's work. That there is a moral purpose is also obvious, for many tales can be read as *exempla.* But in the end it is best simply to marvel at the characters and the way in which the tales fit them. Nowhere, even in Boccaccio, do we find such a slice of genuine life combined with real moral force and understanding of the world.

Chaucer wrote a number of minor works—a treatise on the astrolabe, which is essentially an elementary astronomy book (1391), a translation of the *Consolation of Philosophy* by Boethius, an author he greatly admired, and a few short poems, of which the best is the *Complaint to His Purse* (1399), the poem which secured him a pension from Henry IV.

Chaucer added to the *Canterbury Tales* a retraction in which he asked forgiveness for writing most of his works. He obviously felt, as did many medieval poets, that he should renounce the poetry of worldliness and make his peace with God. We can only be thankful that his zeal did not extend to destroying his works. But such an act would be out of character. He was a well-balanced man.

POETRY AFTER CHAUCER

It was inevitable that a literary figure of Chaucer's stature should exercise great influence on subsequent writings. His forms of verse, his language, his subjects were all imitated. John Lydgate (c. 1370–c. 1450) was his most ardent admirer, to the extent of adding himself to the Canterbury pilgrims in the prologue to his *Siege of Thebes* (1420). He offers this long epic on the famous seven-against-Thebes story as his contribution to the tales! He also wrote the *Troy Book* (1412–21) already mentioned—a 30,000-line version of Guido delle Colonne's prose work. He has two massive allegories, *Reason and Sensuality* (c. 1408), with the usual trappings, of a (this time chaste) love allegory, and the *Pilgrimage of the Life of Man*, 24,000 lines of translation from the French. Lydgate's popularity in his lifetime can be regarded only as proof of the eagerness with which his contemporaries welcomed moralizing and of their stamina. He has no poetic gift and enjoys only one distinction—he is one of the most prolific of English writers.

The poetry of Thomas Occleve (c. 1370–c. 1440) is at least more personal and cheerful, if not much more distinguished. Although he wrote, as did many others, a *Guide for Princes* (1411), most of his work is descriptive of his life as a clerk in the Privy Seal office, during and after office hours, and as such interesting for its topical allusions.

The best "imitators" of Chaucer lived well after his day and were not English but Scottish. In chronological order they are: *The Kingis Quair* (1423), Robert Henryson (c. 1430–1510), and William Dunbar (c. 1460–c. 1520). *The Kingis Quair* ("King's Book") is traditionally ascribed to James I of Scotland, but the ascription has been sharply challenged by recent critics. It is again a dream vision in which a prisoner in a tower sees a fair lady below, falls desperately in love with her, and on his release marries her. Clearly such a poem could be autobiographical but it is also open to any of a number of allegorical interpretations—the triumph of patience, the soul released and joining the beloved, the wheel of fortune reversed. And, as may be expected, it has been thus variously interpreted.

Robert Henryson was a schoolmaster, and it is therefore not surprising that he followed a trend general throughout Europe and adapted the fables of Aesop into his own vernacular, with appropriate local color. In this he was very successful. His continuation of *Troilus and Criseyde*, which he called *The Testament of Cresseid* (c. 1460), keeps Troilus alive while Criseyde slides down the path of sin and finally becomes a leper, begging for her food. Troilus sees her, fails to recognize her consciously but is stirred by a memory of his love. The poem lacks Chaucer's ironical treatment. Henryson also wrote a pastoral poem, the kind in which Robin rejects his shepherdess cruelly and is made to pay for it.

William Dunbar is by far the most vigorous of these poets. His range is very considerable, he has a great comic gift and great power of language. His most serious and noble poetry is undoubtedly his hymns, which have a true lyric quality. Nor is he the least of the "vanity of the world" or *memento mori* writers. He wrote numerous dream allegories and ballads, but his most famous (and most obscene) work is his *The Two Married Women and the Widow*. This satire on courtly love is well constructed. First, it gives us the usual ideal setting, this time a summer evening. Then we hear a debate on love by the women. Although they use the language of courtly love, they are in fact interested in one thing only—sex in its crudest form—and are loud in their complaints of their husbands' incapacity. Clearly, viewing courtly love in connection with such creatures is farcical, and the whole pretense that such love exists is shattered. Dunbar stands out as the greatest of the poets between Chaucer and the Renaissance.

PROSE WORKS

Some important prose works have already been mentioned, among them the greatest of medieval prose works, Malory's *Morte d'Arthur* (see pp. 187f.). Even by medieval standards, however, there is little Middle English prose of note. Needless to say there is a considerable amount of what may be termed "routine" religious prose—sermons, saints' lives, *exempla*, moral sayings—but only one early piece of religious prose rises above the general level: *The Ancrene Riwle* ("Rule for Nuns"; c. 1200), which is a piece of advice for three sisters who were to become nuns. It was originally written, apparently, in the West Midland dialect, but the surviving manuscripts are redactions in English, French, and Latin. The advice given is what one would expect. It is the method which constitutes the work's strength, for it reinforces its moral points with well-expressed, often homely examples which show great understanding of human nature. The pictures of types—particularly bad types—are very effectively drawn.

In the fourteenth century there was in England, as in several Continental countries, a group of mystical prose writers. Of these the most important was Richard Rolle (c. 1300–49), a hermit of Hampole. His more important works were written in Latin, but toward the end of his life he wrote in English such meditative works as *The Bee and the Stork* (an exhortation to activity), *Form of Living*, and *Meditations on the Passion*, a description of mystical feeling about the Passion of Christ. Other mystical writers of the period were Walter Hilton (died 1396), author of the *Ladder of Perfection*, and Juliana of Norwich (last half of fourteenth century), who reveals her own experiences in *Revelations of Divine Love*. *The Book of Margery Kempe* (c. 1436) is the record of visions by a character of rather less delicate sensibilities.

This brief look at religious prose should also mention the English translation of the *Golden Legend* (c. 1438), a translation of the same work by Caxton in 1483, and one of the *Gesta Romanorum* (c. 1440).

Secular prose also exhibits many moral and commonplace books. We should note, however, a few works of real interest. *The Travels of Sir John Mandeville* (c. 1356) was originally written in French and translated into English and Latin. The author came from St. Albans and is hardly likely to have visited all the places he describes, but he makes use of medieval geographies and a vivid imagination to produce a work which is not unlike that of Herodotus. Its range is considerable, for India and China are included! By showing himself as the traveler, he is able to give the feel of authenticity to much that is pure fable.

The *Paston Letters* is a very important collection of family records covering several generations, from 1422 to 1509. Its interest is not, of course, primarily literary, but historical and sociological. They offer one of the finest extant masses of evidence for daily life in any medieval century. History of a different kind is represented by John Trevisa's translation (1387) of Ranulf Higden's *Polychronicon* and by John Capgrave's *Chronicle of England*.

These remarks on secular prose should mention one more of Caxton's translations, his *Historie of Reynard the Foxe* (1481), taken from the Dutch version printed in Gouda.

Middle English literature has fewer outstanding works than the medieval literature on the Continent. Chaucer is a salient figure, equal to the greatest. But only William Langland and

Thomas Malory can be said to approach real genius. There were other writers of talent, and some anonymous works, particularly lyrics, are of importance. Yet it cannot be denied that, in general, the late start which literature in English experienced affected both its quantity and quality.

Celtic Literature

GENERAL

THE LITERATURE of the Celtic countries, principally Ireland and Wales, differs markedly from the works already discussed. Not only is the material of which the literature is composed different, but the types and forms in which literature is cast are not those of the rest of western Christendom. Of course, Ireland and Wales produced their share of religious writings, and lives of saints and Christian hymns are as common there as elsewhere. The secular works, however, go back to a much more primitive period. They are pagan in inspiration, and their form owes very little to classical culture and still less to Germanic, although attempts have been made to magnify what are largely coincidental resemblances.

By far the most important and influential body of literature stemming from the Celtic Middle Ages is the large collection of Irish sagas. We have already noted that these undoubtedly provided many stories for the Arthurian romances, and their heroes can be traced in many romances and lays. Many of the manuscripts in which they appear are relatively late, and there can be no doubt that the forms in which most of them are now extant are the result of many reworkings. This brief account will not attempt to establish the earliest form of the sagas or discuss questions of chronology. The facts generally accepted by competent literary historians will be given, together with an account of the most important sagas and a characterization of the type.

IRISH SAGAS

Most Irish literature is contained in large collections rather than in manuscripts of individual authors. Although the oral tradition goes back to the sixth century, the earliest extant manuscript is the Würzburg Codex of about 700. The works discussed below are to be found in later manuscripts and in particular in the Book of the Dun Cow, written before 1106, the Book of Leinster (Lecan), of about 1160, and in the Yellow Book of Lecan, of the late fourteenth century. There are numerous other writings besides the sagas in each of these manuscripts.

Ulster Cycle

The best known and in many ways the most important of the sagas is the Ulster cycle. It is a long and largely disconnected series of tales about events in Ulster which may be placed in the first century B.C. It is hardly necessary to stress that the events are not in the strict sense historical. Although there may well be a historical basis for many of them, they are interwoven with stories of magic, of folklore, and of mythology. The hero of the cycle is Cuchulain, the son of Lug Lámfada (Lug of the Long Arm). The King of Ulster throughout the cycle is Conchobar, but Fergus is described as having been king before him and as having given up his kingship voluntarily to Conchobar, who is the son of his wife Ness. In some stories Fergus is a king in exile who is torn between love of his native land and enmity to those who now rule it—a common theme in heroic saga. In the Ulster cycle, as in many others, the prose narrative is intermingled with poetry which is used to describe moments of intense emotion. Most of the stories are short and deal with one incident only, but one, the *Cattle Raid of Cooley* (*Táin Bó Cúalnge*) is a long and complex work which contains all the elements which distinguish the saga as a type. The earliest version was probably written in the ninth century, and in the eleventh other redactions were made, from which our present version was evolved. The work shows considerable evidence of learning, even classical learning, on the part of the numerous *filid*, or minstrels, who had a hand in its composition. The work here summarized is that in the Book of Leinster (Lecan).

The work opens with Ailill and his wife Medb comparing their treasures. It appears that they are equal in every respect except that Ailill possesses a bull, Whitehorn, which is beyond compare. Medb cannot rest until she has a bull at least equal to it. She hears of an animal in Cualnge in Ulster which is as good and tries in vain to buy it. Then she gathers her forces for the raid from which the work takes its name. She has on her side many warriors of repute, among them Fergus, who is at this time exiled from his native Ulster. On the side of Conchobar, king of Ulster, Cuchulain is the principal figure. At the beginning of the story Fergus deliberately leads his army astray, for he cannot bring himself to do harm to his own land. All the men of Ulster, except Cuchulain and

his father, are the victims of a mysterious sickness brought on
by the curse of a fairy. Thus they alone are arrayed against
the men of Connaught. Cuchulain shows his prowess by
killing four of the opposition, which provides the author with
an excuse for allowing Fergus to give a long account of the
boyhood deeds of the hero. Cuchulain continues to slaughter the enemy in hundreds and refuses Medb's efforts at nego-
tiation but does agree to a trial by single combat each day.
Cuchulain wins all of these combats, which take place at
a ford (a common Arthurian motif), even when a hundred
men are sent against him at once.

While the hero is pursuing one enemy group, another captures the brown bull, and although he kills its leader, the bull
is driven off. In revenge, Cuchulain lays waste huge portions of Ireland. His divine father, Lug, puts him to sleep for
three days to heal his wounds and while he is sleeping 150
boys from Ulster are killed. Again Cuchulain is fearsome
in his revenge. Then comes the ultimate test—a combat between him and his brother Fer Diad. As so often, a doomed
hero is faced with the alternatives of disgrace or virtually
certain death at the hands of a man he loves. The fight lasts
three days. Not until the hero chooses the "play of the ford"
(a fight in water) and as a weapon the *gae bolga* (with which
he is invincible) does he defeat Fer Diad, whom he laments
in moving verse.

While Cuchulain is recovering from this fight, he sends his
human father, Sualtam, to rouse the men of Ulster. Sualtam
is killed by a curse, but King Conchobar does raise a huge
army. Its coming is described in detail. A great battle rages
in which Conchobar's forces are worsted, and the king himself proves inferior to Fergus. Cuchulain, aroused by the
noise of the king's shield, enters the battle, using a chariot as
a weapon. The opposition is crushed, but Medb and her
remaining men are spared. The brown bull has been taken to
Medb's town. There it meets and challenges the white bull of
Ailill. The fight ranges all over Ireland, but finally the brown
bull runs home with the dead white bull on its horns. There it
too dies.

The heroic elements in the saga are obvious—the dominating hero of both human and divine descent, the frequent
intervention of supernatural and magic forces, the taboo animals of various tribes, the defense of a holy place (the ford),

the fight between dear friends or blood brothers, the exiled king, the woman who causes the destruction of brave men. In the Irish sagas these elements appear larger than life and have been little modified by the more sophisticated views of later ages. As the construction of the saga shows, there is little effort at unity or strict form. It is held together by the personality of the hero. There are clear similarities to the Norse sagas, both in form and content, but less evidence of the conventions of a tightly knit social group. Magic and mythology are far more important in the Irish than in the Norse sagas.

Some of the other stories in the cycle may be mentioned. *The Exile of the Sons of Usnech* (*Longes Mac Nusnig*) is an account of the fatal effects of the love of Deirdriu on Noisi, son of Usnech, and his brothers. They flee to escape the effects of the spell but are treacherously killed on Conchobar's orders after being offered safe return. Fergus was the surety for their safety and in his anger he stays away from Ulster for sixteen years. Deirdriu, captured by Conchobar, kills herself.

Briciu's Feast (*Fled Bricrenn*) is interesting for its resemblances to the story of *Gawain and the Green Knight*. Briciu is the troublemaker in the Irish sagas, as Loki is in Norse mythology. He seeks to cause strife by inviting chiefs to a feast and telling three of them that each is the obvious candidate for a "hero's portion." Inevitably a fight breaks out as each makes his claim. The decision as to whether Loegaire, Conall, or Cuchulain should have the "hero's portion" is left up to Ailill of Connacht. Then the respective wives are brought into the fray. The story becomes farcical with the women racing to be first inside the hall, reciting the praises of their husbands, then being admitted to the hall by gigantic feats of strength performed by the men. Precedence is finally established by a series of tests set by Ailill, in which Cuchulain is victorious. His victory is not recognized by the others until the magician Cu Roi himself appears in disguise and challenges Conchobar's warriors to the beheading test. He allows them to cut off his head, provided that they allow him to do the same to them. Only Cuchulain has the courage to accept the challenge. The magician strikes him with the blunt side of the ax and proclaims him the greatest warrior in Ireland.

The Ulster cycle is full of such stories. They are always interesting as the stories of a primitive people—they are the earliest surviving material in a western vernacular—and sometimes they rise to great heights of art in the depiction of heroism and pathos.

Finn Cycle

The Fenian (warrior) cycle is of a different kind. It lacks any real local association, for its heroes are wandering bands of warriors, of whom by far the most important is Finn. His sons Oisín and Diarmaid also figure prominently. Finn is a semidivine hero, assisted by magic and having many of the characteristics of such heroes as Siegfried and Arthur, Achilles and Gilgamesh—that is, of the hero of light struggling against the forces of darkness. Finn is a hero of Leinster and Munster, and his deeds are considered to have taken place in the third century A.D. Many of the adventures are in ballad form, although some are in prose. There is a long account of Finn's birth, boyhood, and acquisition of wisdom. The longest story of the Finn cycle, *The Old Men's Conversation*, is a kind of frame that provides a pretext for recounting various stories about Finn. St. Patrick is one of the participants. This tale is probably later than the *Cattle Raid of Cooley*, and dates from about 1200 in its present form.

Older than this and of greater significance for the history of literature is the prose story *The Flight of Diarmaid and Gráinne*. Finn, now an old man, has lost his wife, and his son Diorruing suggests that he marry Gráinne, daughter of Cormac. She agrees to follow her father's wishes. Finn, his sons, and some retainers, among whom is Diarmaid, come to Cormac's home. Gráinne sees Diarmaid, puts the others to sleep, and asks him for his love. He refuses, but she puts a curse on him that will take effect if he refuses her requests and thus forces him to go with her. Finn sets out in pursuit and once almost captures Diarmaid, who has refused to make love to Gráinne but does repulse all the attacks on him. Finally, unable to bear Gráinne's taunts about his lack of manhood, he makes her his mistress. After many narrow escapes, peace is restored when Finn marries Cormac's other daughter. In spite of this arrangement, Finn does finally obtain his revenge. Diarmaid joins in a boar hunt, even though he is under a curse which makes it fatal for him to do so. He is wounded, and although Finn could cure him by bringing him water, he refuses to do so until it is too late. It has been shown that this story is almost certainly one of the most important sources for the story of Tristan and Isolde.

Although there is magic and supernatural intervention in the Finn cycle, they are not on such a heroic scale as in that of Ulster. Finn never attains the stature of Cuchulain. Yet the colorful deeds and the fine storytelling remain.

Historical Cycle

The "historical cycle" has many characteristics in common with the stories of the Ulster and Fenian cycles already discussed. The core of each story is a historical event, usually of the early Christian era. Thus the events described are generally later than those of the Ulster or Fenian cycles. The heroes and their actions, however, are much the same. The earliest story in the historical cycle is the *Labraith Loingsech* (*Destruction of Dinn Ríg*), whose events date from the third century, and the latest is the *Brian Bóramha* of 1001–14. The former tells of the vengeance of Cobthach on his brother Loegaire and on Loegaire's son. Loegaire's grandson Labraith allies himself to Scoriath by marrying his daughter, Moriath. He lures Cobthach into an iron house and roasts him inside it.

The *Battle of Mag Mucrama* dates probably from the tenth century. A dispute over a captive leads to the defeat and exile of Lugaid Mac Con by Eogan. Later he returns and defeats Eogan. He becomes king but later is expelled. *The Death of Mael Folhartaig* (tenth century) tells how King Ronan killed Mael Folhartaig on the accusation of his wife. The story closely resembles the Greek legend of Phaedra. *The Battle of Moira* refers to a battle which actually took place in 637 and in which Donnall, the high king, defeated the lords of the Northeast. The first part of the story is called the *Feast of Dun na nGed*, the battle is described in the second part, while the third part is really an independent story about the wanderings of Suibne. Suibne was driven mad in the battle and then wandered under a curse put on him by St. Ronan because of his attacks on Christianity. Other tales of the historical cycle are *The Hostel of MacDareo*, a tale of revolt, *The Expulsion of the Deisi*, *The Battle of Mag Leana*, and the *Fall of Tara*.

Mythological Cycle

In the "mythological cycle," the principal characters are indeed divine but bear little resemblance to the gods of Greek legend. They seem to belong rather to the lower orders of supernatural beings. Their functions are not clearly defined, nor are they shown as superior beings directing the affairs of men. Rather they have adventures very similar to those of mortals, except that they use the powers of magic in their own behalf, and the supernatural generally plays a larger role.

Some of the principal characters in the mythological cycle are: Dagda, king of the fairies, whose son was Oengus Mac Óc; Manannán Mac Lirm ("Son of the Sea"); and Lug Mac Ethnenn or Lug Lámfada (Lug of the Long Arm), who is an important character in several stories and is the divine father of Cuchulain. A wizard Cu Roi also appears fairly frequently. The material is, of course, pre-Christian but the cycle grew during the early Middle Ages and appears in the MSS already mentioned.

In *The Dream of Oengus* the demigod Oengus suffers from a sickness which can be cured only by the love of a girl he has seen in a dream. She spends one year as a swan and one as a mortal. He wins her as a swan. *The Wooing of Etainn* is one of the most important stories of the cycle. Dagda falls in love with Boann, the mortal wife of Elcmar. Their son is Oengus, who lays claim to the lands of his mortal "father" and by supernatural help succeeds in the claim. Later he is visited by Midir, who asks for the fairest girl in his lands. She is Etainn, daughter of Ailill, and hard conditions are set before she is given to Midir. These Midir fulfills, and he takes her home. His first wife, Fuamnach, however, is in a jealous rage and turns Etainn into various shapes. In the form of a fly she is swallowed by the wife of Etar and then reborn as Etainn. In this new existence she marries Eochaid Airam, king of Ireland. His brother Ailill (a different one) falls sick for love of her. She is willing to heal him outside her husband's house, but when they meet, Midir, her husband in a previous existence, puts Ailill to sleep and comes to her himself. On the third such occasion he reveals himself, but she will not go with him without Eochaid's consent. Ailill, however, is cured of his sickness.

Later Midir wins Etainn at a chess game with Eochaid and flies away with her. Eochaid conducts a long search for her and is finally told that he can have her back if he can recognize her among a large group of relations. His choice falls on a girl who proves to be his own daughter by Etainn. His daughter by this girl, conceived before he knew of the relationship, is exposed but reared by a herdsman. She later marries Etarscéle and becomes the mother of Conaire.

This rather confused story has many of the elements we expect in mythology—doubtlet characters, previous existence, abnormal conception, the substitute lover, and the unrecognized child. Even more characteristic is *The Battle of Moytura*. The Tuath Dé Danann (fairy people), in alliance with the Formorians, took Ireland from the Fir Bolg, (sack and bag men), who had conquered it earlier. The Formorians oppressed the people, and their king, Bres, was sent away. He returned with a huge army, but the Tuath Dé, aided particularly by Lug Lámfada, defeated them. *The Battle of Moytura* has numerous digressions describing the persons and deeds of the participants, as well as much magic and sorcery.

The Story of the Children of Lir is a version of the widespread medieval story in which children are changed to swans and suffer in that shape for centuries until they are finally changed back and baptized as Christians. There is also a Christian element in the story called *The Feeding of the House of the Two Milk Vessels*. Here the Tuath Dé have been defeated. Mananánn tells Oengus to expel Elcmar from Bruig na Bóinne. He also tells him of another god who is more powerful than the gods of Ireland—the Christian God, about whom he gives some details. Curcog, daughter of Mananánn, and Eithne, daughter of a steward at the Bruig, are sent to the court of Oengus. Because of an insulting remark Eithne refuses all food except the milk of two cows brought from India. Mananánn finds that she is under the control of the Christian God. She loses her powers as a fairy, becomes visible to men and joins a Christian priest. Later St. Patrick himself prevents her from joining the fairies when they come to look for her.

In this story we see the conflict of the old religion and the new expressed in terms which are still largely those of the old mythology. No other western European culture was so successful in depicting with such grace the conflict (and even the amalgamation) of the two religions.

The Ulster and Finn cycles and the historical and mythological stories have many elements in common. They tell stories of heroes, whether human or divine. Love plays a prominent role, but it is the desire of a man for a woman or vice versa rather than idealistic love. Often the consequences of the passion are of more importance than the love affair itself. No great stress is placed on faithfulness in either sex. When a person is faithful, it is from a taboo or a legalistic sense rather than from deep attachment. The origins of courtly love are not to be sought in Ireland. Nor can we see any traces of the kind of "courtly code" which we associate with the medieval romance in other countries. The society depicted is aristocratic, and its members are of a warrior class, with the virtues of such a class—bravery, physical prowess, loyalty, skill and cunning in war. The ability to make speeches and to deceive the opposition is also important. In the Irish sagas, a man fights essentially for himself and for a good reputation among his peers, as he does in the Scandinavian sagas and in some of the other national epics. The adventures are described in prose with interspersed verse in a style much more colorful than that of the Norse sagas. The works are highly imaginative, often discursive, rejoicing in magic and strange adventures.

Comparison has often been made between the Irish sagas and the *Iliad* and *Odyssey*. Both tell of a relatively primitive aristocratic society, both types were written when this society was already remote in time from the writer. Yet there are equally obvious differences. The element of the fantastic plays a much larger role in the Irish than in the Greek works, and thus the former are at once more colorful and less human. Although there are rules of conduct which the warriors obey, it cannot be said that these rules bear as much relation to our own ideas of morality as do those which mark the conduct of Homer's heroes.

In the end, however, the feeling of unfamiliarity which affects the reader of Irish sagas stems from the fact that, unlike the works of Homer, they did not become part of the general heritage of western European culture, although they contributed many elements to its development.

IRISH ADVENTURE STORIES

There are, of course, adventures and visions in the sagas, but Irish literature recognizes them also as a separate category. They usually tell of the fantastic experiences of men who go on a quest to far-off exotic places or to the abodes of the

dead. These works exercised far more influence on other literatures than did the sagas. Latin works and Latin versions dependent on the Irish forms exist in large numbers, and one
in particular, the *Voyage of St. Brendan*, appears in most of
the western vernaculars during the high Middle Ages. The
adventure (*echtrae*) of Conle dates perhaps from the eighth
century and tells of a meeting with a remarkable woman
whom he alone can see, but others can hear. She tries to tempt
him to her country. Although he resists, he does eat an apple
she gives him and in the end goes with her. This is the well-
known motif of the fairy lover and the fateful meal which
puts the mortal in her power.

The best known of all the adventures is that about Bran,
son of Febal. He also is told by a woman of a far-off and
beautiful land. He travels in a magic boat to the Isle of Merri-
ment and the Land of Women, where he and his men stay
many years. They ultimately return to Ireland, where one of
the men, who disobeys a command not to go ashore, is turned
to ashes. Bran turns away and is not heard of again. This
story of a land where men do not grow old is clearly akin to
the Grail story, which it may very well have influenced.

There are also similarities to the Grail story in the tale of
Art, son of Conn. Bé Cuma, a woman banished by the Tuath
Dé for sinning, wins the love of Art, with the result that he
is banished from Tara, the chief town, and from Ireland. A
curse comes on the country, and the druids declare it can be
expiated only by the sacrifice of the son of parents without
sin. Conn sets out to find such a child. His voyage is like that
of Bran, a fact which makes it clear that the basic material
for the voyage stories was derived from common sources.
Magic feeding again recalls the Grail story. On one of the
islands, the son of the ruler, Segda Saer Labraid, proves to be
the child he seeks, but he is saved from death by the intervention of a woman who proves to be his mother. Art finally
frees himself from Bé Cuma by a long voyage from which he
returns with the fair Delbchaem.

One other adventure, the *Sickness of Cuchulain*—which
again influenced Arthurian romance—must be mentioned. The
version we possess was clearly contaminated from two earlier
ones, since in the extant story the hero's wife at the beginning
of the story is Eithne In Gubai and at the end the more usual
Emer. The story opens with Cuchulain's capture of some

unusual birds for the women at the court. When all are distributed, none is left for his wife. He dreams that two women beat him, and when he awakes, he is unable to speak. A year later he is visited by Oengus and taken to the place of his dream. There he is asked to help Labraid against his enemies. In return he will gain the love of a lady, Fann. He sends his charioteer to investigate. Ultimately he does go to help Labraid and enjoys the love of Fann. His wife, Emer, however, is jealous, and Fann, though in love with him, leaves and joins the divine Mananánn, who gives Cuchulain and Emer a draught of forgetfulness. Again love is a strong motivation, but it is evident that the supernatural elements—a voyage to the other world and a love affair between a mortal and a spirit—are more important.

The voyages (*immrama*) do not differ substantially from the adventures, except that the stress is more on exotic travel than on dangerous expeditions to another world. The best known, the *Voyage of Mael Dúin*, dating perhaps from the eighth century, is probably the source for the voyage of St. Brendan. Mael Dúin sets out to punish the murderers of his father, Ailill Ochair, but he is swept out into the ocean, and a series of amazing adventures follows—ants as big as ponies, magic trees, a cat which burns to death those who attempt to steal the treasure it guards. A pilgrim living on a small island, where the souls of his relations also dwell, is fed miraculously by angels. Again there is an Isle of Maidens from which escape proves difficult, an island inhabited by the disciples of St. Brendan. Ultimately the voyagers return to their starting point.

Two other voyages are similar and indeed borrow from that just described. They are the *Immram Curaig Ua Corra* and the *Immram Snédgusa and Maic Riagla*. The latter is markedly Christian in tone and content and includes accounts of the history of salvation.

IRISH VISION STORIES

The most influential of the vision poems composed in Ireland were those written in Latin—the *Vision of Tundale* and the *Purgatory of St. Patrick*, for instance, which both give accounts of visits to the other world in the form of visions. In Irish we have the *Vision of St. Adamnán*, which was probably

written in the tenth century, although the saint himself was
abbot of Iona from 679 to 704. Like all such works, it employs
rich imagery to depict the delights of the world to come and
the glory of the heavenly kingdom. The reception of the just
souls and the purging of sin are described in detail. A second
section, which may be a later addition, tells of Hell and the
punishment of sinners, many of whom, however, are later
pardoned.

It should be noted here that there also exists a parody on
the visions—the *Vision of Mac Con Glinne*, of the twelfth
century. A wandering scholar and minstrel, Mac Con Glinne,
complains of his treatment at a monastery and is condemned
to be crucified. During the night before his execution he has
a vision, and the abbot announces that the telling of the vision
will cure King Cathal of Munster of gluttony. Accordingly,
the minstrel goes to the court and does indeed succeed in
tempting the devil of gluttony out of the king's mouth, for
which he is richly rewarded. The parody resides in the fact
that the poem is one long paean of praise to food, although
it is allegedly the demon of gluttony who has to be exorcized.

As we have seen, Irish literature, unlike that of all other
countries in western Europe, is largely written in prose, although verse was interspersed in many of the sagas. There
is no epic poetry, but a considerable amount of lyric poetry,
dating from early centuries, is extant. Although it first depended largely on alliteration and assonance for its effects, it
became a syllable-count form by the ninth century. The early
poems have the usual subjects—yearning for home, farewells,
laments for things past. Love poetry is largely absent. From
the time of the Norman conquest professional bards produced
most of the poetry, and that stress on virtuosity of form
which commonly accompanies such an occurrence is very
evident. Panegyric inevitably formed a large part of these
bards' output, since they were dependent on patronage. Some
of their names are known—Gilbride Macnamee (c. 1200),
Muireadach Albanach O'Daly (early thirteenth century), and
Angus O'Daly (c. 1300).

WELSH LITERATURE

Although there are numerous similarities of theme and even
of form between Welsh and Irish literature, the two are re-

markably different in the type of work which has survived. While the most important remains in Irish are undoubtedly the prose sagas, in Welsh the literature is dominated by non-narrative poetry. This phenomenon is clearly due to the preferences of the professional bardic class in the two cultures. Although there is no lack of prose tales in Welsh, it is evident that the production of the highly wrought poetical forms perfected in the early Middle Ages was by far the most esteemed occupation of the Welsh bard. The very complexity of the forms employed and the great subtlety of the style makes it extremely hard to convey to a reader who speaks no Welsh what the peculiar excellence of the poetry is. Summaries of the content convey little or nothing, and even poetical translations give no idea of the original form or of the effects the poet regarded as important.

It has already been pointed out earlier that much of the material found in the Arthurian romances can be traced with great probability to Welsh sources. Yet there are no romances in Welsh which are regarded by scholars as independent of French models. There are some prose stories which contain accounts of adventures of Arthur, but it is not the same king that we find in the romances. We are forced to conclude that the stuff of the Arthurian romances existed in oral form among the Welsh and was passed on to their neighbors without being written down in its homeland.

Early Poetry

Because of the dependence of the poets on patronage, the subjects of poetry in the early and late Middle Ages vary little. Eulogy of a chief, and especially of his deeds in battle, is always one of the principal themes. Coupled with this are the other forms of compliment—on his generosity, talents, and even prowess in love-making. As might be expected, the early poetry was simple in style compared with the complicated forms which were to come later. There is relatively little verbal ornament, and the poems are short. Stress is of little importance in this early verse. Syllable count is observed and there is a good deal of assonance and alliteration, often used to connect two lines as well as to produce effects within the line.

Although the number of poems in the *Book of Taliesin* (thirteenth century) actually written by a poet of that name is disputed—and it is quite certain that he did not write most of them—there can be little question that Taliesin was a poet of the sixth century whose fame was such that his name on a poem gave it distinction. The poems in praise of Urien, father of Owain (Yvain), may well be genuine. They typify the tendency of early poetry to celebrate contemporary events. In *Gododdin*, for example, the sixth-century poet Aneirin describes such an event (that of the attack by three hundred warriors of Mynyddawg on Catraeth) with much color and imaginative detail.

The isolation of the northern Celtic territories in 655 by the influx of Germanic invaders and general social and political upheaval led to a decline in poetry from the seventh to the tenth centuries. There are some elegies—on the death of Cadwallon (c. 630) and on Cynddylan ap Cyndrwyn. About 930 a poem called *The Prophecy of Britain* was written. It is not a real prophecy but a list of events that the poet hopes will happen. He is using prophecy as a patriotic rallying cry against the English. More gloomy are the stories told in the *englynion*, or conversations, which go under the name of Llywarch Hen. They are about heroes, usually men in sorrow and difficulties, and are often hard to follow. They may be verse conversations taken from mixed prose-verse narrations recited by the *cyfarwdd*, or traveling tale-tellers. The fate of Llywarch Hen himself is typical of a minstrel's life. Originally a chieftain, he lost all his sons and ended his life in poverty as the guest of another chief.

As poetry began to revive in the tenth century and later, it assumed many of the forms which we have seen in other countries. There was a great deal of didactic poetry in the form of sayings of a sententious or proverbial nature. There was description of nature which apparently is genuine and not simply a topos description to be attached to love poetry or the like. The landscape described is the local countryside. The most characteristic type of this period, however, is one we have already seen—the prophecy poem. The name of Myrddinn (Merlin) is associated with many of these works, and they take a form readily recognized to readers of later Arthurian romance, namely that a great national hero will return and restore the honor and independence of Wales. The political conditions of the time made such a theme highly popular, and there were other returning heroes besides Arthur.

Myrddinn's ability to prophesy was explained by a story that he took part in the battle of Arfderydd about 575 and went mad. Like many in this condition, he acquired the reputation of a prophet. There are references to contemporary events in several of the poems attributed to him, but most of them are simply appeals for patriotic action in the form of prophecy of the imminent destruction of the enemy. Such is the *Colloquy of Myrddinn and Gwenddydd His Sister* in a manuscript of about 1300. In many of the works the addition of Myrddinn's name is merely an introduction to give authority to a poem purporting to contain prophecies.

Court Poetry

After the first blows of the Norman conquest of England, Wales made a good recovery and for two centuries was ruled by her own princes. This period of relative stability brought with it more attention to poetry, more patronage, and a great increase in the number of court poets. Much of their work has survived, and we know the names of many bards of the twelfth and thirteenth centuries. Their principal themes were still the praise of chieftains, especially their prowess in war, and elegies on the great men of the past. They were not story-tellers, for they preferred to allude to events rather than describe them. Their language is consciously archaic because of a feeling of respect for the past. Thus their poetry is more remarkable for its technical excellence than for its content. Indeed, the forms used demanded great skill and long practice. In the earlier part of the period, the *awdl* or ode was the principal form used. Its distinguishing feature was the employment of the same rhyme throughout. When several were combined into a longer poem, the connection was indicated by the use of the rhyme word of one *awdl* in the first line of the *awdl* following. As in early Germanic poetry, there were many elaborate compounds, particularly descriptive compounds. As the period progresses, the meter becomes even more complicated and culminates in the use of *cynghanedd*— the employment in various ways of syllables which alliterate. They may alliterate internally in definite positions, as a kind of internal rhyme, they may alliterate in groups in two parts of the same line, or they may break the line into three with alliterative and rhyming patterns. These alliterative rules are combined also with a pattern of stresses. What we would call the strophic forms also had strict rules. The *cwydd* consists of seven-syllable lines in rhyming couplets, one of which has a masculine, the other a feminine ending. The *englyn* has four lines containing altogether thirty syllables with ten in the first line, six in the second, and seven in each of the last two. This has one end rhyme throughout, as does the *hir-a-thoddaid*, a strophe of six ten-syllable lines.

The great bulk of the court poetry was, as we have said, eulogy of princes. Gwalchmai (c. 1140–80) wrote in praise of Madoc ap Maredydd, Meillir (c. 1137) composed eulogies on Gryffydd ap Cynan. Cynddelw (second half of the twelfth century), called Prydydd Mawr, prince of poets, wrote on Owain Gwynedd, himself a poet, and others. Most famous of all the poetry of this kind was the *Hirlas of Owain*. A *hirlas* was a drinking cup, and the poet, whose full name was Owain ap Gryffydd ap Maredydd (late twelfth century) uses the occasion of a great banquet and drinking feast to enable each warrior to be celebrated. As the cupbearer brings the drinking horn to each warrior, we hear of the deeds he has performed. Nor are the dead forgotten, even though they are not at the feast. Although the work is basically the same as all the eulogies, it does introduce an element of drama which lends it additional interest.

The court poets do not celebrate love in the fashion of continental Europe. Gwalchmai wrote some poems which are eulogies of a lady rather than true love poetry. The convention of a messenger bearing love declarations is found in the works of Prydydd y Moch ("Poet of the Pigs"!), whose real name was Llywarch ap Llewelyn (c. 1173–1220), and Hywel ap Owain (second half of the twelfth century). The last-named wrote some real love poetry which appears to have true feeling, although the element of praise is still strong. Themes such as the cruelty of a mistress and the power of love appear more frequently toward the end of the thirteenth century and in the fourteenth, notably in the poetry of Iowerth Fychan, Gruffudd ap Dafydd ap Tudur, and Gruffudd ap Maredudd.

Dafydd ap Gwilym

In the literature of medieval Wales, as in that of Germany, France, and Italy, there is one lyric poet who is regarded as far outshining all others. Dafydd ap Gwilym was not a professional court poet but a nobleman who learned the craft of the bards from sheer interest and who so reshaped it that Welsh poetry ever since has depended largely on his techniques. We know very little of his life. He was born about 1320–30 of a family which was long resident in Cardiganshire and was in favor with the English kings. Where the poet himself lived is far from clear. He refers to places in the area of Llanbadarn Fawr and Emlyn, while later poets connect him with Dyfed and Glan Teifi. He probably died about 1380 and was buried at Strata Florida.

Dafydd was a master of all the complications in meter and language which had developed in the poetry of his time, but he carried them much further. It is largely because of the standards he set in the formal use of the *cynghanedd* (see p. 227) that its use became essential in the work of subsequent poets. Furthermore, he raised the status of the *cywydd*, so that it became the vehicle of the most serious poetry as well as that which was less formal. It is, however, the content of his work which most strikes the reader not trained in the complexities of Welsh verse. Like François Villon and Walther von der Vogelweide, he has an eye for the immediate details of nature and humanity, and is not afraid to introduce them into formal poetry. A great deal of his work consists of love poems. These are not the idealized poems of the troubadours but apparently reflect experience and pleasure in sexual attraction. Dafydd does not ponder on the nature of love or the cruelty of his mistress but describes in vivid detail the escapades in which he has taken part and the excitement of the pursuit. He reports his joy at success and his disappointment at failure, and is particularly interested in telling of the obstacles in his way and how he overcame them. Inevitably many of the conventional situations occur—the jealous husband and the physical separation. The pursuit of love is not so serious as to exclude an element of comedy, particularly in Dafydd's descriptions of the difficulties of reaching a mistress on dark nights on poor roads. On the other hand, as was natural in a highly trained bard, he often uses elaborate figures to express his relation to his mistress.

All critics agree that it is in his treatment of nature that Dafydd is at his best. Unlike most medieval poets, he described what he saw, not what was supposed to be there, and hence his descriptions are fresh and lively. Because of the formal restrictions of the verse he wrote, it was not easy for him to link the beauties of nature with those of his mistress, but many of the poems nonetheless contain well observed and sincerely felt descriptions which are a far cry from the formal *paysage idéal* of the majority of medieval lyrics.

The originality of his meters and content is matched by the striking qualities of his language. Many of the stylistic devices he uses are those of the older poetry, but he uses them with the freedom of a great artist. This is particularly true of his figures—metaphors and similes—which show his imaginative power especially. He is not content with mere rhetoric or conventional repetition of compounds.

Many of the poets in the fourteenth century seem to show the influence of Dafydd ap Gwilym, but as Thomas Parry remarks, it is hard to tell how much of the similarity is due to direct influence and how much to the fact that the poets lived in the same intellectual climate. It can, however, be stated with certainty that later Welsh poetry owes more to Dafydd than to any other man.

Later Medieval Poetry

The English occupation at the end of the thirteenth century brought profound changes to Wales, not least in the matter of patronage. The nobles were still the only people who could support professional bards, but they were no longer the independent chiefs of earlier times. The eulogy of nobles continued for some time to be the chief subject of bardic poetry, but it became more and more obvious that description of the great deeds of a chief in battle was not only anachronistic but rather ridiculous in an age when the only battles were minor squabbles among retainers. Thus a shift in emphasis occurred. One change was increasing technical complication, since the bards wished to make their craft difficult of access and to justify by their virtuosity the long years of training they had to undergo. Another was a change or at least modification in the qualities sought out for praise. Bloody descriptions of victories gave way to praise of generosity and wealth and the pleasures of a well-run court. Elegies on the dead praise the same qualities. Closely associated with such poetry is the poem in which the bard requests a gift. Such poems, as might be expected, soon developed a standardized pattern. The love poetry is almost equally formal. Here the new development in the fifteenth century was the detailed description of some feature of the lady's beauty. The best-known example of this type is Dafydd Nanmor's poem on Llio's hair. Elegies on dead ladies also became quite common. There is, too, a certain amount of political poetry, of which the principal theme is, naturally, opposition to the English and the hope of a revival of Welsh sovereignty.

It should be kept in mind that, whatever the subject of the poetry, it was the form which was important. The use of the *cwynghanedd*, the development of new forms of the *cwydd*, were of far more importance to bards obsessed with technical considerations than the discussion of new subjects, and it seems that even their formal meetings were, at first, more concerned with the settlement of technical problems of versification than with competition in poetry writing.

In conclusion the names of a few of the important poets of the later Middle Ages should be mentioned. Iolo Goch (c. 1340–98), Gruffudd Gryg (c. 1360–1410), and Gruffudd Llwyd (c. 1380–1420) were typical of the general run of poets of the period. Less so was Sion Cent (fl. c. 1400–30). His work contains many religious poems, and not only does he write in a less complicated style than most of his contemporaries but he actually attacks them as liars and flatterers. Indeed, he seems much closer in spirit and matter to the English and Continental poets of his day than to his fellow Welshmen.

Prose Works

Welsh literature, like that of Ireland, began to use prose for storytelling much earlier in its history than did the other countries in western Europe. This prose is better known outside Wales than is Welsh poetry, because its subject matter is often closely connected with the matter of Britain—the Arthurian legends. The most famous of the prose collections is that called the *Four Branches of the Mabinogi*, which is found, together with the other prose tales here discussed, in two manuscripts, the White Book of Rhydderch (c. 1300) and the Red Book of Hergest (c. 1400). The whole collection of stories is often called the *Mabinogion*, although the title is strictly speaking inaccurate, since it means "youthful careers," and many of the stories do not fit that description.

In their original form the *Four Branches* were obviously the story of the exploits of Pryderi, son of Pwyll, but they have been so altered in the course of time that the hero's exploits actually take up only a minor part of the present work. In the first branch Pwyll, prince of Dyfed, and his wife Rhiannon have a son Pryderi, who is taken away from them by enchantment but later returned to them when almost grown up. In the second branch Pryderi comes to Ireland to avenge the ill treatment given to Branwen by her husband Matholwch, king of Ireland. Matholwch ill-treats Branwen because her brother, Efnys ien, has insulted him. Only seven men, including Pryderi, survive, and Branwen dies of sorrow at the destruction she has caused. The third branch has nothing to do with Pryderi. It concerns enchantments laid on Manadwyn, Rhiannon's second husband, and his family, and the conditions for their removal. In the fourth branch the hero dies in a war fought over a concubine, Goewon.

There is a good deal of repetition here. The third branch has obvious parallels with the first, and many of the incidents are variants on others found elsewhere in the story. Characteristics which have been noted in Irish sagas are also present—the interference of the supernatural, shape changing, characters from the other world, vestiges of a matriarchal society, such as the close relation between uncle and nephew. The story of Pwyll and Arawn is a good example of the changes which have affected the earliest version. One of the most common motifs in primitive literature is the aid given to a mortal by a king from the other world in exchange for sleeping with the mortal wife. Pwyll and Arawn, king of Annwn, reverse these roles, for it is the mortal Pwyll who sleeps with Rhiannon in exchange for saving the kingdom of Arawn. The number of inserted incidents makes the *Four Branches of the Mabinogi* very hard to follow, but it is an exciting and well-told story, with the same imaginative qualities we found in the Irish sagas.

For Arthurian romance the story *Culhwch and Olwen* (c. 1100) is even more important than the collection already mentioned, for it shows us what might be called an "original" Arthurian story. The title is an indication of the frame in which the various stories are set rather than a true description of the content. Culhwch is doomed by a wicked stepmother to marry no one except Olwen, the daughter of a fierce giant, Ysbaddeden Pencawr, who is himself doomed to die if his daughter marries. The giant sets a large number of impossible tasks for Culhwch, fully expecting him to fail at them. But Culhwch obtains help from Arthur and his followers, and the bulk of the story consists of a description of the carrying out of the tasks. Not all of those set are fulfilled, but Culhwch kills the giant and marries Olwen. The individual tales are drawn from a wide range of subjects. Some are clearly nature myths, some are tales to explain the names of places; there is frequent repetition, whereby the same theme is handled by characters bearing different names. Animals play a considerable role, as does hunting. The tales are by no means all serious. There is much broad comedy in the telling and the work as a whole is far from being a saga of heroes. It should be noted that although Arthur is accompanied by men whose names are familiar in the romances—Gawain and Kay among others—there is no question here of chivalry or the Round Table. Arthur is little more than a brave tribal chieftain of unusual prowess.

Rhonabwy's Dream is a prose tale dating from the middle of the thirteenth century. It seems to be a satire on Arthurian stories; at least it treats many of the elements found in them in an amusing way. The storyteller has a dream in which he meets a knight, Iddawg Cordd Prydain. In company with him he meets Arthur, and the three go on together with their followers. While Arthur is playing a game with Owain ap Urien, his soldiers start to annoy some ravens which Owain has with him, and the king refuses to stop them. Later during a battle Owain's ravens attack Arthur's soldiers and not only injure them severely but prevent them from fighting so that Arthur is defeated. The idea of ravens on a battlefield is by no means unusual, but the author has used it in a very exaggerated and amusing manner. Similarly he parodies the custom of spun-out and lofty description of sumptuous castles and fine clothes. Even knightly prowess does not escape laughter.

The other stories in the *Mabinogion* show at least some influence from non-Welsh sources. The dragon story in *Lludd and Llefelys* is connected with Lludd, the mythical founder of London, indicating the influence of Geoffrey of Monmouth. *Maxen's Dream* draws on late classical history, mixing it a little in the process. There are also several romances in the *Mabinogion*—*Geraint and Enid*, the *Lady of the Fountain*, and *Peredur*—which correspond approximately with the *Erec*, *Yvain*, and *Perceval* of Chrétien de Troyes. These are romances, not stories, and many critics believe that they are actually based on the works of the French author. Others are of the opinion that they drew from other, though similar, sources. In any event, it is clear that they took their structure and milieu from Continental, not Welsh ideas.

Welsh prose also offers translations of some well-known works. Geoffrey of Monmouth's *History of the Kings of Britain* was put into Welsh, apparently on three different occasions, and several copies antedating the fourteenth century survive. A Welsh version of the French *Queste del Saint Graal*, in which the religious element is very marked, was done in the fourteenth century. The Latin account of Roland and Charlemagne which goes by the name of *Pseudo-Turpin* was translated into Welsh about 1270, and a little later versions of the *Chanson de Roland* and *Pèlerinage de Charlemagne* were written. Several of the popular English romances, as well as such favorites as the story of the seven sages, also appeared in Welsh.

There is very little chronicle history in Welsh but a mass of religious literature in the vernacular. Very little of it is at all original. It consists of translations and adaptations of such well-known works as the apocryphal Gospel of Nicodemus, of *St. Patrick's Purgatory*, and of parts of the Bible.

The scope of Welsh literature is relatively narrow. The prose tales are interesting, but the really important contribution is the highly wrought bardic poetry, whose complicated techniques are so much the mark of a specialized professional class. There is no epic poetry, no drama, no original romance. The reason for this lies at least partly in the fact that in Wales there developed a truly native poetry influenced hardly at all by the models of Greece and Rome (although there were many classically educated men in Wales). Its great contribution to literature—the material of the Arthurian romances—was made unconsciously.

Literature of the Iberian Peninsula

GENERAL

SPAIN HAD BEEN one of the most literate provinces of the Roman empire. A large number of the most famous Latin writers of the post-Augustan period were Spaniards, among them Quintilian, Martial, and Prudentius. Like the remainder of western Europe, the area produced little secular literature in the Visigothic period of invasions, and before any recovery could take place, most of the Iberian peninsula was conquered by the Arabs.

Thus social conditions in Spain before the twelfth century were hardly favorable to the production of literature in Spanish. With constant border warfare there was little leisure for writing. Yet in the Arab part of Spain, literature in Spanish was written. More and more Arabic lyrics, dating from the eleventh century, are being discovered, in which there are Spanish or at least Romance refrains. The poems in which such refrains are found are called *zejels* and the refrain itself a *jarcha*. Furthermore, some of these poems, although originally simple dance songs, were developed into sophisticated poetry and have many elements in common with the works of the troubadours, especially with the dawn song. It is very hard to say whether this Arabic poetry, with its vernacular refrains, had any direct influence on Provençal lyric. Again, we have an example of parallel developments in different parts of the western world. It should be noted in passing that rhymed, stressed Hebrew lyric also developed in Spain and may well have been transferred to southern France.

THE CID

The first work that we know of written completely in Spanish was also the greatest work of the Spanish Middle Ages— *Poema del mio Cid*, the poem of the Cid, written about 1140. The word "cid" is a variant of the Arabic "sidi" or lord, and is the title given to Rodrigo Díaz de Vivar, a historical person. Although the poem is a survivor from a number of epics which were inspired by the liberation of Castile and Leon from the threat of Arabic attack, it is not a poem on the wars between Christian and Saracen. In this respect, and in many others, it differs sharply from the *Chanson de Roland*. A considerable number of extant prose chronicles tell of the events of this period, and these accounts can be compared with the poem. They correspond to a very large degree.

The work was probably composed by a Mozarab—a Christian born under Arab rule—from the district of Medina-celi, a district the poem indicates the author knew very well. The story begins with the banishment of the Cid—for actions of which we know only from the chronicles. According to these sources, he had been sent by King Alfonso to collect tribute from the Moorish king of Seville. Learning that this king was being attacked by the king of Granada and some Leonese nobles headed by Count García Ordóñez, he fights the invaders, defeats them, and insults García by plucking his beard. The count persuades King Alfonso to banish him.

The poem as it exists (in a single manuscript of 1307) has lost its first leaf but begins with the banishment, a melancholy scene in which the great warrior can obtain nothing in the town of Burgos and has to take leave of his wife, Ximena, and his two daughters, Elvira and Sol. He is penniless, but his faithful warriors are still with him, and one of them, Martín Antolínez, neatly arranges a loan of six hundred marks, plus a little commission for himself, on two chests allegedly containing the Cid's gold but in fact filled with nothing but sand. With this the soldiers set out on a freebooting expedition. Castejon is taken, with great treasure, Alcocer is captured by a trick, and then a new army of Moors is defeated outside its walls. After more victories the Cid meets and defeats the count of Barcelona and captures him. The count refuses to eat, but the generosity of the Cid prevails—he agrees to release the count if he will give up his hunger strike, and the count relents.

Meanwhile the Cid's army is growing and he is plying the king with presents. He hears of the weakness his three-year ravage has caused among the Moors, calls for volunteers from Castile and Leon, and, after a nine-month siege, captures Valencia. More successes and more presents soften the king. He allows the Cid's wife and daughter to join him and proclaims an amnesty for his supporters. Yusuf, king of Morocco, is the Cid's next victim. Count García and the party of Carrión who represent the Leonese aristocracy bitterly opposed to the Cid now see that the king's favor is shifting.

They decide to ask for the two daughters of the Cid in marriage for two Leonese princes, Diego and Fernando. An embassy is sent, a meeting arranged at the Tagus river, and the Cid and Alfonso are reconciled. Although the Cid is not too happy about the proposed marriages, he yields to the king, and they take place.

The cowardice of the new sons-in-law is revealed when the Cid's lion escapes and they flee in terror. It is further shown in renewed battle with the Moors (an event which has to be reconstructed from the chronicles, since there is a leaf missing here in the manuscript of the poem). The Moorish king Bucár is killed by the Cid, and the booty is huge. Diego and Fernando, mocked for their lack of courage in the battle, now decide to take their wives to their own territories, or rather to pretend to do so. On the way they are well received by a faithful Moorish friend of the Cid but are prevented only by accident from repaying his kindness with treachery. In camp the next night they send their retinue ahead, then beat their wives senseless and leave them for dead. Fortunately, one of the Cid's warriors, Félix Muñoz, has followed, and he finds the badly injured women and takes them back to their father. An appeal is made to King Alfonso for a court of justice. The court is held in Toledo, where the Cid appears in all his splendor. First he demands back the swords, Colada and Tizón, which he had given to his sons-in-law. When they have been returned, he asks for the dowry, and judgment is given in his favor. Then he demands single combat with the princes for the dishonor his daughters have suffered at their hands. The princes say that the women were not fit for them, and a fierce dispute arises. The king decrees single combat between the two princes and two of the Cid's best warriors, Pedro Bermudez and Martín Antolínez. Before it takes place, however, messengers arrive from the rulers of Navarre and Aragón to ask for the two daughters of the Cid in marriage. He accepts, thus gaining even more honor. The combat is set for three weeks later at Valencia. The result is a foregone conclusion. The two princes are ignominiously defeated, and a third supporter of the Carrión party, Asur Gonsález, is defeated by Muño Gustioz, another of the Cid's retainers. The Cid's honor is fully restored, and the poem ends.

It is not hard to see the resemblances between this poem of 3,730 fourteen-syllable lines and the other national epics.

The hero is a hard-hitting fighter, reveling in battle, very concerned for his honor. He is noble and generous to his friends and to defeated enemies, but implacable to those who are treacherous to him. He is tender to his wife and daughters but otherwise unconcerned with love. He is loyal to his king, provided he is fairly treated. The character he most resembles in the *chansons de geste* is William of Orange.

Yet the differences are equally apparent. There is little idealization of relationships, no religious zeal (the Moors are attacked for plunder), no magic or miracles, no pervasive motif of blood guilt and revenge. The Cid is by far the most realistic of medieval epic heroes. He fights for plunder and honor. He is concerned about his social status, is prepared to bribe his king with presents. The fact is that the historical Cid was, even as in the poem, a small knight making a name for himself by his deeds. He also shows a great respect for law, particularly when he can use it to his own advantage.

The Cid is essentially a happy poem. Everything comes out well at the end. Friends remain friends, enemies are defeated, riches accumulate. It is a comedy in the medieval sense of the word and thus very different from most medieval epics.

The style is very straightforward and for that reason very effective. No obvious attempts are made at poetical description, but the clever use of detail and personal observation are equally effective. *The Cid* is very close to history (its hero died in 1099, only forty years before the estimated date of the poem's composition), and this fact is evident throughout. It has the air of great events well told. It was the only one of the no doubt numerous *cantares de gesta* which survived. Of the others we have only prose redactions.

ROMANCEROS

One other type of narrative poetry deserves mention—the *romancero* or ballad. These reached their greatest importance in the sixteenth century, but the events they celebrate date from the mid-fourteenth. They are brief descriptions of historical events, usually a few hundred lines long at most, and they were transmitted orally. The earliest are those of the mid-fourteenth century, about Pedro the Cruel; the best known are those about the frontier wars with the Moors. Another kind was based on older historical material from the time of the Cid, while yet others drew on foreign material such as the Arthurian cycle. It should be noted that the ballads were sung and had some affinities with lyric poetry.

Ramon Llull (c. 1233–1315) wrote in Catalan a poem, *Blanquerna*, which is almost a parody of the *romancero*. The adventures of its young hero consist of the rescue of persons in danger or in sin, and this end is achieved by persuasion. So successful is his way of life that the hero becomes Pope, only to lay down his honors and turn hermit. Clearly this poem is an allegory of the active life in the service of religion carried to its highest point and succeeded by the life of contemplation. The poem is much more successful than most allegories because the author, like Langland (see p. 196), had a sharp eye for the real world.

Arthurian romance in the usual sense fared badly in Spain. Such remains as exist are considered under the section on prose. Other romances include one on Alexander from the thirteenth century and an Apollonius story.

LYRIC POETRY

Early Forms

We have already noticed the existence of fragments of Spanish poetry in Arabic verses. Besides these there was undoubtedly a great deal of popular poetry which flowered later as the *villancico*, which is related to the *zejel* already mentioned, and consists of a theme stanza followed by several narrative stanzas. The earliest *extant* remains of medieval lyric, however, are from Galicia and Portugal and are based on the poetry of the troubadours. Such poetry was of interest largely because of its prestige, and it created a class of *juglares* who sang songs at court. They in turn began to interest themselves in the local popular songs, and they produced the *cantigas de amigo*, songs about a lover, which were put in the mouths of women. They use assonance forms and are often in the "ribbon" form of dance tunes—repetition of a line with slight variation, followed by two more with slight variation. The more sophisticated of these dance songs often play sound repetition against sense repetition. The *zejel*, in an adapted form, was often used for sacred as well as profane poetry— King Alfonso the Wise of Castile wrote four hundred songs to the Virgin in this form, using the Galician dialect, which, throughout the thirteenth century, was regarded as the correct language for lyric poetry. The form was known in Spanish as *estribote*, and it closely resembles the rondeau and ballade forms in French.

Archpriest of Hita

By far the most important lyric poet of the Spanish Middle Ages was Juan Ruiz, the archpriest of Hita. He was born near Madrid about 1280. He became archpriest of Hita, not far from Alcalá, his birthplace, and composed a great deal of lyric poetry, which he collected into a book. In 1343 he was imprisoned in Toledo by the archbishop, for reasons unknown, and while in prison he revised his collection. He probably died about 1350. The book is called *Libro de buen amor* ("Book of True Love"), a title which is susceptible of various interpretations. It may mean true love, or true companionship, or good as opposed to evil love. If it means the last of these, it is definitely ironical. The poet proclaims that it is his intention to show the dangers of worldly love (*loco amor*) and thus inspire his readers to *buen amor*, or love of God. The distinction was a common one—we have already seen it in Veldeke's *Enide* (p. 127)—and the archpriest's words sound remarkably like those of Andreas Capellanus when he apologizes for the content of the first two of his three books on love. Whatever the poet's intention, this is undeniably a superb achievement. After a prayer and a couple of songs to the Virgin, he proceeds to tell in a series of lyric cycles the story of his own love adventures. The forms he uses are varied. One of the commonest is *cuaderna vía*, a four-line monorhyme strophe, each line with fourteen syllables. He used many others also, both learned and popular.

The archpriest assigns to love the same qualities as Andreas. Love ennobles a man and makes him socially better. Yet the archpriest sees love everywhere, not just (as Andreas did) among the nobles. His first two affairs are unsuccessful because of his inexperience, and after a third failure his reproaches conjure up the god of love himself, who advises him to find a good go-between. In his next effort, therefore, he employs an old woman called Trotaconventos to help him lay siege to a widow, Dona Endrina. Although he is successful this time, it cannot be said that the episode shows him in a very savory light. The story has been traced back to a medieval Latin play, but its theme is too common to warrant any final conclusions about sources.

After another failure, the priest goes wandering, and this introduces a string of encounters with female cowherds, each of them uglier than the last, all but one enormously strong and determined to use the poet for her lust. The situation is exactly the reverse of that in the *pastourelle*, for here it is the woman who is powerful and who uses force to obtain her desires. In each episode there is a narrative and a sung portion, the sung lyric being a *cantica de serrana*, or pastoral lyric. There can be little doubt of the poet's intention to pour scorn on the conventional form of the *pastourelle* imported from France, and the result is very funny, even if (deliberately) crude. The mock *pastourelles* are followed by a mock allegory. Gluttony (Don Carnal) is opposed by Lent (Dona Quaresma). After a good supper, the don is unable to resist the dona, but until Lent is over, she resists him. After Lent is over, however, it is a different matter, and Love and Gluttony enter Toledo in triumph, chanting "*Te, amorem, laudamus*" and bearing an image of Venus. It is not really difficult to understand why the archpriest got into trouble with the ecclesiastical authorities.

The poet's last two loves are unsuccessful also. First, he loves a nun, but she insists on remaining chaste and in any case dies soon after. Nor does he have any better luck in his pursuit of a Moorish girl. The book ends, again with songs to the Virgin, after the poet has described the death of Trotaconventos. Clearly the book is, in a way, exemplary. The poet pursues worldly love but it does him little good. Most of his affairs end badly or are discreditable. Sensual love hardly seems worthwhile, and in his encounters with the cowherds it is farcical.

Irony pervades the book. It treats of much more than love, for the poet's format gives him the opportunity to comment brilliantly on the life of his day. The style is relatively simple, generally free from elaborate imagery, and, at times, monotonous. *Libro de buen amor* is in many respects typical of the late Middle Ages. It is realistic and humorous, yet at the same time serious. The character of the author and in particular his attitude to love and other matters is neither clear nor consistent. He tries to give the impression that he took the world as he found it, and to a great extent he succeeds.

The work of the archpriest is the last poetry of the *juglares* which has come down to us. From the mid-fourteenth century on the lyric poetry of Spain is of a different kind. It is formal court poetry, based on Galician and Provençal models, and it is contained in an anthology, composed about 1445, called *Cancionero de Baena*. The poet who had the greatest reputation in his day was Alfonso Alvarez de Villasandino (c. 1345–1425), but his work has little appeal now. The verse form used by these poets is called the *arte mayor*, a strophe of eight fourteen-syllable lines. The subjects are those general ones of love and social satire which abound in the poetry of contemporary France.

Later Lyric Poetry

Another school of poets, of whom the most important were Micer Francisco Imperial (fl. c. 1400) of Seville and Juan de Mena (1411–56) of Cordova, sought to import into Spain features from the Italian lyric, including the new imagery and rhythms of Dante and Petrarch. They were only partly successful, but their influence is shown in the work of the best of the late medieval lyric poets, Inigo López de Mendoza, marquis of Santillana (1398–1458). His father and many other relations were also poets. The introduction to his works is a valuable account of Spanish poetry up to his own time—seen, naturally, from his own point of view. He wrote allegorical and didactic poetry as well as lyrics, but the works for which he is best known are ten pastoral poems and a few lyrics. Although some of his pastorals show the same scenes as those found in the poetry of the archpriest (by whom he was clearly influenced), he never allows his poetry to degenerate into coarse description. Much of his work is purely formal, with the characteristic melancholy inherited from the troubadours, but it is worth noting also that he was the first poet known to have attempted the sonnet in Spanish.

Jorge Manrique (died 1479) was another poet from the nobility. He wrote much, but is famous for one poem—the *Coplas*, on the death of his father. This elegiac poem of forty strophes, each of four octosyllabic couplets with a half line between each couplet, grieves for the death of the poet's father by listing all the fine things which were once splendid and now are gone. Manrique's *Coplas* strikes with great effectiveness that note of plaintive grief for what is past which appears often in fifteenth-century poetry.

One poet who wrote in Catalan should be mentioned here, Auzias March (1397–1459). His attitude toward love is not unlike that of the early troubadours, except that his mistress has yielded, and his ideal love is gone. He laments it bitterly. His imagery shows a typical fifteenth-century ambivalence—death and horror on the one hand and joy in life on the other.

We may end this section on poetry by going back to the work of Gonzalo de Berceo (c. 1198–after 1246), the greatest writer of saints' lives and of works to the Virgin. He wrote verse lives of Santo Domingo de Silos, San Millán, and Santo Oria, all saints of his own area. His poetry on the Virgin consists of three pieces, *Praise*, *Mourning*, and *Miracles*. The last is handled allegorically. Much of the description in these poems is devoted to the everyday life of the saints, and it is to the expressive style in which they are written that they owe their reputation.

PROSE WORKS

The history of medieval Spanish prose begins with a great event—the command of Alfonso X, the Wise, of Castile (1221–84) to collect materials from all sources and write a general chronicle of the history of Spain. It is a superb achievement and was continued by subsequent rulers. One of those who helped in the continuation, Juan Manuel (1282–1349), is also famous for his collection of prose tables called *The Count Lucanor*. Much of the material in this work is from Arabic sources, and the method of presentation is not unlike that of an earlier Spaniard, Petrus Alfonsi, in its posing of questions which are answered by stories.

Arthurian romances appeared in prose in Spain. A chronicle based on the work of Geoffrey of Monmouth had been made as early as the late twelfth century, and the same material was incorporated into the history commissioned by Alfonso the Wise. The story of Tristan was put into Castilian in the early fourteenth century (from French prose), and a second version dates from the fifteenth. The Grail story received considerable attention. There was a Portuguese *Josep Abaramantia* in 1313, a Catalan *Storia del Sant Grasel* in 1380, and the French *Estoire* was translated by Juan Vivas in the late thirteenth century. Lancelot is represented, for example, by the *Lançarote* of the mid-fourteenth century.

Although it is easy to show the influence of French and Italian literature on that of the Iberian peninsula, the fact remains that the poetry of the area stayed outside the main stream of western European development. None of the other national epics is really like *The Cid*, no lyric poet is like the archpriest of Hita. There is always a realistic flavor which is foreign to most of the works produced, at least in the high Middle Ages, in France and Germany.

Drama

CONNECTION WITH THE CLASSICS

IT IS EASIER to discuss medieval drama as a European than as a national phenomenon. There are, of course, considerable variations in the drama of the various western European countries, but the themes treated and the general form of the drama are so much alike that a discussion by countries would involve a great deal of repetition.

The Greek and Latin drama of classical antiquity had little effect on medieval European drama. The Greek classics were known only by name and even then to few people. Manuscripts of the works of Plautus, Terence, and Seneca were available, but only Terence was widely read. His popularity was due to the purity of his Latin, and the general feeling was that the subject matter of his works was something to be tolerated, not admired. It is clear from the remarks of such writers as Isidore of Seville (seventh century) that the idea of drama performed on a stage was alien to the Middle Ages. They thought of the drama in terms of recitation by one or more persons. The terms "comoedia" and "tragoedia" have no reference to comedy or tragedy in the modern sense but meant respectively a story that begins sadly and ends happily and one that ends in sorrow after a happy beginning.

There were a few medieval imitations of Roman comedy. Vitalis of Blois wrote, probably in the eleventh century, a *Geta* and an *Aulularius*, and the twelfth-century *Babio* is a not unworthy attempt at the classical theme of the miserly old man and his discomfiture. Hroswitha of Gandersheim, a nun, wrote in the tenth century a number of works which she describes in a preface as being a kind of counterblast to Terence. She wished to present pieces which, while in Terentian form, would substitute the religious and didactic for the immoral. All her plays are incidents in the lives of holy men and women, and in particular the resistance of Christian virgins and their martyrdom. The milieu is frequently the period of persecutions under the Empire. Actually the "plays" are simply stories in dialogue and lack any true dramatic force. It is ridiculous to call them "imitations" of Terence. *Dulcitius* is the best known, because of a funny scene in which a would-be seducer is deluded into embracing dirty pots in a kitchen in

the belief that they are girls. The works are interesting chiefly
because of the light they throw on the meaning of the word
"drama" for Hroswitha and her contemporaries.

POPULAR DRAMATIC FESTIVALS

There can be little doubt that some forms of popular drama
were alive throughout the medieval period. The mime, a form
of comedy very popular under the Empire, was banned by the
Christian emperors but almost certainly flourished surrepti-
tiously and continued, in simplified form, in the hands of the
strolling players. It is quite certain that popular dramatic performances were given at certain seasons. The majority of
these had their origins in pagan rites such as the midwinter
and spring festivals. The same scenes and characters always
appeared, and the emphasis was on low comedy, with im-
provised dialogue. Such plays are still performed in many parts
of Europe, and they undoubtedly had great influence on the
development of popular comedy and on the insertion of comic
scenes into the religious plays.

Although these popular influences were important and, in
the later Middle Ages, perhaps decisive for the emergence of
comedy, it is doubtful whether any drama could have emerged
in the Middle Ages without the help of the church. Painstaking
research, particularly by Karl Young, has accumulated a great
many texts of works which can, in one way or another, be
called dramatic. These were associated with various feasts of
the church, principally those at Christmas and Easter. They
come from many different countries, but by far the greatest
concentrations are in northern France, Germany, Austria,
and northern Italy. There is one early collection of tropes
from England but otherwise very little. Spain, the Scandinavian countries, and southern Italy are also thinly represented.
It is hard to date these works. Some of them are found in relatively late manuscripts, yet clearly represent an early stage of
development. Often the same piece must have been performed
unchanged for centuries in one region, whereas in another the
simple forms developed rapidly into more complex "dramas."
The summary below traces the course of the development of
the "liturgical" drama as reconstructed from extant works. It
should be clearly understood that we cannot document this
development in any one place and that it varied considerably
according to local circumstances.

LITURGICAL DRAMA

The term "liturgical" is in itself misleading. The verses
which ultimately developed into the drama were never, strictly
speaking, part of the liturgy. They were tropes, short passages
of Latin prose originally designed as mnemonics for the performance of musical additions to a service, either Matins or
the Mass. Later these tropes developed an independent existence. The most important of them for the development of the
drama was a trope inserted before the Introit of the Mass on
Easter Sunday. In its simplest form this trope consists of a
question by one half of the choir: "Whom do you seek,
women?" and the answer "Jesus of Nazareth, the crucified."
Then comes the statement that He is risen. In these early
tropes the music was far more important than the words.
Soon, however, the tropes were expanded, first by the addition
of more words and then by new scenes. The first to be added
was a scene in which the Apostles hear of the Resurrection
and run to spread the news. In the third scene Mary Magdalene meets Christ in the garden. These three tropes form
the basis of the office called Visit to the Sepulchre, of which
a large number of versions exist in manuscripts from the tenth
century on. This office was conducted after Matins on Easter
Sunday, and, being separate from the liturgy, it could be
dramatized and provided with properties and costumes which
would have been inappropriate to a normal service. There
were other ceremonies that included forms of dramatic representation—the Laying Down of the Cross on Good Friday
and the Elevation of the Cross on Easter Sunday.

The subsequent development of the Easter play involved
earlier events closer to the Crucifixion. The material for these
new scenes was drawn in part from the Bible but even more
from the apocryphal Gospel of Nicodemus. From the latter
came the details of the scenes in which guards were set at the
grave of Christ and stricken down by the angel and of those
in which Christ descends into Hell and releases the patriarchs.
Many Latin plays contain some of these scenes. Many also
incorporate comic elements which had little relevance to the
Easter story, among them the boasting of the soldiers at the
tomb and their subsequent discomfiture and the scene in which
the spice merchant sells unguents to the three Marys. This
character, innocuous in his first appearance in a play from
Prague, developed into a full-fledged broad comedy type, who

quarreled with his wife and was deceived by her and an assistant named Rubin, a rascal even worse than his master. Such scenes as the latter are borrowed from the repertoire of strolling players and have little *raison d'être* in the Easter plays. Nevertheless, they were immensely popular, and when the Easter plays began to be performed in the vernacular such scenes dominated the action.

There are relatively few Easter plays written entirely in Latin. Examples exist in the Fleury playbook and from Tours in France and Benediktbeuern and Klosterneuburg in German-speaking countries. The last-named, in particular, has stage directions which indicate a real attempt at stage effects. Most of the good Easter plays are written in either French or German or in a mixture of Latin and a vernacular. Such mixed plays are found in manuscripts from Origny, Trier, and Wolfenbüttel which date from the fourteenth and fifteenth centuries. There are plays where most of the dialogue is in a vernacular with some Latin lines "retained" for the serious "core" of the play. A good example of this type is the Innsbruck play (manuscript of 1391, play of the mid-fourteenth century). The play begins with the request to Pilate to set a watch on the grave. Then follow the scenes with the soldiers and Christ's descent into Hell. In the scenes in Hell one of the main characteristics of the vernacular Easter play appears —the use of the devils as comic figures to harass such unpopular figures as butchers, bakers, and shoemakers. The devils, while horrifying, are usually represented in broadly humorous terms in the Easter plays. More serious treatment of their functions is reserved for the longer Passion plays and mysteries. The Innsbruck play also contains a full-length comedy of the spice merchant, here a quack who sells medicines, his wife Antonia, and their servant Rubin. By far the best of the vernacular Easter plays is that from Redentin. It follows the usual pattern, but after the Harrowing of Hell the devils have a conference on how the place can be restocked. The result is a long and funny scene in which one rascal after another is brought down and made to confess his misdeeds. There are, of course, numerous topical references. The play is in Low German and dates from 1465. *La Seinte Resurrecion* is an Anglo-Norman Easter play written in the twelfth century. It is early and lacks the vigor of the German plays.

The development of the Easter play is closely paralleled by

that of the Christmas play. There were tropes for the adoration of the shepherds and the coming of the wise men, and these became short dramatic offices called respectively the Office of the Shepherds and the Office of the Star. Herod was a normal king in such early plays as that from Nevers, but he later developed the cruel, ranting personality that appears, for example, in the play from Compiègne (eleventh century). The slaughter of the innocents was often dramatized in a separate office, the Order of Rachel. All these, together with prophet plays, were put together into the largest and most important of the Christmas plays, that from Benediktbeuern (thirteenth century). In general, however, the Christmas plays were less popular and less important than those at Easter. Only in England, where they were incorporated into the long craft cycles, did they become important drama.

It is natural for a modern reader to look for those things in a drama which seem to him to be dramatic and significant. Thus he observes the low comedy, the realism, the satire and tends to pass rather quickly over the religious material. Such a view of medieval drama is mistaken. It cannot be too strongly emphasized that the dramatic representations already discussed, and the longer mystery plays, were primarily religious in character. Their purpose was to demonstrate and reinforce Christian beliefs, and many of them were highly sophisticated in their presentation of specific doctrines and in their setting up of dramatic situations which allowed the discussion of articles of faith. Any comic and realistic elements were designed to further this effect. Comedy tends to appear in works in which the theology is less sophisticated, but there can be no valid generalization on the subject. Realism often has the object of intensifying the reaction of the audience to events in religious history and in particular to the agony and crucifixion of Christ. The drama has, in fact, much in common with the popular sermon, and it is this which made it hard for the religious drama to develop into anything resembling, for instance, Greek drama. Suspense, rising and falling action, and character drawing are difficult when so much is predetermined by the Bible and the Apocrypha and when the interpretation is a matter of dogma. Works of great power were produced, but the power came from the religion which lay behind the works.

PASSION PLAYS

It is in the Passion plays that medieval religious drama attains its greatest heights. The term "Passion play" is used very generally and often includes the long mystery plays that covered a great deal more than Christ's Passion. Very little survives of any Latin Passion plays (the only extant one is a fragment from Sulmona), and it is unlikely that the Passion plays developed along the same lines as the Easter plays. Since virtually all Passion plays are in the vernacular, it is probable that their development began when the Easter and Christmas plays, originally sung in the church, were moved outside because of the intrusion of scenes which were unsuitable for performance in the church building.

The extant Passion plays do indeed dramatize the events of Christ's Passion, and a few of them do only this, except that the Resurrection is always included along with the Crucifixion. But most plays cover at least the Incarnation and ministry in addition, and many begin with the fall of Lucifer and end on Judgment Day. Thus even the vague term "mystery" is better than Passion play. The exact origin of the term "mystery," as applied to medieval drama, is obscure. It may come from the Latin *ministerium* (service) or be connected with the Middle English word meaning "specialized craft." Both English and French use the term to mean "a long play on the history of salvation."

The expansion of the Passion play can be traced fairly clearly in France. The *Passion of the Jongleurs* was a narrative of the events of the Passion written before 1300 and was used in several later dramatic works. The *Palatinus Passion* has scenes from the entry into Jerusalem until the Resurrection. The work expands considerably on the scenes of the Crucifixion by introducing such characters as the smith who forged the nails and the torturers Cayn and Huitacelin. Their dialogue and reactions bear chief witness to such dramatic talent as the author possesses. The Harrowing of Hell scene also provides many comic possibilities. The *Palatinus* dates from the mid-fourteenth century. The other great French mysteries are almost a hundred years later and show a corresponding advance in technique. The *Mystère de la Passion* of Arnoul Greban is the greatest of them. Its author was choirmaster at Notre Dame, although he later resigned the position to have more time for his own studies. His *Mystère de la Passion* was very popular and was performed in differing versions in many places, if we may judge by the number of varying extant manuscripts. The prologue outlines the problem of redemption and the conflict of justice and mercy, and then, after a brief glance at the Old Testament, there follow the scenes from the New Testament that appeared in the earlier Passion plays. Great care is taken to bring out in monologue and dialogue the theological implications of various scenes. For example, Judas and Mary Magdalene are juxtaposed, the one an example of the elected man lost by his sin and still more by his inability to believe that God could still forgive him, the other a sinner who acknowledges her wretchedness and is saved by faith. Greban's characters have considerable dimension, and the poetry of his work, including interspersed lyrics, is of a high order. His devotion to the Virgin is apparent throughout, and her role as interceder and mother of mercy is stressed.

Eustache Mercadé's *Passion d'Arras* (before 1440) is 250,000 lines long and required four days to perform. It covers the same ground as Greban's work but makes more use of allegorical figures. Further, it bears the mark of its author's legal training in its careful balancing of the sins of the world against the act of redemption of Christ. The *Sémur Passion* (before 1488) deals with the whole history of salvation, from the Creation through the Old Testament and the prophets to the life of Christ, the Resurrection and Ascension. It took two days to perform.

The French plays were performed on a large stage, with fixed areas (*sedes, mansiones*) for Heaven, Hell, the earthly Paradise, the seats of the prophets, Pilate's palace, etc. There was also a central area in which characters from the different *sedes* or *mansiones* could meet. Thus there were no exits or entrances in the modern sense of the term. Such a stage was not merely a matter of convenience, still less the result of an unsophisticated technique. It represented the eternal nature of the universe, where Heaven, Earth, and Hell, the past, the present, and the future all existed together in the eyes of God. A professional *maître de jeu* or director seems to have put on the plays, often at the request of a city council. He was responsible for finding and casting actors, providing costumes, and producing the play. In all probability he often owned the script of a particular mystery.

It is not clear whether the same system was used in Ger-

many. It is, however, certain that individual towns produced
plays, often at fairly regular intervals, and that they used a
similar type of stage. The important German Passion plays all
date from the fifteenth century, although they continued to
be performed well into the sixteenth in areas which remained
Catholic. In general the German plays are less well constructed
than the French, and their treatment of theological questions
is less refined. On the other hand, there is a greater stress on
scenes of comedy and crude realism. The spice-merchant
scene is longer and funnier than in plays from other countries,
and the devils are given a larger comic role. The plays from
Frankfurt and Alsfeld are very much alike and date from the
last decade of the fifteenth century. The *Heidelberg Passion*
uses Old Testament scenes to prefigure events in the New Testament. There are other Passion plays from Bozen, Lucerne,
and Erlau. The best known and probably best constructed is
the Donaueschingen Passion play (end of the fifteenth century), which stresses, as does Greban's *Mystère*, the contrast
between Mary Magdalene and Judas and the importance of
faith and hope.

ENGLISH CYCLE PLAYS

The French and German Passion plays were thus long, involved works whose intention was essentially didactic, namely,
to represent the salvation of man through Christ and the duties
of a Christian to his faith. The same ends were sought in the
English mystery plays but by rather different methods. The
extant religious plays from England are mostly cycle plays
performed by members of the trade guilds. The works must
have passed through a long process of development to have
attained the form in which they are extant, yet they are still
of very uneven execution. Some scenes are masterly in construction, some still very crude. The unevenness is due at
least in part to the fact that certain guilds seem, at a relatively
early period, to have obtained the "rights" to a particular
biblical scene, and its presentation thereafter would depend
on the vigor of those in the guild who were responsible for
its production, on the writers they used, and the amount of
money they spent. We have lists of the guilds who were responsible for the different scenes, and there can be no doubt that
there was much competition between them—but not neces-

sarily in good writing. Costumes and general magnificence in
staging were at least as important.

The division of a play between different groups hardly made
for unity of construction. Nor did the method of presentation.
The plays were much influenced by the ceremonies at the feast
of Corpus Christi, which were designed to show the holy ob-
jects on procession. The English mysteries were processional,
and hence each scene had to be transported on a vehicle to
various parts of the city. Since a considerable interval might
elapse between scenes, it was necessary to have some form of
narrative to tie the scenes together. Inevitably, it is the individual plays (or scenes) which are memorable in the English
mystery plays, not the plays as a whole. We tend to remember
the cycles as containing such and such plays. Yet the intention
was basically the same as that of the Continental playwrights,
that is, to present the history of salvation and theological
doctrine in a form palatable to the uneducated.

The English cycle encompasses the whole history of salvation from the Fall to the Last Judgment, but the stress is different from that in the Continental dramas. The Christmas
play is treated more sympathetically and at greater length,
and in all the cycles the social and political overtones are very
overt. The shepherds are English shepherds discussing local
grievances, and great lords are treated with scant respect,
whether their name be Pilate or Augustus. Abel is an honest
man who pays his taxes to the church, whereas his brother
Cain is quite the opposite.

We have complete mystery cycles from Chester, York, and
Wakefield and fragments of cycles from Coventry, Norwich,
and Newcastle. Of their early development we know little. A
work called *The Northern Passion*, probably of the fourteenth
century, provided the basis for the important cycles from the
north of England, and no doubt the scenes were constantly
being reworked. The York cycle is probably the oldest, and
it certainly provided the basis for the Wakefield group, sometimes called the Towneley group because the manuscript of
the play was for a long time in the possession of the Towneley
family. Yet the best-known parts of the Wakefield play are
by an author whose style is so distinctive that he is called the
Wakefield Master. This cycle carries comedy to extreme
lengths. The scenes of marital discord between Noah and his
wife may well have a religious and didactic significance, but

the impression on most audiences is that of low comedy. The best-known scene in the Wakefield cycle is that known as the *Second Shepherds' Play*. After the visit of the shepherds to the cradle of the infant Jesus, a sheep stealer, Mak, takes home a sheep, and when the other shepherds (who know Mak's habits well) arrive to search his house, he pretends that his wife has just had a baby and hides the sheep in a crib. Only when one of the visitors wants to kiss the baby is the deception revealed. The play is very funny, but it is also obviously a parody of the Christmas story, and the possibility of deliberate mockery cannot be overlooked.

The scenes in the cycle plays are selected as significant stages in the history of salvation. The Fall is balanced by scenes of the Annunciation and Incarnation; the Noah scenes show the near destruction and partial rehabilitation of God's elect; Christ's baptism at the hands of John the Baptist is the prefiguration of the baptism of Christendom; the raising of Lazarus prefigures Christ's Resurrection.

The religious and didactic elements are more marked in the Chester cycle than in the York and Wakefield cycles, and certain scenes are deliberate expositions of doctrine—Adam's vision of the future of mankind and the fight of Elias with Antichrist, for example. Even more markedly didactic is the so-called *Ludus Coventriae*, sometimes called Hegge or N-town plays. Although there was apparently a tradition that these plays were performed by Franciscans in Coventry (a seventeenth-century marginal note on a manuscript of 1468 indicates this), the actual town where the plays were given is unknown. They were not, apparently, performed by guilds, and although they contain the usual scenes, they seem not to have been designed for continuous performance. The works seem, in fact, to be sermons cast in dramatic form.

The English cycle plays are undoubtedly the liveliest examples of medieval drama, largely because of the popular elements in them. Yet they follow essentially the same form as the French and German dramas. The scenes, their sequence, and to a large extent the treatment were determined by theological, not dramatic considerations. It is hard to see how a play on the history of salvation could have undergone further changes beyond those achieved in England. Better writing of the individual scenes was, of course, possible, but the play itself could not be altered. The Wakefield Master and Arnoul

Greban represent the highest possible achievement in the Passion play, both in comedy and in serious theological construction.

SAINTS' PLAYS

The lives of the saints offered a devotional subject far more susceptible of dramatic treatment and less rigidly bound by convention and sacred writings. Yet there was a curious reluctance to dramatize the lives of all but a very few saints, and those were mostly minor ones. There are long dramatized accounts of the martyrdom of St. Denis and St. Barbara, but the only saint whose life inspired really good plays (apart from the Virgin) was a minor bishop of Asia Minor, St. Nicholas, who became the patron saint of children and students. Four of his miracles were, at one time or another, put into dramatic form—some in Latin in the Fleury playbook of the thirteenth century, one in Latin by Hilarius in the twelfth century, and most important of all, one by the French writer Jean Bodel of Arras. The most popular of the miracles was one in which an unbeliever—Jew or Moslem—does not believe in the saint's powers. He tests his powers by entrusting to him a treasure left at the foot of his statue and is much gratified when it is stolen. The saint, however, lives up to his reputation by recovering the treasure, and the unbeliever is converted. In the Latin versions the emphasis is on the miracle. There is no characterization of the thief or thieves, and no attempt is made to motivate the action. Only the unbeliever is made to express his feelings strongly and then merely to underscore the saint's powers of conversion.

Le Jeu de St. Nicholas

Jean Bodel, already mentioned in connection with the *chanson de geste* (see p. 79), seems to have been a professional *trouvère* and a member of the *puys* or guild known as the Confrérie de la Ste. Chandelle. He died about 1210, but the fact that he contracted leprosy about 1202 and retired to a leper colony seems to indicate that he wrote his play of St. Nicholas before that date, perhaps on the occasion of the removal of the sacred candle from the saint's shrine on the Eve of St. Nicholas, 1199. The plot is much more complicated than that of the Latin plays. A Saracen king of Africa, hearing that the Christians are about to attack him, asks for a sign from his god, Tervagan. The statue both laughs and cries, and this is interpreted to mean that the pagan forces will beat the Christians but later be converted to Christianity. Auberon, the Saracen king's courier, drinks wine in a tavern with one of the thieves, Cliquet, then goes to collect forces for his master. An angel tells the Christian forces of their impending defeat but assures them of Paradise. We are told that they are all killed.

An old nobleman, found kneeling before a statue of St. Nicholas, is told by the king that the saint's powers will be tested by entrusting a treasure to his protection, and that if it is stolen, the nobleman, who believes in him, will pay with his life. Meanwhile he is to be kept in prison. A crier is sent out to announce where the treasure is, and he comes to the inn where the thieves Pincedés and Cliquet are drinking. A third thief, Rasoir, who has already heard about the treasure waiting to be stolen, now joins them, and the three plot to steal it. The innkeeper, eager for a share, offers them receptacles to carry the loot home. They pass the time by playing dice until it grows dark enough to set out. Then they steal the treasure, come back to the inn, and indulge in an orgy of spending.

When the theft is discovered, the wretched nobleman barely obtains a day's grace to pray again to the saint. The executioner regales him with a detailed account of what he will suffer when the day is over. But an angel assures the nobleman that his prayers will be heard by the saint, and sure enough St. Nicholas confronts the thieves (two of them thoroughly frightened but the third defiant) and takes away the treasure. The innkeeper, now loudly protesting his innocence of the whole affair, strips them of their clothing to pay for what they have drunk. The king dreams that the treasure has been returned, and when the fact is confirmed, he releases the nobleman and orders all his liegemen to accept Christianity.

This is one of the very few medieval plays with good characterization. The king of the Saracens, following the usual convention, is a ranting pagan, but his subordinates are carefully differentiated. The Christians are calm and humble, and the nobleman (around whom the play really revolves, since it is his fate which is determined by the saint's miracle) is no calm martyr but a man whose faith is firm despite his human fears and the threats of the executioner. Most effective of all are the low-life characters in the inn. The innkeeper is smooth, avaricious, brutal, and cowardly in turn, and his potboy shows every sign of following in his footsteps. The thieves are no simple types but three completely different men, a fact which appears very clearly in their widely varying reactions to the appearance of the saint. Even St. Nicholas himself is less mechanical than in most versions.

There are two main scenes of action: the pagan king's palace and the associated areas—in which the pagan-Christian conflict is shown—and the tavern scenes, in which the preparations for the theft are made. These tavern scenes are clearly based on Jean Bodel's own experiences in Arras, for there are topical allusions, and local slang is used. Yet we should not think of them as representing Arras. They are simply tavern scenes which the audience would recognize as such, and characters from the other areas frequently wander into them.

The play is an extraordinary combination of lofty sentiment and genuine Christian feeling with realistic comedy of a high order. Few plays at any time have surpassed the scenes in which the three thieves play dice and later spend their winnings. Furthermore, Jean Bodel had a true sense of dramatic structure. He recognized the importance of having a center of interest (the nobleman) and of introducing characters separately. The play is in many ways the best dramatic achievement of the Middle Ages.

Closely connected with the saint's plays are the numerous *Miracles of Our Lady*. These were very popular in France and forty of them, written in the fourteenth century, were collected in a beautifully illustrated manuscript. They all show the Virgin interceding to save sinners from the consequences of their acts—substituting for an abbess who leaves her convent, for example. They all have interspersed lyrics in honor of the Virgin, and the similarity of form seems to argue some attempt at uniformity.

Two plays which show the intervention of the Virgin to save sinners are *Theophilus* and *Frau Jutta* (the female Pope). The first of these was written by the *trouvère* Rutebeuf about 1261. It tells of an official in Asia Minor, who, on the death of the bishop he had served, refused to succeed him but was then ejected from his position by the bishop's successor. In his anger he makes a pact with the devil (in writing) to recover his office. But he soon repents of his deed and is saved by the Virgin, who wrestles with Satan and recovers the written compact. Rutebeuf dramatizes only the part in which the agreement is made and the subsequent action. And although he is sympathetic with Theophilus, the play suffers from poor construction and motivation. German adaptations start the action earlier and are generally more effective.

The play of *Frau Jutta* (1490) by Dietrich Schernberg tells of a learned woman who disguises herself as a man to obtain high offices in the church. Ultimately she becomes Pope, but a love affair leads to her discovery, for she gives birth to a child in public. She dies and devils seize her soul and torture her in Hell (with the usual comic overtones). The Virgin hears her genuine repentance and saves her. The play is vigorous and original.

OTHER RELIGIOUS PLAYS

Some other events in the history of salvation received special attention. The story of the wise and foolish virgins, often called the *Sponsus*, was several times dramatized. It is peculiar as the one story in which the Virgin's intercession is ineffective. A good example of the type is a play written in Limoges in the early twelfth century, where the virgins are several times warned to be prepared for the coming of the bridegroom. The foolish virgins try desperately to buy oil at the last minute, fail, beg Christ's mercy, but are dragged off by devils. There is also a German version of the play dating from the third quarter of the fourteenth century. It was almost certainly a version of this which so horrified Friedrich, margrave of Thüringen, that he died five days after seeing a performance of it in 1321.

There were several prophet plays beside those that were incorporated in cycles. The most popular of them was the play of Daniel, largely because the descent of Daniel into the lion's den was widely regarded as a prefiguration of the descent of Christ into Hell. By far the best known of the Daniel plays is that preserved in a manuscript of Beauvais dating from the early thirteenth century. The music has fortunately been preserved, and the whole play offers a brilliant representation of the secular splendor of the court of Belshazzar and of God's support of his prophet. Virtue triumphs in the face of overwhelming odds.

Plays about Antichrist were also very popular. They were

included in the cycle plays, because, according to the Book of
Revelation, the appearance of Antichrist would be one of the
signs immediately preceding the Day of Judgment. Although
the nature of Antichrist is vague in the Bible, in medieval
accounts and especially that of Bishop Adso, he is a worshiper
of worldly goods who has the power to perform miracles and
even delude good Christians into thinking that he is Christ
come again. By far the most interesting of the Antichrist plays
is the Latin version from Tegernsee, written probably in the
last decade of the twelfth century. The play shows the Roman
emperor triumphant over the whole world and his yielding of
his secular power at Jerusalem. All is ready for the triumph
of Christianity when Antichrist appears. Personifications such
as Hypocrisy and Heresy help him to win over all the powers
except the king of Germany. Even he is converted when Antichrist proves his "divinity" by miracles. After a struggle between Elijah and Antichrist, the avenging angel of God finally
strikes Antichrist down. The work is more remarkable for its
form and for its political overtones than for its religious
teaching. It is a lively and well-written work which shows
considerable skill in balancing Antichrist's utterances against
Christ's own words.

The allegorizing tendency of the late Middle Ages appears
very strongly in the drama. The best-known examples are the
English moralities, although there were examples from most
western European countries. The English moralities are concerned with the fate of the human soul and resistance to
temptation. *Mankind* (c. 1475), *Mind, Will, and Understanding* (c. 1425), and the fragment *Pride of Life* (c. 1400), are
much inferior to two really important plays, the *Castle of
Perseverance* (c. 1425) and *Everyman* (c. 1500). The former
depicts, in allegorical form, man's temptation, his yielding to
vice, his repentance, and temporary security in the Castle of
Perseverance. The virtues guard him there, but the vices
besiege the castle and are successful, because Avarice lures
Humanity out of his fortress. His soul is seized by devils but,
as so often happens, the pleas of the Virgin result in his
rescue.

Everyman, probably based on the very similar Dutch
Elckerlijk of Petrus Dolandus, uses the same techniques but
with far greater effect. Again we see the man suddenly sum-
moned by death. His pleas for more time are unavailing. All
the pleasures and friends of the secular world prove their

fickleness and ineffectiveness. Only Knowledge and Good
Deeds stay with him until the end. The author characterizes
the various allegorical figures very well, and he is aware of
the necessity for a dramatic climax. The audience is neatly
involved in Everyman's misery, for the universality of the
situation is made clear by personifications readily recognizable
to anyone.

The French moralities have a wider range than those in
England. Their titles give an idea of their subjects—*The Men
of Good and Bad Counsel, The Sinful Man*, and the *Condemnation of Feasting*.

The Italians never developed religious drama such as that
which appeared north of the Alps. There were semidramatic
performances of religious themes, but they were dramatized
preaching rather than true drama. Italy was already writing
works in the classical tradition by the time the great medieval
plays were being produced in France and Germany.

SECULAR DRAMA

Secular drama was slow to emerge, at least in written form.
Two early and very successful comedies were both written by
Adam de la Halle (Adam le Bossu) of Arras, a professional
trouvère who died after 1288. He seems to have continued
the tradition of Jean Bodel, for he had a good sense of the
dramatic and of dramatic structure. *Le Jeu de la Feuillée*
(literally, "Play of Foliage," but it alludes to a spring
festival) is a fairy play. Adam (the author, himself on the
stage) says that he is tired of married life and must go off to
Paris to study. His father agrees but says that he cannot provide
any finances because he is too ill. A doctor diagnoses the
disease as avarice, and the play goes on to reveal the weaknesses
of several elements of the population. A fairy procession,
with Queen Morgain la Fée and Harlequin, visits the
town and grants wishes to many of the people. Adam, however,
is made to stay with his wife, which, it turns out, is what
he wanted anyway. The realism and satirical description found
in Jean Bodel's St. Nicholas play are again present here, and
with the same lighthearted touch. The work is amusing, not
didactic, and the plot, such as it is, is merely a framework for
the author's ironic comments.

Robin and Marion, the second of Adam de la Halle's plays,
is a dramatized *pastourelle*. It tells the usual story of the

attempted seduction of a peasant girl by a nobleman, but in
this case the girl has a lover, Robin, who receives a beating
from the nobleman when a lost falcon is found in his possession. In the resulting confusion the knight is able to abduct
Marion, but the elaborate plans made by Robin and his
friends to rescue her prove to be quite unnecessary because
she returns unharmed. She has merely asked the nobleman to
let her go and he has agreed, unable to understand the stu-
pidity of one who prefers Robin to himself. There are many
songs in the work, which is clearly closer to operetta than
drama. *Aucassin and Nicolette* (1210/20) is a pleasant story
of the trials of two lovers who are in much the same position
as Shakespeare's Romeo and Juliet. It is partly dialogue and
partly narrative with interspersed songs.

In the late Middle Ages France and Germany produced a
considerable amount of farcical comedy, the extant versions
of which date mostly from the sixteenth century. In the French
sotties and the German *Fastnachtspiele* the subjects and treatment are those of the French fabliau (see p. 115)—the
foolish husband, the unfaithful wife, gossips, cheats, and
boasters. *Maître Pierre Patelin* (last half of the fifteenth century) is the best known of the French *sottie* type of play.

A few other plays on secular subjects are extant. In France
there was the four-day play called *The Mystery of Troy the
Great*, written by Jacques Milet between 1450 and 1452. It is
a dramatization of Guido delle Colonne's long-winded account
of the siege of Troy and seems almost too huge to perform.
The *Abele Spelen* (Preludes; strictly the word Abel = Latin
habilis, fit or suitable) of the Netherlands were serious works
whose subject matter was often taken from romances.

The most important achievement of medieval drama is in
works connected with religion. It should never be forgotten
that the primary purpose of the religious plays was didactic,
and that they were intended to recount the history of salvation and strengthen faith. All other features are subordinated
to this purpose. The greatest of the dramas achieve this end
by a blend of theological instruction and deep humanity. Yet
to those who think of drama in terms of the post-Renaissance
theater, there can be little effective drama except in such
works as that of Jean Bodel, where the religious elements,
although present, are subordinated to the interest which the
spectator feels in the plot and the human characters.

Conclusion

THE FOREGOING CHAPTERS give some idea of the scope of medieval literature. Great works were written in almost all the countries of western Europe, and each contributed in some measure to the general development of literature. Although many works of great technical excellence were written in medieval Latin, it must be admitted that it was only in the vernaculars that works appeared which can be said truly to be works of genius—the *Divine Comedy*, Wolfram's *Parzival*, Gottfried's *Tristan*, the lyric poetry of France and Germany, the *Canterbury Tales*. It must be admitted too that France played a decisive role in the determination of literary types and their development, even though she may not always have produced the greatest individual work in a given period or genre. Still, the *Chanson de Roland* is probably the greatest of the national epics and set the tone for subsequent developments, the *Roman de la Rose* is the greatest of the allegories, and the French mysteries stand above most other plays.

Medieval literature generally reached its greatest heights when patronage was still in the hands of a noble élite. The transfer of the power of patronage to lesser nobility and bourgeoisie was, in general, fatal to the ideals of medieval literature.

Recommended Reading

GENERAL

Artz, F. B., *The Mind of the Middle Ages*. 2d ed. 1953.
Cambridge Mediaeval History, ed. Tanner, Previté-Orton, and Brooke. 8 vols. and maps. 1911–36. Shorter version in 2 vols.
Cantor, N., *Medieval History*. 1963.
D'Entreves, A. P., *The Medieval Contribution to Political Thought*. 1939.
Evans, Joan, *Life in Medieval France*. 1957.
Haskins, C. H., *Renaissance of the Twelfth Century*. 1927.
————, *Studies in Medieval Culture*. 1929.
Huizinga, J., *Waning of the Middle Ages*. Eng. trans. 1924.
Jackson, W. T. H., *The Literature of the Middle Ages*. 1960 (with bibliography).
Lewis, E., *Medieval Political Ideas*. 2 vols. 1954.
Painter, S., *French Chivalry*. 1940.
Powicke, F. M., *The Thirteenth Century*. 1953.
Reese, G., *Music in the Middle Ages*. 1940.
Runciman, S., *Byzantine Civilization*. 1954.
Southern, R. W., *The Making of the Middle Ages*. 1953.
Stenton, Doris M., *English Society in the Early Middle Ages*. 1951.
Stenton, Frank M., *Anglo-Saxon England*. 2d ed. 1947.
Stephenson, C., *Medieval Feudalism*. 1956.
Strayer, J. R., *Western Europe in the Middle Ages*. 1955.
Taylor, H. O., *The Medieval Mind*. 2 vols. 4th ed. 1925.
Vossler, K., *Medieval Culture*. 1925. Eng. trans. 1958.

INTRODUCTION

Baldwin, M. W., *The Medieval Church*. 1953.
Copleston, F., *Medieval Philosophy*. 1952.
Deanesley, Margaret, *History of the Medieval Church*. 3d ed. 1934.
De Wulf, M., *History of Medieval Philosophy*. 3 vols. 6th ed. 1934–47.
Gilson, E., *History of Christian Philosophy in the Middle Ages*. 1955.
Owst, G. R., *Preaching in Medieval England*. 1926.
Smalley, B., *The Study of the Bible in the Middle Ages*. 1952.

EARLY GERMANIC LITERATURE

Blair, P. H., *An Introduction to Anglo-Saxon England*. 1956.
Bostock, J. K., *A Handbook on Old High German Literature*. 1955.

Bowra, C. M., *Heroic Poetry*. 1952.
Chadwick, H. M., *The Heroic Age*. 1912.
Chadwick, H. M. and N. K., *The Ancient Literature of Europe*. 1932 (*Growth of Literature*, Vol. I).
Einarsson, S., *History of Icelandic Literature*. 1957.
Heusler, A., *Die altgermanische Dichtung*. 2d ed. 1941.
Ker, W. P., *Epic and Romance*. 2d ed. 1908.
Schroeder, F. R., *Germanische Heldendichtung*. 1935.
Wardale, Edith E., *Chapters on Old English Literature*. 1935.
Wilson, R. M., *The Lost Literature of Medieval England*. 1952.

MEDIEVAL LATIN LITERATURE

Hélin, M., *A History of Medieval Latin Literature*. 1949.
Manitius, Max, *Geschichte der lateinischen Literatur des Mittelalters*. 3 vols. 1911–31.
Raby, F. J. E., *A History of Christian Latin Poetry*. 2d ed. 1953.
———, *A History of Secular Latin Poetry*. 2d ed. 1957.
Wright, F., and Sinclair, T., *A History of Later Latin Literature*. 1931.

FRENCH LITERATURE

Cohen, G., *Littérature française du moyen âge*. 1951.
Crosland, Jessie, *Medieval French Literature*. 1956.
Holmes, U. T., *A History of Old French Literature*. 1948.
Remy, P., *La Littérature provençale au moyen âge*. 1944.
Voretzsch, K., *Introduction to the Study of Old French Literature*. 1931.
Zumthor, P., *Histoire littéraire de la France, VIme-XIVme siècles*. 1954.

GERMAN LITERATURE

Bostock, J. K., *A Handbook on Old High German Literature*. 1955.
De Boor, H., and Newald, R., *Geschichte der deutschen Literatur*. Vol. I (to 1100), Vol. II (to 1250), both in rev. eds. 1957; Vol. III, Part 1 (to 1350) 1962.
Schwietering, J., *Deutsche Dichtung des Mittelalters*. 1938.
Walshe, M. O'C., *Medieval German Literature*. 1962.

ITALIAN LITERATURE

De Sanctis, F., *History of Italian Literature*. 2 vols. Eng. trans. 1931.

Storia litteraria d'Italia by various authors for the different periods.
Wilkins, E. H., *A History of Italian Literature.* 1954.

MIDDLE ENGLISH LITERATURE

Bennett, H. S., *Chaucer and the Fifteenth Century.* 1947.
Chambers, E. K., *English Literature to the Close of the Middle Ages.* 1945.
Literary History of England, ed. Baugh. 1948. Old English period by Kemp Malone, Middle English by A. C. Baugh.
Wilson, R. M., *Early Middle English Literature.* 2d ed. 1951.

CELTIC LITERATURE

Dillon, Myles, *Early Irish Literature.* 1948.
Parry, T., *A History of Welsh Literature.* Eng. trans. 1955.

LITERATURE OF THE IBERIAN PENINSULA

Brenan, G. F., *The Literature of the Spanish People.* 2d ed. 1953.
Prat, Angel Valbuena, *Historia de la literatura Espanola.* 3 vols. 3d ed. 1950.

DRAMA

Chambers, E. K., *The Medieval Stage.* 2 vols. 1903.
Craig, H., *English Religious Drama of the Middle Ages.* 1955.
Creizenach, W., *Geschichte des neuren Dramas.* 5 vols. 1893–1916. Vols. I and II cover the Middle Ages.
Frank, Grace, *The Medieval French Drama.* 2d ed. 1960.
Kindermann, H., *Theatergeschichte Europas.* Vols. I and II, 1957–, are concerned with the Middle Ages.
Prosser, E., *Drama and Religion in the English Mystery Plays.* 1961.
Young, K., *The Drama of the Medieval Church.* 2 vols. 1933.

Index

This index contains the names of the authors and works mentioned in the text. The names of important characters in major works are also listed, as well as types of literature, technical terms, and commonly occurring motifs. The titles are generally in their English form, but very well-known works, such as the *Divina Commedia*, are listed in the original language. All italicized words are titles.

The following abbreviations have been used:

A/S	Anglo-Saxon	OF	Old French
Ca	Catalan	OHG	Old High German
Ir	Irish	ON	Old Norse
It	Italian	OS	Old Saxon
L	Latin	Pr	Provençal
ME	Middle English	Sp	Spanish
MHG	Middle High German	We	Welsh

These are general indications of the language area in which the works are to be found, not precise descriptions. Thus OF includes all northern French medieval dialects up to 1450, even Anglo-Norman, and Sp all the romance languages of the Iberian peninsula.